THE COMBINED BOMBER OFFENSIVE 1943 - 1944: THE AIR ATTACK ON NAZI GERMANY

L. DOUGLAS KEENEY

PUBLISHED BY PREMIERE

Acknowledgments

Original manuscript found at the Air Force Historical Research Agency, Maxwell Air Force Base, Alabama
All Photographs: Courtesy The National Archives

CONTENTS

FOREWORD

During a dinner party on the evening of November 28, 1943, Russian Marshal Joseph Stalin raised his glass to toast President Franklin D. Roosevelt during their first Big Three conference in Tehran, although one might have wondered what on Earth there was to celebrate. The war against Hitler was at a stalemate. The Germans had just defeated the British on Leros and the Allies were now stalled in Italy below Rome. British manpower was taxed to the limit and Prime Minister Winston Churchill now feared the end of it all if he launched D-Day and it failed. He had in fact become so despondent about its prospects that he had a change of heart and was now insisting that D-Day be completely canceled. If it was, said U.S. Army General George Marshall, he would resign.

But one thing was going very, very well, and Stalin saw it and he brought it to everyone's attention as he rose to toast the President. "Machines," said Stalin. "I want to tell you, from the Russian point of view, what the President and the United States have done to win the war. The most important thing in this war are machines. The United States has proven that it can turn out from 8,000 to 10,000 airplanes per month. Russia can only turn out at most 3,000 airplanes a month. England turns out 3,000 to 3,500 airplanes a month which are principally heavy bombers. The United States therefore is a country of machines. Without the use of Lend-Lease, we would lose this war."[i]

It was just what the leaders needed to hear and it turned around the war. Yes, combat had stalled in Italy and Churchill had his fears but there was America and behind the scenes were more than a million fresh American soldiers coming into combat — and tens of thousands of American bombers and fighters. Churchill had no reason to fear D-Day. What would have sent chills up and down his spine was how poorly these machines were being employed. Until now, the United States' Eighth Air Force had failed to use their machines against Nazi Germany with any degree of effectiveness whatsoever. Through November of 1943, American B-17s and B-24s were being destroyed at rates that made the completion of 25 missions statistically impossible. The October raids into Germany had been so thoroughly savaged by the Luftwaffe that we had decided to halt deep mission altogether. Barring something new, the prospect of getting soldiers ashore on the Normandy Beaches seemed dim indeed, Churchill's cold feet notwithstanding.

But then came January 1, 1944 and with it a complete overhaul of the air war and the creation of the United States Strategic Air Forces. General Carl A. "Tooey" Spaatz came in from North Africa to take over, General Jimmy Doolittle was give command of the Eighth Air Force, and a firebrand named Pete Quesada arrived and honed his Ninth Air Force into a killing machine. Strategic bombing was validated. Air-to-ground interdiction was pioneered. Bridge busting was pioneered. Air photo reconnaissance was pioneered. The air war turned around and in just five months the Luftwaffe was so beaten down that they could scarcely mount a single mission against the landings. It would go down as the most effective air campaign in the history of military aviation. And D-Day was saved.

But none of this happened the way we remember it today.

On D-Day the Germans completed every single attack on the D-Day beaches with just a few dozen combat losses. One German squadron shot up the soldiers on the beaches then spent that afternoon beside a pool working on their tans. That morning, the bombers of the Eighth Air Force missed 100% of their critical targets and left the soldiers on Omaha beach exposed to German coastal batteries and pillboxes that had been untouched by bombs.

But that was a mere blemish on what had already been accomplished through the Combined Bomber Offensive. The greatest air campaign had already so badly defeated the German Luftwaffe and its supply of aircraft that on the day of its greatest failure, the German Air Force was in such tattered remains that it scarcely mattered.

Stalin toasted the machines but it was The Pointblank Directive that saved D-Day and made June 6, 1944 the crowning achievement of air warfare, a victory on a scale of air combat never before seen, and never seen since. For five solitary months the airmen of the Eighth, Ninth and Fifteenth Air Forces combined their more than 20,000 bombers and fighters to create an arc of destruction 130 miles wide around the D-Day beaches. The flew treetop-level reconnaissance missions, bombed radar sites, aircraft factories, more than 100 German airfields while freeing their fighters to engage in air-to-air combat that cost the Germans 90% of their frontline European airplanes.

And it culminated on D-Day. Allied Supreme Commander General Dwight D. Eisenhower summed up what the Combined Bomber Offensive meant as he and his son John walked on Omaha Beach one week after D-Day. Armored trucks and tanks crawled bumper-to-bumper in a traffic jam as thick as rush hour traffic in Manhattan. Said the young Eisenhower to his father, "You'd never get away with this if you didn't have air supremacy."

His father didn't miss a beat. "If I didn't have air superiority, I wouldn't be here."[ii]

In restoring this set it was impossible to decipher every word but it was possible to maintain the original integrity of the documents so that historians and buffs can read what was written about the war as it was written fresh from the victory over Nazi Germany. Mistakes will be obvious to the well trained eye and many spellings have changed over the years and some small villages have simply been swallowed up by the larger metro areas. History even refutes some of the numbers and conclusions contained on these pages – aerial kills are but one glaring example – but there's more to this than that. In today's world of quick answers and Wikipedia reporting, it's rare to find an original manuscript with the original voice and the old feelings – but through that old voice events take on a substance the bare facts – and time—have erased. It is impossible to write without some emotion, some bias, some inflexion points and the restoration of old documents allows us to immerse ourselves in those old emotions today as we examine events so far back in our history.

There is also a sense of a war evolving. As of the writing of this document, there was no formal name given to the "ski" sites bombed by the Eighth but we now know they were rocket launch sites. Additionally, the now well known V-1 and V-2 rockets were then called "pilotless aircraft."

We sense the evolution of war in other ways, too. Blind bombing sometimes worked and sometimes didn't work and often worked best on coastal targets because the radar could easily paint the land-sea divide. But coastal targets were relatively unimportant and often the radar simply failed to work. The experiments continued and we sense the evolutionary nature of it all although the author refrains from casting judgment. We now know, however, that it went on to become a significant technology for Curtis Lemay in the Pacific.

It is clear that deep penetration bombing missions into Germany were failing to do significant damage and, worse, that they were sustaining horrific losses. Through November of 1943, these missions were simply death traps for our bomber crews. The author sees this but continues a conceit that ultimately doomed Ira Eaker. The answer to the horrific losses of bombers wasn't a larger bombing force or multiple bombing missions on one day. The answer also wasn't drop tanks alone. The true answer was a complete change in one's mindset about the role of fighters — and that only came about with the removal of Eaker and the installation of the new leadership team – Doolittle, Spaatz and so on.

There are gems here too. Many of the quotes from Hap Arnold or Tooey Spaatz have been simply lost to history but we have new ones here, quotes that give us insights into how they felt about the evolution of the war including the horrible Schweinfurt-Regensburg raid.

All-in-all, *Lost Histories* make for thoroughly satisfying reads and this installation is an important addition to the series and enjoys a prominent place on my bookshelf.

L. Douglas Keeney
Series Editor

[i] Foreign relations of the United States, The President's Log at Tehran, p. 469

[ii] Ambrose, Stephen. . New York: Touchstone, 1995, p. 239n*.

1

TARGET SELECTION FOR THE COMBINED BOMBER OFFENSIVE - Early Planning: 1941-1942

The history of the combined bomber offensive (CBO) in Europe is, in the main, an account of strategic air warfare. In a letter written to the Commanding General of the Army Air Forces in January 1943, Maj. Gen. Ira C. Eaker, Commanding General of the United States component of the CBO forces, made a significant distinction between two of the most important military applications of air power. In the course of a comment on the enemy he said:

```
The Germans never had an Air Force. They had a great Air Support Command.
Goering designed and built their airplanes to support  ground armies in
continental conquest. They never had an Air Force of  long range bombers
with a defensive fire power to carry destruction outside the continent … .
They had not the means, perhaps, to build the overpowering Air Force and
the overpowering Air Support Command. Quite rightly, therefore, by their
lights, they built the latter …
```

War Department doctrine on the employment of air power makes the same distinctions of mission and composition in more conventional terms.

According to this doctrine the over-all mission of a strategic air force is the defeat of the enemy nation, the implication being that such a force can wage war on an enemy independent of the action of other forces. The strategic air force comprises bombardment, fighter, and photographic aviation, but heavy bombardment aircraft constitute its backbone. Its objectives are to be found in the vital centers of the enemy's communication lines and his economic system. The tactical air force, on the other hand, lacks the emphasis on heavy bombardment aircraft and normally functions in a theater where ground forces are operating. Its missions are principally to gain air superiority within the theater, to prevent movement of hostile troops and supplies, and to participate with the ground forces in a combined effort to gain objectives on the immediate front.

The joint and separate U.S. and British planning for the defeat of Germany contemplated from 1941 forward the strategic application of air power as one of the means of bringing that end about. The British-United States Staff Conversations held in the first quarter of 1941 and reported on 27 March of that year proposed "a sustained air offensive against the German homeland and all territories under her control" as one of the measures against Axis Europe. The War Department plans, which followed these staff conversations and provided for the defense of the Western Hemisphere and action in the Pacific ad European theaters, proposed the conduct of "offensive air operations from bases in the British Isles ... against German military power at its source."

The AAF plan APD-1, drafted in August 1941 in pursuance of a presidential directive dated 9 July and in consonance with the United States-British Staff Conversations of 1941 and RAINBOW NO. 5, stated clearly a strategic doctrine for the defeat of Germany I these words: "The center of the Axis system is Germany ... . The basic conception on which this plan is based lies in the application of air power for the breakdown of the industrial and economic structure of Germany. The purpose was further elaborated in a "Plan for Initiation of U.S. Army Bombardment Operations in the British Isles." 20 March 1943, which stated that after our bombardment force had been built up sufficiently it would "commence operations against the strategic objectives, facilities and establishments which support the operations of enemy forces and the enemy national, economic, and industrial structure.

The air plan known as AWPD-43, dated 9 September 1942 and prepared by the Army Air Forces in compliance with a letter directive from the President to the Chief of Staff, declared that our air force must depleted the German Air Force and undermine the economic structure that supported the surface forces of the enemy. The accomplishment of these tasks was to be through the combined efforts of the U.S. AAF and the British RAF. The AAF would conduct precision bombing in daylight and the RAF would make mass area attacks at night for the purpose of cutting down production and weakening morale.

It is thus quite evident that the strategic air force mission was understood and clearly stated well in advance of the drawing up of the final Combined Bomber Offensive Plan.

Strategic warfare with heavy bombardment aviation involves three phases: the preoperational or planning phase, operations and attack, and the assessment of results. The planning phase is considerably different from that for other types of warfare and even unlike that required for other applications of air power. The strategic plan calls for two essential stops – the selection of targets and the calculation of the force necessary to destroy these targets. It is primarily in the selection of targets that planning for strategic air war differs most from other types of war planning. Since the strategic force aims to destroy the economic sources of military cover, the selection of target systems is of paramount importance. Their selection requires a kind of intelligence of the enemy and a type of personnel different from other military preparations.

The air planning for war against Germany that preceded the CBO Plan paid a great deal of attention to the matter of target selection. AWPD-1, mentioned above, selected a set of industrial system for destruction and arranged them in order of priority. The plan called for:

1. Disruption of the German electric power system
2. Disruption of the German transportation system
3. Destruction of German oil and petroleum supplies
4. Undermining morale by attacks on centers of population

To aid in the accomplishment of these objectives it would be necessary
to neutralize the German Air Force by attacks on

1. Its bases
2. Engine and airframe factories
3. Aluminum and magnesium factories

The "Plan or Initiation of Air Force Bombardment Operations in the
British Isles" selected some 144 targets within four categories in the following order of priority:

1. Munitions industry
2. Electric and water-power industry
3. Petroleum and fuel industry
4. Rail and water transportation

AWPD -43, mentioned above, went into considerable detail in selection
of systems and individual targets, and in the calculation of the forces and
munitions necessary for achieving the destruction of these targets. The size
of the forces planned was based upon the bombardment accuracy that had
been observed in early Eighth Air Force operations. The plan provided
seven target systems for the attention of the Eighth while the RAF bombers
were to be engaged in mass area attacks. The systems for the AAF bombers
included:

* First priority, the facilities supporting the GAF – including eleven fighter
  factories, fifteen bomber factories, and seventeen engine plants.
* Second priority, twenty submarine building yards.
* Third priority, transportation system – Individual targets (36) were to be
  found among building shops, repair works, marshaling yards, and canals.
* Forth priority, electric power – including some thirty-seven major plants.
* Fifth priority, oil – which required destruction of twenty-three plants.
* Sixth priority, fourteen aluminum plants.
* Seventh priority, rubber – The destruction of the two principal plants
  was called for.

Since during the course of 1943 the German submarine had become a serious threat to our successful waging of the war, the facilities supporting underseas craft were moved to top priority in a list of target categories given to the U.S. Eighth Air Force by the theater commander in October 1942:

❋ First priority, five submarine bases
❋ Second priority, aircraft factories and fields
❋ Third priority, twelve railroad "marshaling yards"

THE CASABLANCA CONFERENCE

From the above it seems quite evident that definite progress had been made in the sphere of target selection in the planning prior to the drawing of the final blueprint for the combined bomber offensive in 1943. It was true, nevertheless, that certain things were lacking in the preparations for the air offensive against the Western Axis. No directive emanating from the top policy levels had been issued to control the combined operations of the two Allied air forces that were operating against Germany; no directive of sufficient clearness and definiteness and been given to the U.S. Eighth Air Force; and no unified analysis of enemy economy had been made that was sufficiently thorough to serve as a basis for the best target selection.

Two of these defects in strategic planning were eliminated by the work of the Casablanca Conference in January 1943: a directive was issued by the Combined Chiefs of Staff, and this directive proved to be quite clear and definite. There had apparently never been any disposition on the part of the Combined Chiefs to depart from the intention to use strategic air power as one of the primary offensive measures against Germany, but there had been some pressure exerted to have the U. S. Eighth abandon daylight precision bombing and join with the British in night bombing.

The Commanding General of the Eighth was called to Casablanca and given opportunity to defend the United States doctrine of day bombing. His defense emphasized the greater accuracy of this type of operation which permitted small targets like factories to be found, seen, and hit. Day bombing, he declared, was more economical in the employment of forces, for a smaller number of bombers could destroy a given target. This meant reduced exposure to enemy action and consequent lower losses for a given result. Also, day attack was more economical because all forces could carry bombs, whereas at night large numbers of pathfinders and target illuminators were required. It was stated, in addition, that day bombing used in conjunction with British night bombing would heavily tax German defenses by allowing no rest during the daylight hours, and would prevent congestion and provide more economical use of English airdromes. The general's defense of precision bombing likewise stressed the fact that American training and equipment would require modification if successful night operation was to be possible, for American crews would need a long period of additional training to make them capable of coping with English weather at night and U.S. planes would have to be flame dampened, thus reducing their power and range. Furthermore, the point was made that day bombing provided an excellent means of cooperating with the RAF night effort, in that the AAF bombers could find difficult targets and mark them by setting fires, whereupon the RAF could complete the job of destruction at night. Moreover, day bombing would permit the destruction of the enemy's day fighters, thus causing the greatest reduction of his air force. Finally, it would (as a complement to night bombing) result in the greatest havoc to the enemy's industrial system.

General Eaker spent an hour with the British Prime Minister at Casablanca and was assured by the latter that he would be given an opportunity to prove his case.

The Casablanca directive that was issued by the Combined Chiefs of Staff on 21 January 1845 is noteworthy because it governed the operations of both U.S. and British bomber commands in the United Kingdom, because of its excellent statement of the mission of strategic bombardment, and because of the target systems that were selected for attack.

The mission of the bomber offensive from the United Kingdom was "the progressive destruction and dislocation of the German military, industrial and economic system, and the undermining of the morale of the German people to the point where their capacity for armed resistance is fatally weakened."

The target systems to be attacked in the accomplishment of this mission were in five categories in the following order of priority:

1. German submarine construction yards

2. The German aircraft industry
3. Transportation
4. Oil plants
5. Other targets in enemy war industry

The directive stated that strategical developments might vary the order of the five categories and that there were other targets of military and political importance, such as submarine operating based on the Biscay coast and the city of Berlin, which were worthy of attention. Attacks were to be made in the Mediterranean theater when the occasion demanded, and the units of the German fleet were to be hit when opportune. Daylight attacks were to be pressed against targets within Germany in order to maintain continuous pressure on German fighters, and to take enemy fighter pressure away from the Soviet and Mediterranean theaters.

The Report of the Committee of Operations Analysts

The target selection in the Casablanca directive was not, however, much different from nor perhaps any better than that in the earlier planning. The thing that had been lacking in all this planning was a thorough study of the enemy economy by a single agency, such a unified analysis being necessary for the proper selection of strategic objectives. This phase of planning had developed its own principles and techniques, which involved a detailed knowledge of the enemy's productive system and a careful balancing of economic and military factors; but no agency had been created to apply these techniques in preparing a comprehensive report.

Not all of the intelligence of the enemy necessary for target selection can be obtained directly by an air force or a bomber command. Such intelligence is obtained by many regular and special governmental agencies and by a variety of individual experts. Its sources are as varied as its collectors. Aerial reconnaissance photographs, ground reports, captured weapons, interrogations of refugees and prisoners of war, current and prewar enemy technical publications, the prewar experience of Allied technical experts abroad, our own production practices and Allied data on bombing effectiveness are but some of the courses used in making a selection of targets for strategic bombing.

Before industrial systems can be ranked in target priority a number of economic and military criteria must be applied. Most important, perhaps, is the military use of the products of a system. Some of the economic factors which must be considered are the depth of an industry (measured by the time required to get products from industry to the front line), the cushion (idle capacity that can be brought into production), the reserve stocks, the attrition rate, the existence of substitutes, the possibility of exercising economics, and the ability of an industry to recuperate.

Military factors relating to the vulnerability of targets and the capabilities of the attacking air force must be applied. The structural characteristics and concentration of buildings, their susceptibility to various types of munitions, the dispersal of plants, and distances from bases all govern the possible destruction of a telling fraction of an industry by an air force.

The appointment of a body to make the analysis of German economy that was necessary before further progress in target selection could be achieved was made on 9 December 1943 by the Commanding General of the Army Air Forces. This body, known as the Committee of Operations Analysts (COA) and placed under the direction of the Assistant Chief of the Air Staff, Management Control, was instructed to submit a report which would show the rate of deterioration of the German war effort that would result from air operations and which would indicate an approximate date when invasion of the Continent would be possible. This was the body that filled the gap that had existed in the strategical planning before 1943 by making a thorough-going study of German economy upon which a dependable choice of target systems might rest.

The first meeting of the Committee of Operations Analysts was held on 10 December, and it immediately went to work with the appointment of subcommittees to study enemy industrial systems.

Although it was desired that the committee submit a report before the Casablanca Conference, that could not be accomplished in the time available. An interim report was submitted on 23 December 1943 in which the committee's methods and courses of intelligence were described and in which the principle of concentration of effort was stated thus: " ... it is better to cause a high degree of destruction in a few really essential industries or services than to cause a small decrease of destruction in many industries."

The next few months were spent in the study of various target systems. Assistance was given by A-3, G-2, the Board of Economic Warfare, the Office of Strategic Services, the War Production Board, and certain other government agencies and experts in private industry. Certain members of the committee went to England where methods and materials were reviewed with the Eighth Air Force, the Royal Air Force, the Air Ministry, and the Ministry of Economic Warfare.

The final report of the OCA was submitted on 6 March 1943. The overall results of the researcher of the various subcommittees were presented in a bound volume which surprised data on 10 different German industrial systems – all that appeared to have bombardment significance. Under a separate tab the various production units in each system were listed. The distance of each unit from London and its percentage of total axis production were set forth. For security reasons the committee did not rank the 19 systems in order of priority, but it did announce a set of principles of strategic selection which apparently constitute one of its chief contributions to the planning chase of this type of warfare.

Although the report did not recommend definite target priorities or find it possible at the time to forecast a date on which invasion would be possible, it did arrive at two important conclusions:

1. The destruction and continued neutralization of some sixty targets would gravely impair and might paralyze the Western Axis war effort.
2. In view of the ability of adequate and properly utilized air power to impair the industrial sources of the enemy's military strength, only the most vital considerations should be permitted to delay or divert the application of an adequate striking force to this task.

The Combined Bomber Offensive Plan and Directive

A committee composed of Brig. Gen. Heywood S. Hansell, Jr., Brig. Gen Orvil A. Anderson, the plans personnel of USAAF, the Royal Air Force, and the Eighth Air Force, was set up under General Eaker for the purpose of drawing up an operating plan to accomplish the desired result. The committee had as its task the establishment of target priorities and the calculation of the size of U.S. forces necessary to accomplish their destruction.

This committee completed its work in April 1943. The finished plan restated the mission of the strategic air forces as defined in the Casablanca directive and recommended the destruction of 76 specific targets that were to be found in the following systems:

1. Submarine construction yards and bases
2. German aircraft industry
3. Ball bearings
4. Oil
5. Synthetic rubber and tires
6. Military transport vehicles

It further stated that the destruction of the selected individual targets within those systems would achieve the elimination of commanding fractions of enemy production within the affected industries:

1. Destruction of the selected submarine yards would reduce German construction by 89%
2. German fighter capacity would be reduced by 43% and bomber capacity by 65%
3. Ball-bearing capacity would be reduced by 76
4. Destruction of Ploesti refineries and German synthetic oil plants would reduce production by 45%
5. Destruction of 50% of synthetic rubber production and nearly all of that for tires would be accomplished.
6. Destruction of seven plants producing motor vehicles would fatally weaken the capacity of the German people for armed resistance.

The German aircraft industry was placed second in the priority list of target systems, but the plan stated that German fighter strength was an intermediate objective of the bomber offensive second to none. That is to say that the German fighter force and to be destroyed before the combined bomber offensive, especially the American part of it, could b successful. It was pointed out in this connection that German fighter production had increased 44% and fighter strength on the Western front had nearly doubled since the entry of the United States into the war.

The plan emphasized the fact that the bomber offensive was in integrated RAF and USAAF effort, and that the capabilities of the two sources were complimentary.

A time schedule was worked out calling for AAF and RAF missions against a certain number of targets within certain systems in each of four three-month phases. The first phase was scheduled to run to 30 June, the second to 20 September, the third to the end of 1943, and the fourth to go into the early months of 1944. The specific targets for the Eighth during the first three phases were set forth in charts b category, and the distance from bases and the productive importance of each was shown. The RAF was given a certain definite assignment of cities in each phase for attack. In general, these coincided with the location of the USAAF targets. The precision targets of the Eighth and the area targets of the RAF were shown on maps using different symbols.

The Eighth Air Force penetrations of enemy territory were to become deeper as the offensive progressed. First-phase operations were to be relatively shallow and were to be concentrated against the submarine yards and bases along the coast. Second-phase range was to increase to approximately 400 miles, and about three-quarters of the effort was to be concentrated against German fighter aircraft factories and other German Air Force facilities. The third phase was to see attacks against all the principal objectives with continued effort to neutralize those previously attacked but capable of repair. Fourth phase was to witness the continuation of these operations with provision made for attacks against installations associated with a cross-channel invasion.

The calculation of the size of U. S. forces needed was based upon the experience of the Eighth in operating in the theater. It was stated in the plan that this force had conducted about 20 missions in the three-month period from January to April 1943, and that approximately 12 of these missions had been successful. It was stated also that the average number of aircraft dispatched by the Eighth was 86. It was assumed, therefore, that a force of about 100 bombers would be sufficient to destroy a target about 1000 feet in radius, and that about two-thirds of the missions could be expected to reach and strike their objectives. It was further assumed on the basis of Eighth Air Force experience that about 37.5% of the airplanes in the theater could be dispatched on missions at any one time. That percentage made allowance for airplanes in reserve., in depot repair, and being modified. Contemplating about 19 important operations during each three-month phase, of which 12 were expected to be successful, the heavy bomber force build-up for the U. S. continent called for in the plan was:

1. At the end of the first phase, 30 June 1943 : 944
2. End of the second phase, 30 September 1943 : 1192
3. End of third phase, 31 December 1943 : 1746
4. By 31 March 1944 : 2702

The plan also called for the build-up of the U. S. forces in medium bombers which were to be used in attacks on German airdromes and to aid in the heavy bomber raids by missions designed to divert enemy fighters. It was pointed out that medium bombers would also be required to support combined operations in 1944. The build-up program for the medium was set at:

1. By the end of the first phase : 300
2. End of second phase : 400
3. End of third phase : 600
4. By 31 March 1944 : 800

The plan did not provide a schedule for the build-up of fighter forces. It did, however, call attention to the need for extensive U. S. fighter strength both to protect the bombers and to help reduce the German fighter strength. It also called attention to the necessity for the creation of a tactical air force in the European theater in order to be ready for combined operations in 1944.

This rather complete air plan, which restated the strategic air mission with respect to Germany, listed target priorities, contained a detailed schedule of operations by phases, and provided for the build-up of United

States heavy and medium bombers, received the approval of the U. S. Army Commanding General of the European Theater of Operations and of the Chief of the British Air Staff. The plan was taken to Washington by the Commanding General of the Eighth Air Force and presented to the Combined Chiefs of Staff, who granted approval in May. The Combined Bomber Offensive directive based upon it was issued through the British Air Staff to the Eighth Air Force and to RAF Bomber Command and Fighter Command on 10 June 1943. The directive reaffirmed the strategic air mission as it had been given in the Casablanca directive; it listed target priorities in the light of the then existing strategical situation; it assigned tasks to the British Fighter Command and to the American fighter forces, and provided for coordination of British and U. S. efforts.

Target priorities were assigned to the Eighth under three heads: intermediate, primary, and secondary objectives. The intermediate objective was stated to be the German fighter strength. Calling this an intermediate objective implies that it was something that had to be accomplished before the rest of the offensive could be effectively concluded. It was pointed out that any delay in the attack on German fighters would make the prosecution of the rest of the task progressively more difficult. Enemy fighter strength was to be cut down by attacks on airframe, engine, components, and ball-bearing factories; by area disorganization attacks; by strikes against repair depots and storage parks; and by the destruction of fighters in the air and on the ground.

Primary objectives of the heavy bombers were to be:

1. German submarine yards and bases
2. Facilities supporting the German air forces other than fighters
3. Ball bearings
4. Oil

It was directed that the German submarine yards and bases receive maximum effort whenever tactical and weather conditions precluded attacks on German fighter objectives. The offensive against oil was stated to be contingent upon attacks against Ploesti from the Mediterranean.

Secondary objectives of the bomber offensive were to be:

1. Synthetic rubber and tires
2. Military transport vehicles

The directive called for the British Bomber Command to be employed in the general disorganization of German industry, with all action designed as far as practicable to be complementary to that of the Eighth.

Judgments Concerning the Selection of Targets

Before proceeding with the account of operations in pursuance of the Combined Bomber Offensive directive, it might be well to examine tentatively, in the light of the strategical situation and the intelligence of the enemy available in 1943, some of the questions that have been raised concerning the wisdom of the target selection in that plan.

Basing a judgment upon subsequent events, the giving of high priority to submarine yards and bases as primary objectives might be questioned. We now have the testimony of Grand Admiral Doenitz to the effect that the bombing of these facilities was not very damaging. He declared that the U-boat assembly places were never hit until 1945 and that the turn-around time in the pens was not increased by bombing. Eighth Air Force studies made in late 1942 and early 1943 concerning the effectiveness of bombing submarine installations had already indicated that such action was none too effective. There was great doubt about the vulnerability of submarine pens; in fact a study mad by VIII Bomber Command on 5 December 149 expressed the opinion that none of the U. S. bombs available at the time were capable of penetrating the roofs of the pens from any practical bombing height. Another study on the target value of submarines concluded that because of the cushion of excess productive capacity an attack on components would have at best only a very long-term effect. Submarine yards, moreover, were not considered profitable targets unless the then current sinking rate by air and surface craft could be doubled. "Even total destruction of all yards would produce no decrease in the number of submarines operating in the Atlantic for the 12 months succeeding the destruction. The COA report of 8 March 1945 explained this lag in military results with the statement that the number of submarines under-going trials and nearing completion was sufficient to make good the sinking rate at the time.

This report also said that there was no conclusive evidence that the bombing of bases would substantially reduce the number of submarines operating at any one time.

It seems, therefore, that neither submarine yards nor bases met the tests of a good target for strategic bombing. One must conclude, however, that the U-boat was such a menace in early 1943 that any method that offered any promise at all should have been used. Fortunately, the strategic bombardment of yards and bases was but one of the methods employed against this enemy weapon. The inclusion of the Aircraft Industry in high-priority target position is not open to so much questioning. It is true that testimony of German prisoners of war has indicated that our bombing was not nearly so damaging as we believed it would be or thought it was at the time. The reason seems to have been found in the ability of the enemy to effect dispersal of the industry. Of course, the degree of effectiveness of the bombing as it developed did not to any great extent invalidate the wisdom of selecting the aircraft industry as a target system in 1943. One of the fundamental tasks of an air force is the destruction of hostile air forces by attacks in the air, on the ground, and against all installations which support air cover. The aircraft industry met the economic and military criteria for a target system in 1943 and it would have been a violation of fundamental principles of air warfare not to have given it high priority. Moreover the effects were by no means negligible.

The ball-bearing industry was accorded third priority among primary objectives of the bomber offensive, immediately after submarines and aircraft. Some of the testimony by German prisoners of war seems to minimize the effectiveness of the bombing of this industry also. That its effect was not more marked was due to several factors: the dispersal that was achieved, the ability of the enemy to cut down on the delivery time of the finished product from the factory to the consumer, the fact that in the aircraft industry ball bearings could be replaced by other appliances, and that the German army had accumulated in the vicinity of Magdeburg several months supply for emergency purposes. Allied information on the ball-bearing industry rated it an excellent target system from both the economic and military standpoints. On the basis of American and British knowledge and practice it was believed impractical for the Germans to have accumulated any great stock of bearings. Nearly half the German supply was turned out in three plants around the one city of Schweinfurt, and 10 of the product came from two plants near Paris. The damaging of the ball-bearing industry would be crippling to all other industry which used high-speed moving parts. The bearing industry was too valuable to the German war effort not to have accorded it high priority in 1943.

The information concerning the effect of Allied strategic bombing in Europe that has been obtained from the German prisoners of war indicates that attacks on oil and transportation did more damage to German effort than any other bombing. The target priority list which according to Hermann Goering would have been most effective reads as follows:

1. Synthetic oil
2. Communications
3. Aero-engine factories
4. Airframe factories
5. Ball-bearing factories
6. Airfields

Albert Speer, former German Minister of Armaments and War Production, ranked objectives in order of relative importance from the point of view of armament production. His first two categories were:

1. Key points in the basic industries or supplies.
2. Transport and communications although the effect of attacks on these was long delayed because of the density of the transport network.

Speer said that the attacks on the chemical industry were the most difficult to deal with, and he included synthetic oil production in the chemical industry. The former Minister of Armaments even went so far as to say that the attack on the chemical industry, without the impact of other military events, would have rendered Germany defenseless.

Field Marshal William Keitel rated the destruction of transportation as the most decisive influence in the defeat of Germany, and the demoralization of the Wehrmacht and the nation was of second greatest influence.

General Galland rated the bombing of transport facilities and oil targets in first and second places in his scale of effectiveness. He ranked transportation facilities first because of their direct importance to military operations and war production, oil targets second because of their relation to the function of air and armored forces and military and industrial transport.

There is slight point in introducing further evidence concerning German opinion on the ranking of target systems. Oil and transportation run like a chorus through a considerable portion of their testimony. This raises two questions: why oil was not given higher priority, and why transportation was not included among primary or secondary objectives of the Combined Bomber Offensive Plan. As far as oil is concerned, this amounts to asking why it was not tanked above ball bearings. The oil industry (synthetic and natural) aside from Ploesti was much more dispersed than was the bearing industry. Synthetic production, which accounted for about 31% of Axis output, was scattered among some 13 plants. Only two of these plants were estimated to turn out as much as by each of the total Axis product. One was at Leuna, 570 miles from London, and the other at Ploesti, which was 640 miles from London. It was recognized in 1943 that the German oil position was serious, but it was also known that much a large portion of the Axis requirement was supplied by the refineries located about Ploesti that an attack on this complex would be necessary before attacks on the dispersed synthetic producers would show telling results.

The question of the exclusion of transportation targets from the early phases of the combined bomber offensive is relatively simple. It will be recalled that AWPD-1 (Plan for Bomber and Constituent Units to Arrive in the United Kingdom in 1942), AWPD-42 (the target directive given to the Eighth Air Forces in October 1942), and the Casablanca directive all placed transportation in relatively high priority. Transportation had never been forgotten in strategic planning, nor was it neglected in the Combined Bomber Offensive Plan. One of the chief ends of the strategic mission was to weaken Germany to such an extent that successful cross-channel landing operations could be undertaken by the Allies. It was just before and during such operations that attack on transportation would be most profitable. In the early stages of the CAO before the force war built up and before the timing would help ground forces, the transportation system did not present a telling target. Limited and scattered attacks would do little good because of the ease of repair. There was no small number of points whose destruction would prove decisive. It would be necessary to hit a great many targets within a relatively short time in order to do the enemy the same harm as an attack on one of his other systems would accomplish. The wiser course in regard to this category was to wait until the air offensive was well advanced and combined cross-channel operations were at hand.

Questions concerning the judgment to be made of the target selection for the CBO call for examination of several other systems. One, a question of exclusion, involves electric power. It will be recalled that the 1941 and 1943 target planning included this in high priority. It was not included in the directive of 10 June 1943. Field Marshal Goering, in his interview of 29 June 1945, stated that an attack on electric power had been feared. He also declared that the Germans had planned attacks on 21 power plants in the U.S.S.R. Field Marshal Keitel has stated that an attack on electric power plants, while dangerous, would not have stopped transportation on electric railroads because of the possibility of the switch to steam locomotives. The key to the thinking back of the exclusion of this category from the CBO targets may be found in the COA Report of 8 March 1943. This stated that while German industry as a whole was in large measure dependent on electrical energy for continued operation, in almost no instance was a single industry dependent upon a single plant. It rather depended upon a network which pooled the electrical power within an area. As a bombing problem, then, an attack on electric power resolved itself into the deprivation of a given region rather than an assault upon the whole industry, which was too big and too dispersed to entirely destroyed. There was also some doubt about the vulnerability of electric power plants.

The wisdom of the inclusion as target systems of industries manufacturing rubber, tires, and motor vehicles is evident upon examination of some of the data collected about them in 1943. The German position in rubber at that time was thought to be precarious, since one-third of her supplies was provided by blockade running and the reclamation of scrap, and the other two-thirds by synthetic production. Nearly one-half of the synthetic rubber was turned out by two plants, one at Huls, and these plants were responsible for an even larger fraction of the synthetic suitable for tires.

Tire-manufacturing plants particularly those for manufacturing airplane tires, presented a fine target system from the standpoint of concentration and vulnerability. Four plants located produced practically all the aircraft tires. The destruction of six other plants (including ones in Aachen, Harburg, Clermont-Ferrand, and Munich) was deemed sufficient to deprive Germany of more than 50% of all tires (truck, passenger vehicle, aircraft, etc.) Rubber tire plants were believed to be especially susceptible to incendiary attack. All these factors made the rubber and tire industry too lucrative a target system to be neglected.

The motor vehicle industry well met the tests of military significance, concentration, and vulnerability. Furthermore, attrition was supposed during the winter of 1942-43 to have been twice as great as production. The German vehicle position was such that it was assured that scarcely any vehicles could have been withdrawn from industrial and other uses for the military service. Although there were about 35 truck-assembly and manufacturing plants, it was believed that above 35% of the total truck output was concentrated in seven plants (Ford-Cologne: Opel-Brandenburg; Daimler-Benz, Stuttgart; Matford-Paris; Matford-Bourges; Citroen-Clichy; and Fiat-Turin) four of which were less than 450 miles from London.

On the face of the thing it would appear that any attempt to undermine the economy of a modern industrial nation would involve attacks upon the very foundations of that economy, namely, iron and steel, coke, and machine tools. The conclusions of the COA on these industries as strategic targets are pertinent.

Concerning the steel industry the conclusion was that the Western Axis position was strong and the destruction of one-half the plants would not produce such military effect for more than a year. Moreover, because of their ruggedness of construction the vulnerability of steel plants was not high. The Western Axis was thought to be more vulnerable in high-grade alloy steels, but even here the result of attacks was considered questionable because of the existence of a number of alternate facilities.

Coke ovens were considered vulnerable to air attack, but their number was so great that they did not represent a profitable target for achieving decisive results in the crippling of the German military machine.

The COA conclusion in regard to machine tools was that the industry did not constitute a high –priority target because it lay too deep in the industrial process. There was, however, a recommendation that the plants making machine tools for a particular industry should have a high priority I order to prevent recuperation when that industry was successfully attacked.

2

THE FIRST PHASE OF THE COMBINED BOMBER OFFENSIVE APRIL – JUNE 1943

SIZE OF THE UNITED STATES FORCES

The basic measure of strategic bombardment has been the unit weight of bombs on target. The chief vehicles employed by the Eighth Air Force in carrying bombs to enemy targets were the B-17 and B-24 heavy bombers. The carrying capacity of these aircraft changed somewhat during the course of the 39-odd months the Eighth operated in the European theater, and the number of trips per unit time (sortie rate) also changed, but the quantity of bombs delivered always depended in a definite way on the size of the force of heavy bombers and upon the crews available to fly them.

Behind the sortie rate of the operational aircraft are very many highly important factors which are beyond the scope of this examination of the forces available to the Eighth Air Force for conducting the combined bomber offensive. Here the concern is to be primarily with the size of the force in terms of combat nits in too large for treatment at this time. The aim is to set forth the effective combat strength available to the Eighth during the first three months of the combined bomber offensive, and to make a brief inquiry as to why it was not larger.

The Eighth Air Force had been sent to the United Kingdom in the spring of 1942 as a part of the so-called "BOLERO Task Force." BOLERO was the plan for the build-up of a force in the British Isles which was to launch an invasion of the Continent. This invasion was to be preceded by an air offensive designed to gain the necessary degree of air superiority. After that was accomplished, air forces were to disrupt the German industrial machine by strategic bombardment and to operate in conjunction with ground forces. As long as the invasion of the Continent was planned for the summer of 1943, the Eighth had a definite mission. But a change in plans occurred in July of 1942 when the decision was made to invade North Africa (TORCH project). The Eighth was, in consequence, left without a clear-cut mission for some time, or perhaps it is better to say, with its mission postponed for an indefinite time. Nevertheless, it continued to carry the fight to the enemy as best it could.

The size of the forces available was, of course, adversely affected by the strategical decision. During the last five months of 1942 the Eighth really served as "a giant replacement pool" for the Twelfth Air Force in North Africa. During that time the Eighth dispatched to the new air force more than 1050 aircraft, practically all its organizational equipment, and huge quantities of supplies. It supplied three P-38 fighter groups in October, one heavy bomb group in November, and two in December. In addition it provided training for other Twelfth Air Force groups.

During these last months of 1943 the Eighth never had more than seven heavy bomber groups operating at any one time, and after September it had but one fighter group (Spitfire). Its average number of operational heavy bomber aircraft was less than 100 during every month except December; its average number of heavy crews available was never much above 100; and its greatest average effective heavy bomber strength, attained in December, was only 114. The Commanding General of the Eighth was not exaggerating when he described his command at this period as "our piddling force of Fortresses."

The U. S. air arm in the British Isles had its mission restated in clear-cut terms at the Casablanca Conference in January 1943, but that did not immediately raise the size of the effective forces. During the first quarter of that year there were operational no more than six heavy bomb groups, one fighter group, and one photoreconnaissance group. The effective heavy bomber strength was even lower than it had been during the last quarter of 1942.

The failure of the Eighth Air Force to build up to greater strength was not due to lack of planning by the Army Air Forces. Back of our air strength in Great Britain there was planning of two general types. In the first place, such over-all plans as AWPD-1 (1941) and AWPD-42 had made theoretical calculations of the size of forces necessary to do a certain kind of strategical job against Germany. In the second place, considerable attention was given to the very practical matter of allocating what was available among the various theaters and charting the rate of flow of units and replacements. The Arnold-Towers-Portal agreement of June 1943 specified a definite build-up plan for the Eighth to be achieved by the first of April 1943. In September of 1943 the so-called Peabody Flow Chart set forth a rate of build-up for the air forces in the United Kingdom as well as in other theaters. A variety of other factors governed the flow of aircraft and crews to the Eighth. Over-all strategical decisions, as that to invade North Africa before Western Europe, continued to affect the build-up of force, and demands of the Mediterranean and other theaters were again to draw strength from the United Kingdom. As important as any other factor was the rate of production of aircraft and equipment, and closely parallel to this was the state of training of combat and service units. The limitations of shipping moreover, were constantly threatening to upset any planned flow of units and material to a theater.

Despite these difficulties there was an understandable demand from the European theater for definite commitments. The British wanted a reliable plan for the flow of new units in order that they might prepare the airdromes and accommodations for their reception. The air force commander wanted a chart of the arrival of new units in order that he might plan his operations accordingly. His forces sank to such a low point in February 1943, that he pleaded for just the air echelons of groups even though there was no shipping available for ground echelons. He needed to know the rate at which replacements, particularly crews, would arrive, for these determined the rate at which the old units could conduct operations. The theater commander needed to know the dates on which units and certain types of equipment would be ready in order that he might properly assign shipping priorities.

The AAF expended great effort in the preparation of flow charts for the United Kingdom, both to meet the needs of the European theater and to aid in the planning of allocations to all theaters. During the first quarter of 1943, and even thereafter, they were produced in quantity but all were subject to change without notice and none could be carried out on schedule.

At the Casablanca Conference of January 1943 General Arnold gave to Air Vice Marshal J.M. Slessor, RAF Director of Plans, a table showing the build-up of the VIII Bomber Command for 1943. It had a goal of 39 heavy groups and 10 medium groups, and indicated that the command would be maintained at this strength during 1944. Later in January Air Vice Marshal Foster received from Maj. Gen. George Stratemeyer, U. S. Chief of Air Staff, another chart which forecast the rate of build-up of the Eighth in all types of combat aircraft, but projected the expansion to 30 June 1944, at which time the heavy bomber strength was to reach 45 groups; medium bomber, 11 groups; and fighter, 35 groups. Strength was also forecast for 30 June 1943, and 31 December 1943. According to this chart, heavy bomb groups were to have 48 aircraft per group; medium groups, 64; and fighters, 100. About a month later General Arnold stated that changing circumstances made it impracticable to forecast the flow of aircraft with any degree of accuracy. The Commanding General of the AAF explained that the situation in the Mediterranean theater had occasioned the revisions of the Stratemeyer program of January.

General Eaker complained on 1 March to General Arnold that he was greatly embarrassed in his conferences with the British Chief of the Air Staff by not having accurate figures on the proposed build-up of his air force. General Arnold relied on the 24th with another chart that forecast the flow of all types of aircraft as of 30 June and 3 December 1943, and 30 June 1944. He told the commander of the Eighth, however, that the figures were not sufficiently reliable to be used as definite commitments. They were simply the best estimate that could be made at the time on the basis of the training and activation schedule and the expected availability of aircraft. That was all that any flow chart could be because it was impossible to predict with exactness the rate at which men and airplanes would arrive in any theater.

Another flow chart taken to Europe in April by the Chief of Air Staff, and called in the theater the Stratemeyer Flow Plan, seems to have had more significance during the first phase of operations than any of the others. It evidently was the basis for planning on both sides of the Atlantic until it was amended by the Bradley Plan in May.

The latter plan, named for Inspector General of the Army Air Forces. Maj. Gen. Follett Bradley, was the most significant step taken in the build-up of the Eighth Air Force and deserves somewhat detailed consideration. It had much greater scope than simply the charting of the flow of units or aircraft to the United Kingdom. It made recommendations for fundamental organizational changes in the strategic air force, provided for the organization of a tactical air force, and set up a troop basis for both of them. It had a difficult time in the War Department and was finally approved only after it was out of date. It did, however, serve the theater, the AAF, and the War Department as a basis for planning and therein lies its significance.

The Combined Bomber Offensive Plan which was drawn up in the theater in April 1943 and approved by the Combined Chiefs of Staff in May, provided for the build-up of heavy and medium bomber forces by three-month intervals beginning with 30 June 1943. There was drawn up at the same time by General Eaker's staff a troop basis incorporating the combat and service units for the strategic air force as well as for the tactical air force which was to support the invasion. All the units included in the troop basis were standard War Department units designed to operate in any theater. This troop basis was not accepted because it was believed that in a stabilized theater where bases were located in a highly industrialized nation a considerable saving in manpower could be effected by organizing certain units under manning tables. General Arnold realized that the air build-up plans for the United Kingdom current in April of 1943 called for more personnel (691,051) than could ever be shipped or than would ever be approved by the War Department. On 14 April he sent a cable to General Eaker directing that he initiate a study with the purpose of determining what economics could be exercised and telling him that he was sending General Bradley and two other officers to the theater for the investigation of the same problems.

Somewhat later in the month the Commanding General of the AAF gave definite instructions to General Bradley for his important assignment. The

Air Inspector was to: (1) find whether the ultimate planned strength of 120 groups for the United Kingdom could be operated and maintained with no more than 550,000 personnel, and if that could not be done, to determine what strength could be operated with that number; (2) study certain proposed adjustments in organization and maintenance with the view of incorporating them in other theaters; (3) make an estimate of the operational saturation point of RAF and USAAF numbers in the theater; (4) obtain the preferences of the theater commander concerning the ratio of AAF ground to combat troops; and (5) collaborate with Generals Andrews and Eaker in preparing a troop basis to implement the plan for the bomber offensive.

The Bradley Committee visited a number of typical RAF and AAF installations, interviewed the agencies concerned, and on 23 May made its recommendations which were based upon the following assumptions: (1) that since strategic bombardment was the mission of the Eighth during 1943 and 1944, rapid build-up of the bomber command was necessary to success; (2) that there was to be a separate tactical air force to operate initially from fixed bases in England and eventually from the Continent; (3) that both tactical and service units on a station should be under the group commander, who was to have the assistance of competent air and ground executives; (4) that approved method by which technical control of service functions by the Air Service Command could be accomplished was through the establishment of control areas to operate sub-depots on tactical stations.

Important recommendations were made concerning the organization of the bomber command and the air service command, a troop basis and rate of build-up were set forth for both strategic and tactical air forces, and manning tables were drawn up for a variety of units in order to effect the saving in manpower that had been directed by AAF Headquarters.

The most important organizational recommendation for VIII Bomber Command was that there be activated the administrative units known as air divisions. A recommendation for such units had already been made by the Commanding General of the Eighth Air Force. This departure from the conventional AAF organization was based partly upon the RAF Bomber Command model, partly on the signals arrangements of British Airdromes, and partly upon the need for some decentralization in the administration of so large an organization as the VIII Bomber Command was destined to become. The air division was to consist of five or six combat wings, each of which in turn would be composed of three heavy ground. A heavy bomb group, made up of four squadrons, would occupy a single airdrome. The combat wing was not to have administrative functions but was to be entirely a tactical organization. Thus the VIII Bomber Command was a counterpart of the RAF there the bomber command is divided into groups, each composed of a series of bases, each base controlling three (3) stations with two (2) squadrons on each station with an I. E. [initial equipment] of twenty-four (24) aircraft each.

Other organizational recommendations affecting tactical units were (1) that there be air and ground executives at each station responsible to the station commander who would normally be the tactical group commander, and (2) that station complement organizations (for housekeeping functions) and guard organizations be provided for each station.

Important recommendations of the Bradley Committee also affected the VIII Air Force Service Command. The details of this mater cannot we covered here and need not be since the history of the Service Command is available. The significant recommendation was that decentralization should be achieved in the operation of this command through the creation of subdivisions known as control areas. There was to be a Base Air Depot Area to control the base air depots, an Air Service Strategical Control Area for advance air depots serving the heavy bombardment stations, and Air Service Tactical Control Area to supervise the units serving tactical aviation.

The Bradley Committee recommended that troop allocation for the air forces in the United Kingdom should eventually be:

Strategic Air Force	354,996
Tactical Air Force	330,347
Total	435,843

It was intended that the air force strength should grow during 1943 at the following rate:

Total by 30 June	110,000
Added during third quarter	80,000
Added during fourth quarter	58,000
Total by end of 1943	250,000

Strategic air force units were given priority over tactical units in the planned build-up, which was envisaged during 1943 as:

	June	September	December
Heavy bomber groups	19 ¾	25	38
Medium bomber groups	4	7	9
Light and dive groups	--	1	3
Fighter groups	5	9	16
Night fighter groups	--	--	¼
Photo Recon. Groups	--	½	½
Troop carrier groups	½	4 ½	7 ½
Observation	1	1	3

The so-called Bradley Plan was favorably indorsed by the Commanding General of the Eighth Air Force on 30 May, and by Lt. Gen. Jacob L. Devers, Commanding General of ETOUSA, on 8 June 1943. The plan was promptly approved by AAF Headquarters, and after much study, by the War Department, tentatively on 18 August, and finally on 8 November 1943. The over-all troop basis as finally approved was cut to 407,333.

The Commanding General of the Eighth stated that the Bradley Plan met the organizational and personnel problems of both the strategic and tactical air forces. He felt hat the rate of build-up and the flow of replacement crews and aircraft would permit six to eight maximum missions per month which would enable the Eighth to carry out the task set for it in the CBO Plan. He pointed out that the rate of operations was controlled by the flow of replacements, especially of crew replacements. This was to remain the controlling factor until fairly late in 1943, for the Eighth's position with respect to operational heavy bombers was better than that for available crews until December of that year.

Headquarters AAF set about fulfilling the requirements of the Bradley Plan in June of 1943, some months before it was finally approved by the War Department, and this also thus became the principal guide for the build-up of the air forces in the United Kingdom, even during the summer of 1943.

The fact that the Army Air Forces and the theater had a build-up plan did not mean that unit and replacement flow would follow it automatically. The same matters of inter-theater competition, training and activation schedules, production of equipment, and shipping were still to govern. The question of balance between training and production was very troublesome. In fact, the deficiency of the Eighth in replacement combat crews became so serious before the first phase of the bomber offensive was over that it was to slow down the arrival of new units because AAF Headquarters set a goal of 1 ½ crews per aircraft unit equipment in order to be sure that groups could operate at full strength.

The demands of the Mediterranean theater, which had so depleted the strength of the Eighth in 1943, were again to make inroads during the first phase. Planned in that theater were two important operations which required more heavy bombardment then was than was there available. These were the invasion of Sicily (operation HUSKY and the attack on the Ploesti oil refineries (SOAPSUDS). Although they were not to be undertaken until later in the summer, the presence of the aircraft and crews was required for training. Consequently, the War Department ordered bombs groups scheduled for the United Kingdom, diverted to North Africa, with other bomb groups sent from the United Kingdom. .

Despite the drain of heavy group strength at the end of June, the Eighth had more than doubled its unit strength during the first phase of the bomber offensive. In the matter of operational groups the growth experienced was indicated by the total on hand at the end of each month:

	31 March	30 April	31 May	30 June
Heavy bomb groups	8	6	12	13
Fighter groups	1	3	3	3

The effective combat strength in terms of bombardment aircraft and crews was not so great, however, as the increase in units might indicate:

Daily Ave.	Aircraft (HB)		Crews		Effective
By Month	In Tac. Units	Fully Opnl. in Tac. Units	Asgd.	Avail.	Strength for Combat
March	190	112	151	87	87
April	231	153	187	140	140
May	340	200	318	178	178
June	459	237	419	222	222

An examination of the above table makes it at once evident that the controlling factor in effective strength during all the first phase was the availability of crews and not the maintenance of aircraft. The wide difference between assigned and available crews is explained by the fact that most of the crews arriving in the theater had to undergo a considerable period of training before they were ready for combat.

The growth in personnel during the first three-month phase was more than 150%, the total climbing from 40,860 on 31 March to 101,349 on 30 June. It will be recalled that the Bradley Plan troop basis forecast the growth of the Eighth to reach 110,000 by 30 June.

GENERAL NATURE OF FIRST-PHASE OPERATIONS

The combined bomber offensive was a joint undertaking of the United Staten and British air forces. The plan for the offensive that was drawn up in the theater in April 1943 and presented to the Combined Chiefs of Staff stated that the capabilities of the two forces were complementary. The Eighth Air Force was the racier attacking precision targets by daylight. The RAF was the bludgeon destroying German material facilities and undermining the morale of the German worker. The coordination of the two forces was not left to chance. Moreover, the problem was not simply one of coordinating the efforts of two bomber commands. Much of the fighter support provided for the U. S. heavy bombers during the first phase (April-May-June 1943) was by the RAF Fighter Command. It was necessary to assure the closest cooperation among bomber and fighter commands of both forces and with RAF Coastal Command in connection with air-sea rescue.

The chief agency for coordinating the efforts of the forces involved was called the Combined Operational Planning Committee (CCPC). It was established about April 1943, shortly after the VIII Fighter Command but three groups of P-47's into operation. This committee was composed of representatives of VIII Bomber Command, VIII Fighter Command, RAF Bomber Command, and RAF Fighter Command. After 15 October 1943 the Ninth Air Force representative was included. The committee was charged with the function of planning the operations against major targets. The plans, after completion, were submitted to the commanders concerned, and after approval by the Eighth Air Force Commander, they were given code names and filed at each operating headquarters against future need. When the VIII Bomber commander, at his daily operational conference, selected one of these targets for attack, the code name was immediately passed to all related commands and the operational plan previously prepared was put into effect.

The CCPC received the sanction of the Combined Chiefs of Staff in the directive of 1 June 1943. Certain terms of reference under which this committee was to operate were set forth in an enclosure to this directive which formally launched the combined bomber offensive. Not only was the CCPC given a planning function; it was instructed to "observe critically the tactical execution of these plans and to report to their Commanders of the four commands concerned.

The operations of the combined bomber offensive made full use of the scientific method in the application of air power to destruction, and this subject merits consideration. Air warfare, employing so man of the products of scientific research, might have been quite unscientific in its operations had these operations been controlled merely by the opinions of commanding officers, even though the latter possessed great experience. The Eighth Air Force agency for the scientific study of all phases of air operations was known as the Operational Research Section (ORS). There were, of course, agencies in the United States which mad valuable studies of the tactics of air warfare. The AAF School of Applied Tactics made many contributions to the solution of the problems of the Eighth and other air forces, but the Operational Research Section functioned in the field, secured its data at the sources, and drew its conclusions on the facts as they were found. As General Eaker's report later pointed out, "Operational research was originated in the VIII Bomber Command ... It is composed of a group of scientists who study every phase of our operations and of enemy reaction, catalogue results and draw conclusions. It has now been definitely demonstrated that the studies of this organization are invaluable to air force commanders and that operational research has a staff function and staff agency in modern aerial warfare and fills a requirement not supplied by any other staff section." The results of some of the studies of ORS will presently be examined.

The scale of Eighth Air Force operations during the first phase does not now seem consequential. During the eight months prior to April 1943, General Eakers "piddling force of Fortresses" had engaged in 45 missions, flown 3364 sorties, and dropped 4715.7 tons of bombs on targets. April, May, and June were to see that eight-month record beaten badly on the sortie and tonnage counts. It took but 33 missions (two of there were wholly recalled) during these months to pile up 4267 sorties and drop 6435.4 tons on targets. Yet that first-phase effort was itself "piddling" when command with the over-all achievement of the Eighth During its 33 months of operations against Germany. Even though this effort of the second quarter of 1943 was small when compared with what was to follow, it did constitute the first experience with an expanding force and it did help to make succeeding efforts more effective.

April 1943 was a slack month for VIII Bomber Command, its operations falling considerably short of the record piled up in March. The reasons were two. It has already been noted how small were the effective forces; furthermore, the conduct of operations was greatly hampered by bad weather. During this month there were but four missions flown by the heavy bombers; and on only one of the four (17 April, Bremen) were there as many as 109 aircraft reported attacking the target.

Reasonably good bombing weather and the expansion of the force combined to make May the best month the VIII bomber Command had ever seen. The heavy bombers were out nine days during the month and dropped approximately 2800 tons of bombs on 18 different targets. Three of these were attacked by more than 100 bombers each. The last operation in May (on the 29th) saw the Eighth break all its previous records, for a single day as well as for a month, dispatching 272 heavies of which 239 actually attacked. The May operations cost 6 heavy bombers against claims of 389 enemy aircraft destroyed.

The month of May witnessed also the initial experimental operations of the medium bombers of the Eighth Air Force. The Combined Bomber Offensive Plan had provided for medium bombers as necessary adjuncts to heavy bombers and as a vital factor in the support of combined operations scheduled for 1944.

The first U. S. medium bomb group to become operational in the United Kingdom was the 322d, which had arrived in the theater on 8 March. Before its May effort it was given eight weeks of training in low-level operations. This type of training indicated the tactics that were contemplated to capitalize on the speed and ruggedness of the B-24. Since these tactics were changed after but two missions, it is appropriate to inquire into the reasons for their adoption. In the first place, since mediums were to be used to support surface operations, low-level tactics would be needed, and training in them would be of great value. In the second place, the B-26's were not equipped with bombsights for medium-altitude attack. Furthermore, it was desirable to learn whether a well trained force could utilize the element of surprise on an important objective.

The strategical directives for the Eighth Air Force were delivered through the British Air Ministry, so in March when the commander of the Eighth was planning the operations of the mediums, he wrote to Air Chief Marshal Sir Charles Portal and asked that certain targets in occupied Europe be cleared for attack. These targets required very shallow penetration of the Continent and included airdromes as first priority, marshaling yards, power stations, and port facilities in France, Belgium, and Holland. Mediums were also to be used on targets in Germany.

Air Marshall Portal's reply suggested that the most important matter to consider in planning the operations of the medium bombers was to see that their activities were coordinated with other daylight operations. It was his idea that the Eighth's mediums should give first priority to transportation targets rather than to airdromes. This was the policy of the RAF light bombers, and was in accord with the directives of the Combined Chiefs of Staff. (In March the bomber offensive was functioning under the Casablanca directives which placed transportation targets in third priority.) The change to airdromes against priority for mediums, in his opinion, might prove profitable later if it were decided to shift the main effort of the entire bomber attack to the German Air Force.

Eventually, during the first week in May when the 322d Group was well advanced in its low-level training, certain industrial installations were cleared as freshman targets" for the 34 Wing which contained this medium bomb group.

The objective actually selected for the initial medium mission of 14 May was the power station at Ijmuiden, Holland. The same objective was hit three days later on the ill-fated second operation that finally convinced the Eighth Air Force commander that the low-level technique was not feasible in Western Europe. One intelligence officer of the 3d Bombardment Wing had been convinced of this for many months before the attack. This officer, Major Von Kolnitz, had advised the commander of the 3d Wing in December 1943 that in his opinion low-level attacks on heavily defended targets would be disastrous. Between the 14 May and 17 May missions the same officer made strong representations to the commander of the 322d Group about the dangers of the operation. It certainly would seem, however, that the first attack on Ijmuiden was not a fair test of the ability of the B-26 to surprise the defenses for the RAF had hit it on the 2d and 5th of May.

On the 14 May Mission, 13 B-26's had taken off and 11 of them dropped 10.75 tons of high-explosive bombs from an altitude of between 200 and 300 feet. The bombs employed had 30-minute delayed-action fuses. Apparently very little damage was done to the power station. The one medium that failed to bomb had an engine shot out by flak as it crossed the enemy coast and was forced to return to base. No enemy fighters were encountered, but nine of the bombers were damaged by flak. One ship crash-landed at its base and killed the pilot after the reminder of the crew had bailed out. Since this test was inconclusive, the second attempt was made three days later. Twelve B-26s got out on the 17th, and again one turned back, this time because of engine failure. The attack was again made from minimum altitude employing 30-minute delayed-action fuses. Of the 11 attacking, not one returned, although one of them, badly shot up, was abandoned by the crew near its base. The remainder were lost to flak, ground fire, collision and unknown causes. This was enough to convince the Commanding General of the Eighth that a change in policy for mediums was required:

> The simple truth appears to be that worthwhile targets on the coast of Western Europe are too heavily defended to make low-level attack feasible and economic … . I am now convinced that we must discontinue low-level attack except for that against surface vessels. We have a plan to get some training and experience of the latter category. I am going to put the medium bombers in the Air Support Command and give them maximum training was part of the tactical air force to support any ground forces invading the Continent. Their crews will get their fighting experience by medium altitude attacks heavily defended by fighter aviation. This will necessitate the installation of some bomb sights, at least for lead aircraft.

The 322d Group was removed from operations, and the mediums got no more action against the enemy until July.

June operations by the Eighth fell somewhat short of the record achieved in May, for the weather kept both the USAAF and the RAF grounded during the first 10 days of the month.

The geographical pattern of the Eighth Air Force operations during the first phase of the bomber offensive calls attention to what has been one of the great tragedies of World War II – the necessity of fighting over and destroying so much in territory belonging to peoples who were enemies of the Axis powers. Of the 6,435.4 tons of bombs dropped by United Kingdom-based U.S. heavy bombers during the second quarter of 1943, just slightly more than half (51.4%) fell on Germany. France received 37.3% Belgium slightly more than 10, and Holland the remainder.

Bombardment policy in Allied or neutral territory occupied by the enemy was carefully regulated. Only military objectives (these were narrowly defined) were to be bombed and such bombing was subject to certain principles. The bombing of civilian populations as such was forbidden. The military objective had to be clearly identified and the attack made with reasonable care to avoid undue loss of life to civilians in the vicinity of the target. If doubt existed as to the possibility of accurate bombing, the attack was to be withheld. All Red Cross conventions were observed. Despite the fact that both RAF and AAF took every possible precaution to reduce the risks to civilian populations in occupied countries to a minimum, casualties could not be avoided. The protest of the subject peoples and their representatives to the Allied powers did not make the tasks of the air leaders any easier. They were faced with the fact that many of the facilities in occupied countries were contributing to German war effort, and they had no choice but to attempt to destroy them.

The efficiency of daylight precision bombardment is difficult to assess, but one can hardly study the operational site without becoming aware of the tremendous effort necessary to achieve even a small result. Some notice has already been given to the size of the forces available to the Eighth during the first phase of the bomber offensive, but it must be remembered that only the planes in commission can engage in operations. During April, May, and June more than two-fifths of the heavy bombers were unserviceable because they were undergoing repair, being modified, or awaiting parts. Planes in commission, even planes airborne on operations, are of slight offensive account unless they can get over the target. Of the sorties flown in April, May, and June, only 60 actually accomplished the mission assigned (effective sorties) of dropping bombs in the target area. The question as to the accuracy of the bombing is very difficult, particularly in the early period of operations. The scant evidence available indicates that first-phase daylight bombing accuracy was low, even lower than during the first quarter of 1943. This may have been due in part to the lower level of experience resulting from the sudden expansion of VIII Bomber Command in May.

THE DEFENSE OF THE DAY BOMBER

Presently the effectiveness of first-phase bombardment is to be examined from another point of view, but first one of the most important problems of first-phase operations deserves some attention. As a statement from an Eighth Air Force intelligence report indicated, the U. S. heavy day bomber posed a formidable problem to the German Air Force:

The first operations of Flying Fortress formations in high altitude daylight precision bombing attacks over Europe opened a new chapter in the oldest conflict in warfare. That conflict is the perpetual struggle between offensive and defensive technique. Our Fortresses, as used here, were a new offensive weapon.

Against them the Germans confidently pitted the three-fold mechanism of defense which aerial bombing has itself generated: Radar detection and counter attack by both flak and highly maneuverable heavily armed fighter planes. This defensive technique as developed by both Germans and British was believed to have precluded large scale daylight bombing in this theater forever.

But the Fortress brought to its work two unique features. The first was its ability to operate effectively above the maximum effectiveness of light flak. The second was its formidable armament of .30 caliber machine guns, which, compounded by the mutual support of close formation flying, provided withering air power against conventional fighter plane attack.

It is true that the countermeasures taken against the Fortresses and the Liberators threatened to restore the balance between the offense and the defense which the first operations had upset. The complete redress of the balance would have nullified the bomber offensive. Our air leaders were forced to great efforts in the defense of the day bombers to keep the offensive going. It is necessary to note some of these efforts as they developed during the first phase.

The simplest statement of the problem is presented in the figures for the heavy bombers. The operations of the last five months of 1942 cost 31 heavies missing in action, 26 attributed to enemy aircraft and 5 to flak or a combinations of flak and enemy aircraft; and the first quarter of 1943 saw 59 of our bombers lost on operations. During the first month of the period under review, April 1943, 20heavies were lost; in May there were 69, and in June 85, giving a total of 161 for this first phase of the CBO. Of these losses, 9 were due to the action of enemy aircraft, 98 to flak or a combination of flak and enemy aircraft, and the remainder to accidents and unknown causes.

The rate of loss is more revealing than the absolute loss. Taking these planes that were lost due to combat (lost in action or to operational salvage) as a percentage of planes attacking (completing effective sorties) we find the following:

Last five months of 1942	4.5
First quarter, 1943	7.1
Second quarter, 1943	7.6

Another side of the bomber loss problem is seen in the attrition rate. This considers all kinds of lost aircraft (operational and nonoperational) as a percentage of unit equipment. During 1942 the attrition rate for the B-17's was 3.3% and for B-24's was 2.1%. For the first quarter of 1943 for both types of heavy bombers it was above 7.2% That the attrition rate turned sharply upward for B-17's is evident from the figures for April, May, and June. It is to be remembered that the Fortresses constituted the bulk of the bomber force during this period. Attrition as a percentage of unit equipment was:

	B-17	B-24
April	11.7	5.2
May	16.3	7.3
June	15.9	---

Another measure of the severity of the opposition encountered by the day bombers is found in the amount of battle damage sustained by aircraft which were able to return from missions. During the 1942 operations, 27% of heavy bombers completing "credit sorties" (that is, sorties entering areas where enemy action was normally anticipated) were damaged in varying degrees of severity; in the first quarter of 1943 the rate was 31% and for April, May, and June it was approximately 30.7. That meant that three out of every 10 heavy bombers entering enemy territory were damaged.

Loss and damage figures can be interpreted in various ways. "The Statistical Summary of Eighth Air Force Operations in the European Theater, 17 August 1942-9 May 1945" and various studies by the Operational Research Section are excellent sources for these figures. The interest here is in that these date tell about the intensity of enemy opposition. The evidence indicates that the effectiveness of that opposition was increasing during the first phase of the bomber offensive.

It is evident also that the defensive problems presented by this severe opposition were recognized by AAF leaders and that energetic steps were taken to overcome the formidable efforts of the Germans to halt the day bomber offensive.

It had been noted that the three principal German defense were the radar installations for detecting the approach of hostile forces, the German fighter force with its elaborate control system, and antiaircraft artillery (flak). Since the principal defensive efforts of the Eighth during the first these were concerned with fighters and antiaircraft fire, those measures will be considered here. Radar countermeasures are treated in connection with the third phase when they were first used.

The plan for the bomber offensive which was drawn up in the European theater in April called attention to the growth of the German fighter force and the changes that had taken place in the composition of that force. The GAF was increasing its fighters at the expense of other types, and it was concentrating these on the Western Front at the expense of other theaters. Both these trends were to continue for many months.

The German fighter force was not only increasing its numbers and concentrating then against the bomber offensive; it was improving its standard pursuit tactics and even making some rather startling tactical innovations. Two of these innovations began to appear during the first half of 1943. The first was air-to-air bombing, both dive and level, by individual planes and in formation. Apparently the first use of this tactic against the Eighth's heavy bombers was on 16 February 1943, in a mission against St. Nazaire. Reports of its use were made in March, and the four April heavy missions encountered it. Air-to-air bombing was met on at least nine missions in May and several times in June. This German measure was never successful because of the great difficulty of insuring the detonation of a projectile at just the right instant sufficiently near a rapidly moving target. Undoubtedly the reason for its use was that the size of the lethal burst of a bomb was very great – perhaps six times as large as that of the best flak.

The other new tactic of the German fighters which was initiated during the first phase was the employment of 21-cm. rockets by both FW-190's and Me-109's. Their use was first reported positively on 21 May 1943 during the raid on Wilhelmshaven, but there is some evidence that they were used earlier. The danger to the heavy bombers from the rocket projectiles lay in the fact that the rocket gun could be carried to 35,000 feet by either of the enemy's two best single-engine fighters, and once at that altitude could fire an 80-pound shell very accurately at ranges well beyond those of the .50-caliber machine guns carried by U S. bombers. Another great danger from the rocket projectile lay in the fact that it had a lethal burst of 150 feet and its detonation could be well controlled.

The greatest danger from enemy fighters during the first half of 1943 was not due to these innovations but to improved pursuit tactics and that these fighters were armed with larger caliber guns. During 1943 there were 40 cannon hits for every 100 machine-gun hits; during the first half of 1943 there were 77 for every 100 machine gun hits. The hits by heavier guns helps to explain the increased loss rate of bombers to fighter action. The damage rate due to enemy fighters became particularly formidable during the first two months of expanded VIII Bomber Command operations (May-June 1943) than more than 15 of the bombers crossing into enemy territory were damaged by fighters. This was approximately one and one-quarter times the rate for all operations prior to May.

An indirect product of damage from enemy aircraft was self-inflicted damage to the heavy bombers. This was caused both by the guns on the damaged planes and by guns on friendly planes in the same or near-by formations. This category of battle damage became prominent first in May 1943. On missions 55 through 60, carried out between 13 and 21 May, 24 of 125 aircraft damaged by machine-gun fire were reported damaged by their own guns. Most of the self-inflicted battle damage came from empty shell cases falling from higher planes. Most of the self-inflicted machine-gun fire damage occurred to B-17's and was caused by waist gunners firing into the horizontal stabilizers and elevators on their own planes.

The other German weapon for combating the day bomber was flak. Although the damage rate from flak was higher than from enemy fighters, the damage from the forger was generally less severe. It was often true, however, that flak damage was a contributing factor in many cases of aircraft reported lost to enemy aircraft, for an initial hit by antiaircraft frequently caused a bomber to straggle behind its formation and make it easy prey for fighters. All important German targets were heavily defended by flak; these included the submarine yards and airdromes that were the particular targets during the first phase of the offensive. In France, the most heavily defended areas were around Paris and St. Nazaire, both of which were attacked by the Eighth during the second quarter of 1943.

Defense of the day bomber involved both materiel and tactical developments. Two of the more outstanding materiel problems that demanded attention during the first phase were the modification of the heavy bomber to increase fire power and the development of escort for the bomber formations.

During the early months of the bomber offensive certain complaints were voiced against the armament of the heavy bombers. The most serious was that the forward fire power was entirely inadequate. B-17d's and F's came to the European theater with a single hand-held .39-caliber center nose gun or with no center nose gun at all. B-17E's had no side nose guns and some F's had two hand-held side nose guns. B-24D's generally had one . 50-caliber gun in the nose. Such armament was not a sufficient deterrent to the German fighter armed with 30-mm. cannon.

When Marshall Goering was interviewed as a prisoner of war, he said that tail attacks on the day bombers were preferred to head-on attacks because the closing-in speed involved in the latter allowed too short a firing time. Tail attacks were the rule during the period from August 1942 to November 1942, but head-on attacks predominated in December 1942, and during the whole first half of 1943. The evidence is quite clear, and it was recognized in the theater at the time.

Modifications were performed on the heavies throughout the first half of 1943 in order to increase their forward fire power. On the B-17's either one or two .30-caliber guns with ring-and-post sights were installed in the center nose section. On B-24's an additional .50-caliber nose gun was mounted.

These hand-held guns were the best answer the Eighth found to the problem during the first phase. They were recognized as a temporary measure, for the manufacturers of the B-17 were working on a power-driven chin turret for the aircraft. Turrets possessed several advantages over hand-held guns in field of fire, accuracy, and fire power per gunner. Since the chin turret was not expected until late in 1943, another temporary experiment in the form of a reworked Bendix lower turret was tried out during the first

phase. An airplane with one of these experimental turrets arrived in the theater on 27 June and was given thorough tests. The preliminary results indicated some superiority over the hand-held guns, but combat tests proved
the later better. The reworked turret would not react quickly enough on
simultaneous attacks from several directions. Orders were given from Headquarters, AAF to stop installation of the makeshift lower turret and to continue with the development of the regular chin turret. Meanwhile it should
be remembered that the chief dependence for forward fire cover by heavy
bombers during the first phase was upon the hand-held .50caliber gun pro-
vides with direct sighting. Other armament modifications were performed
on the heavier but those designed to increase forward fire power seen most
significant.

Coupled closely with the effort to increase the firepower of the bomb-
carrying heavies was the attempt to convert a member to an escort cruiser
by substituting fire power and armor for bomb-carrying capacity. In the
spring of 1942, Maj. Gen. Carl A. Spaatz had speculated on the possibilities
of such an aircraft: "Auxiliary (expendable) tanks offer the only immediate
solution for extending the range of fighters, unless it can be developed that
the bomber, with its fire-mover, can substitute ammunition for bomb-load
and act as an accompanying fighter. The escort cruiser which was developed
– a heavily armed and armored B-17 – was designated the XB-40. This craft
had the chin turret, upper turret, ball turret, direct-sighting power-boosted
twin .50's on each side of the waist, twin .50's in a Martin electric upper
turret in the radio compartment, and twin .50's in a power-boosted tail gun
mount with reflector sights. It carried 40,000 rounds of ammunition. General Eaker was quite interested in the development and in mid-March 1943
expressed a desire to try it out against the Germans, but at the same time
voiced doubt about the economy of taking bombers that did not carry
bombs on combat missions. In the operating groups there was more enthu-
siasm for the escort airplane, particularly for the chin turret which was one
of its most promising features.

In mid-April, when the German fighters were concentrating on the lead
formations of his bomber forces, the Eighth's commander became very anxious to get some of the YB-40's as quickly as possible. He was told that 13

YB-40's were to be sent to the United Kingdom just as soon as the crews had completed their gunnery training.

These heavy cruisers arrived in the theater in the first part of May and most of them were assigned to the 92d Bomb Group (II). After additional training and modification they embarked on their first mission on 29 May, when seven were dispatched to St. Nazaire. The initial dictated the necessity for modification of waist and experience tail gun feeds and ammunition supplies, and indicated the basic defect of the craft, which was its inability to keep up with normal B-17's – especially after the latter had dropped their bombs. Modifications were complete by 15 June, and YB-40's took part in five missions during the last half of the month. On the 22 June raid on Huls, 11 were dispatched and one was lost. On the 25th, only four of the seven dispatched were able to accompany the formations to Northwest Germany. Five took off on the 26th, but not one was able to complete the attack. Their record was better against St. Nazaire on the 23th, when all six dispatched completed the mission. The mission to Le Mans on 28 June found the two that were dispatched abortive.

Although the YB-40's were to see further action in the theater, the June experience was sufficient for the Eighth's commander to form an adverse judgment on this version of the escort cruiser. His report condemned it because it had different flight characteristics (it was tail-heavy) and was so much heavier than the normal B-17 that it could not fly formation with them. And 40's had been tried in their own formations and on either side of the lead ship in a combat wing, but in neither case were they successful. The crews of the YB-40's did not like the planes because they had to occupy the hot spots in the formation and because they carried no bombs. General Eaker was strongly sold on one feature of the YB-40 – the chin turret – which was presently to be placed on all operating heavies. He did not entirely condemn the whole idea of such an escort, but the June experience convinced him that such a craft required two features that the 40's did not have: the ability to carry bombs and the same flight characteristics as other bombers.

At the same time that the development of the heavy escort was taking place, attention was given to the build-up of a fighter force and the extension of the range of our fighter craft for escort purposes.

The fighter situation in the Eighth Air Force during the first quarter of 1943 was pitiful. It has been noticed that three P-38-equipped groups had been sent from the Eighth to the Twelfth Air Force in October 1942. Four additional fighter groups were trained by the Eighth for the North African theater during the last part of 1942. There was but one operational group left to the Eighth and that was the 4th ("Eagle") Fighter Group, equipped with Spitfires. This situation prevailed until 3 April 1943, when three groups became operational. These three (4th, 76th, and 56th) were all using the P-47 Thunderbolt at the time. The 4th first had had some P-47's assigned to it in January, and was converted to this craft in March. The 78th camp to the theater equipped with P-38's but was presently reequipped with the P-47. The 56th came to the United Kingdom on 13 January 1943, already out-fitted with the Thunderbolt. The tardiness in getting the P-47 into operation was due partly to radio and mechanical difficulties in the aircraft and to the necessity for "selling" it to the pilots. Moreover, the Fighter Command had to proceed cautiously, for it did not want to run the risk of a serious setback in making a new airplane operational.

Three operational groups of fighters were all the Eighth had during the first phase of the bomber offensive. Although the 353d Group arrived in the theater in June, it did not become operational until August.

Inquiry as to why VIII Fighter Command was no better off in the early part of 1943 is not very profitable. Inter-theater competition drained the groups away and there seems to have been some weight of opinion that the B-17 could carry out daylight operations without escort. The CBO Plan had provided no build-up rate for fighters as it had for bombers, although it had called attention to the need for the latter craft. General Bradley, chief author of the build-up and troop basis for the Eighth, had made the assumption that strategic bombing would generally be unsupported by fighters because of the fighters' deficiency of range. Whatever the reason, VIII Fighter Command was sadly lacking in planes all during the first phase.

The realization that they were needed, however, became strongly impressed upon the minds of the air force leaders on both sides of the Atlantic. The attrition and damage figures were easy to read. In April the Commanding General of VIII Fighter Command expressed the need for 30 groups and the opinion that opposition to the bomber offensive would grow heavier unless the German fighters were neutralized by an American fighter force. The German fighter tactics of concentrating against the bombers during the bombing run made it clear that protection would have to go all the way to the target. This was set forth by Assistant Secretary of war for Air Robert A. Lovett after a trip to the United Kingdom in June. He declared, "The greatest single factor differentiating the 8th AF operations from those in other theaters is the extremely high proportion of battle damage resulting from combat with the best German fighters ... . There is an immediate need for long range fighters. This may be met by tanks for the P-47s for now but ultimately P-38s and P-51s will be needed."

The story of increasing fighter range by use of drop tanks is well covered in the histories of VIII Fighter Command and VIII Air Force Service Command. Here all that is necessary is to note the progress that was made in this development during the first phase of the bomber offensive. Expendable tanks were not a development of the European theater, but had been used for some time for ferrying purposes. One of the first tanks used by the P-47 was a 200-gallon-capacity paper ferry tank. The tests which were made on this tank in March 1943 were only partially satisfactory because fuel could not be extracted above 20,000 feet. Moreover, its structure was much that it was not capable of pressurization, and it was not good aerodynamically. However, the range of the Thunderbolt could be extended by using fuel from this tank while climbing to altitude. Such tanks were employed on the first escort mission in which VIII Fighter Command used droppable tanks. This event did not take place until 28 July.

Besides the test on the 200-gallon ferry tanks, there were two other developments in the expendable tank problem during the first phase. One was the testing and provision for procurement of a smaller paper tank of British design. VIII Air Force Service Command's maintenance division designed a steel tank which was approved by Fighter Command on 29 May. British agencies were asked to manufacture these, but because of production difficulties, the British proposed the substitution of 103-gallon paper tanks which could be pressurized and which had been successfully used on the Mustang. Tests were run on the tank and it was officially approved by the Fighter Command on 26 June. The British began delivery of this tank on 13 July. The third development in the range-extension problem was experimentation with a variety of metal tanks raging in capacity from 75 to 150 gallons. All these were capable of leak-proofing and pressurization but required the installation of certain fixtures on the P-47. Although the solution to the fighter range problem was not reached during the first phase, the need for extending the range was thoroughly realized and progress in design and production was made on both sides of the Atlantic.

The fighter protection given to the heavy bomber operations during the first phase was provided by both RAF Fighter Command and VIII Fighter Command. As a matter of fact, the latter was under the control of RAF Sector Controller until 30 June 1943. All four of the April missions of VIII Bomber Command were given fighter support by Spitfires of the RAF.

The first escort of heavy bombers by P-47 Thunderbolts was furnished on 4 May during the mission against the Ford and General Motors plants at Antwerp. On this mission six squadrons of P-47's and six of RAF Spitfires were used. The Bomber Command described the support as excellent and attributed the mediocre enemy fighter opposition to the presence of the P-47. During May and June the Thunderbolts escorted the day bombers on at least five other occasions. The other operations of VIII Fighter Command consisted of sweeps, or forays into enemy territory, and diversions designed to give indirect support to the heavies. The P-47's flew 4727 sorties in 31 operational days during the fires phase and about 30 of them were in support of heavy bombers.

Defense against enemy fighters involved tactical deployment of bombers as well as material developments. Principal tactics were the use of the formation, the diversion, and the feint.

The formation as a defensive measures witnessed much experimentation and development in the ETO in 1943. In the early operations bombing was done by elements of three aircraft in formation and later by squadrons of six. The intensity of enemy fighter attacks forced the bringing together of more aircraft to secure mutual fire support. From January to April 1943 the formations flown were boxes of 12 to 14 aircraft rather widely spaced. The formations were generally loosely flown, for individual evasive action was encouraged. After May the basic group formation was a combat box of 18 to 21 aircraft flown much more tightly than in the earlier period. Such a box ideally flown would occupy 1,200 feet in altitude, 900 feet in breadth, and

600 feet in trail. Actually it was always much larger in breadth and trail. Two or three combat boxes stacked together constituted the combat wing. Experience indicated that three groups was the maximum number that could be practically flown together in a defensive formation. The combat wing was not maintained during the bombing run, since bombing was done by groups. After bomb release the combat boxes would reassemble for support on the route to base.

Formation flying required great skill on the part of the pilots, and the Eighth constantly emphasized the necessity for better training in this specialty at operating altitude. The use of group bombing also influenced another aircrew position. One or two bombardiers in a group became very important because generally all planes released bombs on one sighting operation, that of the bombardier in the lead aircraft. Others simply toggled their bombs on his signal.

The diversion as a defensive tactic was employed by both fighters and bombers. The chief defensive value of the diversion lay in its proper timing to attract enemy fighter action to itself from the main bombing effort of the day. The diversionary force was at times dispatched ahead of the main effort in order to arouse the enemy ahead of time, have him use up his fuel, and so find his fighters grounded when the main attack was delivered. It was also dispatched after the main effort had gone out in order to lessen enemy pressure on a withdrawing force. The diversion was employed at least five times by VIII Bomber Command and several times by VIII Fighter Command during April, May, and June. During the raid on the Erla aircraft plant at Antwerp on 5 April, a force of 25 B-24's conducted a diversionary sweep over the North Sea and toward the French and Belgian coasts. This measure brought up no fighter opposition, but a similar venture on 4 May was highly successful. On that occasion the bombing objectives were the Ford and General Motors plants at Antwerp. Seventy-nine B-17's were dispatched on the main effort and 20 B-1's and 13 B-24's were dispatched on a diversionary feint toward the French coast. The diversion as well as the main effort was provided with fighter cover. The feint attracted more than 100 fighters (about half the Germans had in the region) and kept many of them airborne so long that they could not attack the main effort. The principal force encountered out 30 enemy aircraft.

VIII Fighter Command engaged in diversionary indirect support of heavies even before it undertook direct close support. On the 17 April raid against Bremen, 76 P-47's carried out a sweep of the Holland coast while the bombardment mission was in progress.

The diversion not only had defensive value; it gave excellent training to participating air crews. The bomber diversion was but a variation of what has been called the "split-target" technique. This involved the dispatch of strong forces to several different objectives at the same time, thus causing the enemy to disperse his forces. Although practiced during the first phase, the best use of the tactic had to await the build-up of the Eighth to greater strength.

Another defensive variation of the diversion was the feint or fake by the main attack force toward one target with a sharp turn toward the intended objectives at the last moment. Route to and from the target was not left to the groups but was carefully prescribed by higher headquarters.

Except for radar countermeasures, the defensive tactics against flak were fairly well developed by the time of the first phase. These involved selection of operating altitude and route, reduction of bombing run, control of the number of groups bombing together, and evasive action. Further protection from flak was provided by armor plate and the development of special flak curtains and flak suits for crews.

Bombing altitude of heavy bombers during the first phase was generally above 20,000 feet. The lowest reported bombing altitude was 19,000 feet on the Le Mans mission of 20 June, and the greatest, 27,590 feet during a June raid against northwest Germany. Although it is not possible to state an average, it is safe to say that most of the day bombing was from about 23,000 feet. This was high enough to take the planes out of the range of the enemy's light flak. Bombing altitude, as is the case with many other operational policies, was a compromise. Much better bombing accuracy could have been achieved and many operational problems could have been eased at lower levels. On the other hand, the damage from heavy flak could have been greatly decreased by operating at greater altitudes. The Commanding General of the Eighth stated that the reasons for not going higher were that above 25,000 feet increasing difficulties were experienced with oxygen equipment and with propeller and supercharger action. Operations above

20,000 feet brought to the Eighth a host of problems connected with oxygen, electrically heated flying suits, machine guns, and the functioning of internal combustion engines. Many of the complaints in the United Kingdom about the lack of training of new crews and replacements were due to the altitudes to which the enemy forced operations.

Intelligence and antiaircraft officers played a prominent part in the planning of routes designed to avoid as much flak as possible. With the enemy's chief emplacements known, not only the best route from base to target could be selected but the best angle of final approach could be charted. Angles of approach and departure were determined by calculating the effectiveness of all possible AA batteries along each 30-degree direction about the target. Charting of such courses became a very important and exacting portion of mission planning. Likelihood of flak damage was also diminished by making the turn along the predetermined axis of attack at the last moment and the production of the bombing run to the shortest possible time commensurate with accurate bombing.

The common method of AA fire control used by the Germans were the predicted barrage and the continuous-following method. In the predicted barrage each gun fired at a particular spot in the sky through which the formation is due to pass; hence the Allies sought protection from barrage fire by increasing the spread of the entire formation in altitude and breadth. Protection from continuous-following fire control was secured by closing up the units in trail and thus saturating the enemy's flak defense at a particular time. This tactic reduced the risk to any single unit.

Various types of evasive action were taken by the bombers to reduce the likelihood of hits by flak. One was a change of altitude by at least 1000 feet on the approach to the bombing run or after bombs were released. Another was the making of irregular changes in course of at least 20 degrees every 20 to 40 seconds except on the bomb run. Such tactics gave protection because of the tracking time necessary in continuous-following fire control and because of the time required for a projectile to reach operating altitude.

In addition to protection offered by armor plate, further protection was given to air crewmen by the development of flak suits and flak curtains which were capable of stopping low-velocity projectiles. In the autumn of 1943, an analysis of the wounds to crew members on combat missions had showed that 70 were due to missiles of relatively low velocity. The Surgeon of the Eighth Air Forces, Col. Malcolm Crow, was of the opinion that many of these wounds could be prevented by body armor. As a result of researches by the medical department and by the British, had the Wilkinson Sword Company of London make up simple suits of body armor. These were made of laminated (20 gauge) manganese steel plates 1/16 inch in thickness, approximately two inches square, which overlapped 3/8" on all sides. This armored suit covered the vital parts of the trunk, and was designed with a quick release mechanism to facilitate removal in case the wearer was required to abandon the aircraft. The armor as used formed a loose fitting outer garment which weighed about 20 pounds. By the end of May enough of these were being manufactured in the theater to outfit some 30 Heavy crews, and orders were to be placed in the United States for additional quantities.

Defensive measures and devices constantly called for the best efforts of air leaders. That these efforts brought forth both makeshift and very clever contrivances is already evident. Subsequent defensive developments will be taken up as they appeared in later phase of the offensive.

DAY OPERATIONS IN ACCORDANCE WITH CBO TARGET SYSTEMS

During most of the second quarter of 1943 the bomber offensive was conducted under the Casablanca directive of 21 January 1943. This had made submarine construction yards the first-priority target system. The directive had also called for experiential attacks on submarine operating bases on the French coast in order that an assessment of their effectiveness might be made. The January directive made the German aircraft industry second priority, transportation third, oil plants fourth, and other war industries fifth.

After 10 June 1943 the Eighth Air Force operated under the Combined Bomber Offensive directive issued on that date. As has been noted above, this had given submarine yards and bases first priority along primary objectives; but another target system, consisting of the German fighter forces and their supporting installations, was given even higher rating by calling these an intermediate objective of first importance. After the German fighter force installations and submarine yards and bases, the 10 June directive called for attacks on the remainder of the aircraft industry and on production of ball bearings, oil, synthetic rubber and tires, and military motor transport, in that order.

It was the policy of the Eighth Air Force, commanded by General Eaker, and of VIII Bomber Command, under Brig. Gen. Newton Longfellow until the end of the first phase (1 July 1943), to attack CBO targets at every opportunity. The working out of this policy was controlled to a considerable degree by weather conditions, particularly those prevailing in target areas. When Bomber Command was ready to run a mission, the first step called for a check on Continental weather to determine the areas available for operations. That known, the highest priority target or targets were selected within the open regions. This decision was usually reached the afternoon preceding the day set for the operation. The commanders of wings (later called divisions) were notified of the operational decision and told target designations by code numbers. Bomber Command then issued the field order, which usually reached the wings in the early evening. The field order left some details to be filled in by the wing commanders. These were supplied by their orders to group commanders. The groups kept a file of target folders (such target designated by a code number) in which all pertinent information was kept up to date. Using this information and that supplied by the field order, the antiaircraft, intelligence, weather, and other staff officers could immediately make final preparations for briefing the participating crews before the take-off next morning. All the dramatic details of briefing, take-off, assembly, flight to target, return, and interrogation have been told and pictured too many times to need attention here.

Submarine Installations

The Eighth was not expected to make deep penetrations into every territory during the first phase. More than half of the German submarine construction was done in yards that were more than 400 miles from British bases, but about 32% of building capacity was located at Emden, Bremen, Wilhelmshaven, and Bremerhaven could be reached by flights of less than 400 miles. Hamburg and Kiel, two of the most important German cities in the German U-boat industry, were both outside that range, as were Flensburg and Lubeck, cities of lesser importance.

Of the principal operating bases on the Bay of Biscay, Bordeaux at 470 miles and La Rochelle at 450 involved more than a 400-mile range. St. Nazaire and Brest could be reached by shorter flights of 300 to 370 miles.

Submarine yards and bases absorbed more than 69% of the AAF effort during the first quarter of 1943, but during April, May, and June only slightly more than one-half the tonnage of bombs dropped fell on these installations.

In general, high-explosive bombs were used against yards, bases, and port areas. However, some incendiary bombs were employed against building yards. The most commonly used high-explosive bomb against yards was the 500-pound variety, although some 100-pound missiles were used. The bases with their thick concrete pens called for heavier munitions. Two-thousand-pound bombs were employed.

In April there were two small-scale attacks made on French ports, Lorient and Brest, both on the 16th of the month. Fifty-nine out of 83 Fortresses dispatched raided Lorient, doing some damage to a power station and other facilities. Liberators were used in the attack on the port areas of Brest. This small force, which served as a diversion for the main operation of the day, was hindered in its bombing by a very effective smoke screen. The B-24's were escorted by RAF Spitfires on both penetration and withdrawal. The bombers encountered from 10 to 15 single-engine enemy fighters and the escort about 20. The B-17's on the Lorient raid encountered 20 to 25 fighters, some of which attempted air-to-air bombing.

During the first half of May two attacks on U-boat installations were achieved. The latter raid to Kiel combined Fortresses and Liberators (125 attacked) in the deepest penetration American bombers had made up to that time. The long trip (430 miles) to Kiel was completed without escort and aroused intense fighter opposition both to and from the target. The enemy attacked the bombers from all directions with machine-gun and cannon fire and tried aerial parachute bombing. These enemy aircraft and moderate to intense flak brought down nine heavies, five of them B-24's. The weather conditions were excellent, and the bombing was the most successful accomplished by the Eighth to that date despite the strong resistance.

The last half of May saw the bomber war on the submarine increase in size and weight. On 17 May good weather in western France enabled the heavies to strike hard blows against Lorient and Bordeaux. This was the first American raid on the latter, more distant French port. The Lorient mission was carried out by 118 B-17's of the 1st and 4th Wings. Eighty 1st Wing craft concentrated on the submarine pens and bombers of the 4th Wing put the north power station out of action. The Bordeaux raid was carried out by a small force (34 bombed) of B-24's which swept in on the port from the sea to achieve complete surprise. The lock gates to the U-boat pens were badly damaged.

On 19 May good weather in North Germany permitted 101 B-17's to return to Kiel and a smaller force (56) to hit the U-boat building yards at Flensburg just south of the border. The Kiel raid was not as satisfactory as the one on 14 May, and there is some doubt about which of the three yards was the target.

During the final 10 days in May five submarine targets, including two yards in Germany and three bases in France, were attacked on two operational days. The German yards at Emden and Wilhelmshaven were raided with indifferent success on 21 May by medium-sized forces. On 29 May the Eighth dispatched 273 heavies against a naval storage depot at Rennes, the base at La Rochelle, and oft-bombed St. Nazaire. The latter target called for the big effort of the day with 140 B-17's dropping 277 of the 2000-pound bombs on locks to the U–boat basin, workshops, and various dockside buildings. The results were described as fair. Seven B-40's completed the St. Nazaire mission and withdrawal cover against fighters was supplied by 10 Spitfire and three B17 squadrons.

During June the U-boat construction facilities were attacked on the 1th and 15th. A big force of B-17's (167) hit the Marinewerft at Wilhelmshaven on the 11th, while a smaller force (30) was delivering a blow to the port area of Cuxhaven. Two days later on 13 June, a two-pronged attack was delivered at Bremen and Kiel. Bremen's Beschimay U-boat yards called for the bigger effort (102 B-17's dropped 254 tons) and the Leutsche Werke at Kiel received about 85 tons. The cost of the raids was in inverse proportion to their size, for the Kiel raid stirred up the strongest fighter opposition the Eighth had ever met.

The first-phase attack on submarines was completed, appropriately enough, by the 23 June raid on the St. Nazaire base. A large force (150) of B-17's in two waves dropped 300 ton-size bombs in an effort to destroy the one serviceable lock entrance to the U-boat basin. Strike photographs indicated that the mission was successful.

GAF Facilities

Eighth Air Force operations against German Air Force facilities are thoroughly covered by another AAF Study, The War Against the Luftwaffe, April 1943-June 1944, and these operations are considered here only briefly as an integral part of the first-phase of the CBO. Missions against GAF installations absorbed about one-fifth (21%) of the entire first-phase bomb tonnage dropped by the Eighth and involved attacks on nine operational days. Assembly plants, engine works, repair facilities, and airdromes were included among the GAF objectives.

During April two attacks were delivered, one against the Erla aircraft and engine repair works at Antwerp on the 5th, and the other against the Focke-Wulf assembly plant at Bremen on the 17th. In the Antwerp mission 64 B-17's dropped 245 tons on the Erla works and stirred up a hornets' nest of enemy fighters (50-75) which pressed their attacks halfway across the Channel on the route home.

The enemy fighter reaction to the important brazen mission was twice as severe (150 encounters and cost 16 heavy bombers, four times as many as the Antwerp operation). The Bremen mission was one of the most important of the first phase. The Focke-Wulf assembly plant at this city a major producer of all enemy single-engine fighters and of all the FW-120's. Marshal Goering still remembered the raid in his interview as a prisoner of war in June 1943. The attack was made by 107 B-17's dropping 1000-pound high-explosive bombs. The Fortresses met a prepared defense that seemed to indicate the enemy had advance warning. German fighters concentrated on the bombing run and the ferocity of the air battle is attested by the loss of 15 of the B-17's to fighters (one was lost to flak). The bombers, however, claimed 65 fighters destroyed, 15 probably destroyed. The bombing of the assembly plant was considered successful.

The first June attacks on the facilities of the GAF were not impressive, and it didn't develop too much until late in the month. An airdrome and repair depot were attacked in adverse weather conditions by a handful (13-16) B-17's on the 20th, and a somewhat larger force (39) hit another airdrome the same day. Bomber Command reported the results were negative. Somewhat better results were achieved two days later on another airdrome. Next day, 29 June, B-17's were able to bomb the aero-engine works at Le Mans. Most of the bombs that were dropped did little or no damage.

Rubber

There was but one operation by the Eighth during the first phase on synthetic-rubber production, the 23 June attack on Huls near Becklenhausen in northwest Germany. The plant at this city was one of the two most important synthetic producers and was the source of a considerable portion (1) of axis supply.

The Huls attack was, for the time, a large-scale effort. It involved 11 operating groups dispatching 330 B-17's of which 170 actually dropped bombs on Huls. Eleven of the planes participating in the mission were YP-40's, one of which was lost to flak. Although the Huls raid was the main show for 30 June, the Eighth dispatched two other missions on the same day, one to hit Antwerp and a diversion over the North Sea. The RAF contributed another small diversionary attack on Rotterdam. The diversions, which were strongly supported by AAF and RAF escort, contributed greatly to the success of the main effort by disorganizing the enemy opposition and drawing off a number of his fighters estimated at 180.

The Huls mission was considered a success despite the loss of 15 heavies. It prompted RAF Fighter Commander Sir Trafford Leigh-Mallory to say it opened "a new chapter in aerial warfare."

Motor Vehicles

The Axis industry producing military motor vehicles was right after the production of rubber and tires on the target-systems list in the directive of 10 June 1943. Most of the first-phase effort against motor vehicles took place prior to the issuance of the Pointblank directive, but it was justified under the Casablanca directive which, although it did not specifically name the

vehicle industry as a target category did call for attacks on industries supporting the Axis war effort.

The first blows against motor vehicles were small to medium-sized
efforts against plants in occupied countries. The mission of 4 April against
the Renault-Billancourt works two miles southeast of Paris was the most
important. It involved 6 attacking B-17's, which aroused 75 German fighters
to vigorous resistance and the use of serial dive bombing. This technique
did not destroy any bombers, but other tactics brought down four. The 351
tons placed on the Renault works did severe damage to this facility.

The May operations against motor vehicles were carried out on the 4th
and 14th of the month against the Ford and General Motors truck plants at
Antwerp. The first of these involved 65 attacking B-17's dropping 161 tons
of bombs and was the main effort of 4 May. The small-scale second mission
(23 B-17's) was but one of the attacks delivered on 14 May, which also saw
raids on Kiel, the Courtrai airdrome, and the first B-26 mission of the
Eighth against Ijmuiden in Holland.

On 22 June, 39 B-17's were used to bomb the Antwerp Ford and General
Motors plants and to divert enemy fighters away from the main effort of the
day, which was the bombing on synthetic rubber at Huls. Four days later six
B-17's droped on a motor transport plant at Polsay to wind up the first-
phase attack on motor vehicles.

There were no first-phase attacks by the Eighth on either oil or ball bearings, both of which were high on the priority list. Already noted are the facts
that more than half the weight of bombs during the second quarter of 1943
was on submarine facilities and 21% on GAF supporting installations.
Rubber received? And motor vehicles 9%. Only a little more than 10% of
the effort was focused on other than CBO targets. Even this small diversion
was due to circumstances beyond the control of the leaders of the Eighth. A
mission aimed on 15 May was so hindered by cloud that most of the participating planes bombed targets of opportunity in northwest Germany.
Cloudy weather was also responsible for failure to bomb CBO targets on 11
June, and again on the 25th. On the latter date when the submarine facilities
at Bremen and Hamburg were scheduled objectives, the bombers' crews
showed great persistence in seeking targets and provoking battles with
enemy fighters. Their bombs were dropped on half a dozen towns in north-

west Germany. The fight they sought was provided by 100 to 150 enemy aircraft and the score was 18 heavies lost against claims of 62 enemy fighters destroyed, 11 probably destroyed, and 40 damaged.

The USAAF part of the combined bomber offensive was small during this period, and it neglected two important target systems entirely. Nevertheless it did exhibit strong adherence to its cardinal principle of daylight bombing.

THE RAF ATTACK ON THE RUHR

RAF Bomber Combined operations during the second quarter of 1943 were on a far larger scale than those of the Eighth Air Force. While the Eighth was dropping 6435 tons the RAF bombers, particularly the Halifax and Lancaster heavies, unloaded more than 39,000 long tons (Equals 1.12 U. S. tons) of bombs of which 30,731 long tons hit Germany. Relatively small fractions of the effort were devoted to targets in France and other occupied countries. This great RAF attack was delivered at a cost of 811 aircraft, and 718 of these were lost over Germany.

The RAF bombardment of Germany was facilitated by the use of new navigational aide which allowed reasonably accurate bombing in weather which formerly would have stopped operations. The conquest of weather obstacles made the battle much easier against German night fighters, which found it difficult to operate on some of the nights chosen by the RAF for attacks.

. RAF Bomber Command's air war on Germany was particularly concentrated against three types of objectives in the Ruhr and Rhineland:

1. The industrial centers of the Ruhr valley.
2. The great Rhineland centers of commerce – Dusseldorf and Cologne.
3. Subsidiary targets not primarily concerned with heavy industry but important for the production and transport of other badly needed war materials.

The RAF leveled three strong attacks against Essen during April and May which were designed to finish the destruction that had been started in that city in March 1943. Various industrial and transport centers suffered two heavy attacks in May, which involved nearly 1300 attacking bombers.

Bochum, a coal-producing center was attacked once in May (night of 13-14) and once in June (night of 12-13) by more than 800 aircraft dropping high-explosive and incendiary bombs. Its extensive coke, gas, benzyl, iron, and steel plants were apparently damaged.

One of the most spectacular accomplishments of RAF Bomber Command during the first phase was bombing of dams on the night of 16 May by 19 Lancasters equipped with special mines. The dams controlled the level of the Ruhr River. The breaching of these dams was a severe blow to the water supplies of many Ruhr towns.

Dusseldorf and Cologne, the great cities of the Rhine were both attacked twice during the second quarter of 1943. The first attack on Dusseldorf (22-26 May) employed blind-bombing methods and was not successful. The second (11-13 June) used visual methods and achieved good concentration. The two June attacks against Cologne were made to destroy the progress achieved by the Germans in their attempt to rehabilitate the city since the 1000-plane raid of May 1943 and to round out the RAF Bomber Command's campaign against the Ruhr.

Other towns in this important industrial region attacked during this phase.

Outside the Ruhr and the Rhineland regions the RAF war on Germany included large-scale attacks on Kiel, Frankfurt, Stuttgart, and Stettin in April. Smaller forces hit Rostock and Mannheim during the same month. The Kiel and Frankfurt attacks did not do great harm but Stettin suffered heavily. Both of the two smaller attacks (Rostock and Mannheim) were quite successful. The Manheim raid was made as a diversion for a heavier blow which was designed against the Pilsen plants in Czechoslovakia, on the night of 16 April. This attack on Pilsen and another on the night of 13 May did little damage.

Only twice during May and June did any large force hit targets outside the Ruhr. A formation of Lancasters successfully attacked Friedrichshafen on the way to North Africa. Berlin underwent a series of nuisance raids and was attacked 12 times by Mosquitoes.

THE TENTATIVE RESULTS OF FIRST-PHASE ATTACKS

The assessment of so small a segment of the combined bomber offensive as was encompassed in the second quarter of 1943 can have very little value in the measurement of the part played by strategic bombing in the victory over Germany. An assessment that was made at the time does have value in an operational story, however, for it tells something about what the air leaders who were doing the strategic job believed their efforts were accomplishing.

The best strictly first-phase assessment of the bomber offensive, made shortly after the close of that period, was the work of the British war Cabinet Joint Intelligence Committee, "Effects of Bombing Offensive on German War Effort", dated 22 July 1943. Given here is a brief summary of the effects reported.

The bombing offensive had forced Germany to adopt a defensive air strategy. That strategy involved strong efforts to increase the fighter force and to so distribute it that more than half was employed on the western front at the expense of the Mediterranean and U.S.S.R. fronts.

German aircraft and maintenance facilities suffered very little damage from first-phase attacks. The Eighth Air Force raid on Bremen in April seems to have been partially nullified by a previously effected dispersal.

The judgment of the effectiveness of U-boat yard-bombing was uncertain, but it was estimated that the Germans had been deprived of 12 to 13 submarines, which would show up in decreased output between September 1943 and March 1944.

It was believed that the bombing of submarine bases had caused delay in the sailing of submarines from the Biscay ports, and that valuable stores of ammunition and other supplies had been destroyed. The towns and docks of Lorient and St. Nazaire had been severely damaged, but it was not believed that their concrete-covered submarine pens had been put out of action.

The examination of the results of the attacks on the synthetic rubber plants led to the belief that the targeted plants had been put out of action for several months. This meant a further tightening of an already difficult situation for the Western Axis.

The bombing of Axis motor-vehicle production may have deprived the German armed forces of an output of between 3000 and 5000 motor trucks. This was equivalent to the full motor-transport establishment of three to four infantry divisions.

The RAF heavy attacks on the Ruhr had caused grave effects in the production of solid fuels, iron and steel, and alloy steels. Evidence of falling off in deliveries of Ruhr coal to Italy, to North German ports, and to Berlin was found. Rate of operations in the Ruhr iron and steel industry had been curtailed by the second-quarter bombings. Steel production at the end of June in that region was estimated at 30 of capacity as contrasted with the start of 1943. It was not clear in July that the shortage of steel had affected the armament industry.

The effects of bombing of rail transportation appeared to have caused the enemy to step up his locomotive construction programs. This meant a diversion of some resources from the production of armaments.

Diversion or dislocation of effort was believed to have been one of the very important results of bombing. Prominent examples of diversion were the removal of skilled manpower from other jobs to improve radar and fighter defenses. It was also necessary to keep men from other employment part of the time in order to maintain air-raid protection and fire services at a high level of efficiency.

It was judged that the destruction of housing had caused some decrease in the willingness of the people in heavily bombed areas to hold out. This same kind of destruction was believed responsible for some deterioration in the morale of the armed forces.

This summation of the results of the first-phase offensive is intended to do no more than to describe the estimate of those results as they appeared at the time. There was enough evidence available of "the softening" of Germany to warrant the continuance of the effort and to step up the rate of strategic operations.

3

THE SECOND PHASE OF THE COMBINED BOMBER OFFENSIVE, JULY – SEPTEMBER 1943

ORGANIZATION AND BUILD-UP PROBLEMS

In the proceeding chapter it was stated that the principal guide for the build-up and organization of the strategic and tactical air forces in the United Kingdom was the Bradley Plan. This plan had been drawn up primarily to achieve the maximum economy in the utilization of manpower in the U. S. air forces in the ETO. The plan was promptly approved by the theater commander and by the Commanding General of the Army Air Forces. It was given conditional approval by the War Department in the third week of August 1943 and did not receive complete approval until 3 November, after the end of the second phase of the bomber offensive.

The reason the Bradley Plan failed to secure complete approval by the War Department was that it was believed the plan did not accomplish the purpose for which it was drawn – the cutting down of air force personnel to the smallest number with which the offensive could be carried out. The War Department and the Army Air forces manpower position was such that no single force and no single unit of a force could be staffed fully without taking from some other force or some of other unit.

Specifically the chief conditions set up by the War Department for its approval of the Bradley Plan were:

1. The theater was to requisition only standard number of Organization units, which were somewhat different from the units provided for in the Bradley Plan. The difference between the two was to be supplied by shipping technically trained "fillers" to the theater, were they were to be incorporated into the proper units, which would be reorganized in the theater and reported to The Adjutant General.

2. Certain overhead organizations provided for in the plan were to be eliminated. General Marshall thought that the Eighth Air Force was top-heavy with headquarters. Especially did he object to certain features of VIII Air Forces Service Command organization –namely, the area commands through which the command aimed to decentralize its operations. Under the Headquarters of the Service Command were the Base Air Depot Area Commands for controlling the three base air depots, and the Strategic Air Depot Area Command for supervision of the depots serving heavy bomber stations, and the tactical Air force. The War Department believed that the base air depots and the strategic depots could be supervised from the VIII Air Force Service Command headquarters. Only the Tactical Air Service Area commanders approved at first, probably because this organization was designed to become the service command for the tactical air force when it assumed its separate existence.

3. The troop strength figure of 485,543 set up in the plan was accepted for planning purposes only. The War Department did not commit itself to this figure but rather reserved judgment in order to determine whether it could be whittled down.

Theater dissatisfaction with conditions laid down by the War Department was strongly expressed. The organization of the various area commands had already been set up as provided by the Bradley Plan without waiting for War Department approval. The recommendation for the elimination of certain parts of a going organization was resented as unnecessary thrift by people who were too far removed to understand the problem. The Commanding General of the Bradley Plan actually nullified it, for it was regarded as an integrated whole. It was felt in the theater that the elimination of the strategic and base depot control areas was unsound, for there was as much reason for them as for the tactical control area which was approved. The opinion in the VIII Air Force Service Command was that the failure to secure unconditional approval definitely hindered the improvement of its maintenance and supply functions.

Eventually the Air Force got its way in the matter of the service command organization. The control areas, which were not strictly geographical regions but really functional subdivisions, had been provisionally approved on 1 August, and were somewhat more formally launched on 4 September, after General Marshall stated that the War Department accepted the Bradley Plan as an "integrated whole." In the theater this statement was taken to mean that the earlier conditions were withdrawn. Although this theater interpretation of the statement of the Chief of Staff went somewhat beyond his intentions, apparently no further objections were raised and the control area commands carried out their supervisory functions long before they were finally sanctioned in November.

The functional organization of VIII Air Force Service Command was but one of the problems in the implementation of the Bradley Plan. One of the important parts of that program was a schedule of the flow of combat and service units into the United Kingdom. This schedule proved impossible to fulfill in either category.

In the matter of combat units it was found necessary during the third quarter of 1943 to postpone the sending of four heavy groups and six medium groups because the AAF training program could not meet both the demand for replacement combat crews and the scheduled flow of new units. Some attention has already been given to the problem of replacement crews. Shortage of these constituted the chief limiting factor on the rate of heavy bombardment operations during most of 1943. During the phase under review in this chapter the problem was not principally by two measures. The crews of about six groups in the United States that had been trained in the ZI were converted to heavy bombers, and four new heavy

groups scheduled for the United Kingdom during the summer were withheld in order that their crews might be used as replacements for groups
already in the theater. In July the AAF goal for heavy crews had been set at
two per airplane assigned to the ground, with a sufficient flow of replacements to care for a 24% attrition rate per month. Meeting this goal was such
a difficult task that the scheduled flow of new heavy units could not be met
until after 1 October.

The problem of meeting the Bradley schedule of service units was even
more difficult than that pertaining to combat units and replacement crews.
It was the opinion in the War Department that the build-up plan called for
an excessive number of service units. It seemed also that these generally
arrived in the theater in the wrong order. Air echelons of combat units
would arrive first, and somewhat after them would come the service elements designed for their support. This practice places a very heavy burden
on the service forces already in the theater, for they had to do double duty.
The build-up of service units had lagged so far behind schedule in August
1943 that General Marshall's office made it the subject of a special memorandum for the Commanding General of the Army Air Forces. The latter
was told: "It is desired that positive and immediate action be taken to eliminate this deficit and bring into balance the AAF program for Tactical
Service units and combat units. If this cannot be accomplished by other
means at your disposal, the activation of additional combat units will be
deferred until the structure of the AAF is balanced."

The lack of balance between service and combat units was due to a
variety of factors. Shortage of personnel and training equipment slowed
down the training program and shortage of shipping delayed the dispatch to
the theater. Combat units usually had higher priority on the shipping lists
than service units and consequently arrived in the theater first. Even when
supporting units were not available or when there was no shipping to transport them, leaders in the theaters were reluctant to stop the flow of combat
units simply to preserve balance. They preferred to have their forces
increase as rapidly as possible and to resort to improvisations to support
them.

In the Eighth Air Force the unbalance was due in part to the great variety
of units (especially nonstandard units) that was required. Before the end of

the third quarter of 1943 it became evident that the AAF could not meet the requirements for many of the units. Rather than delay the build-up too much, the decision was made to ship large numbers of individuals in various stages of training to the theater as "fillers" with the understanding that certain units would thereafter be activated. These fillers were charged against the troop allotment as set up in the Bradley Plan. The procedure placed an added burden on two forces in the theater, but it seemed to be the wisest solution of a difficult problem. This was one of the most important decisions made in the build-up of the air forces in the United Kingdom. General Marshall's proposal o the theater commander is worth quoting:

```
Our suggestion is that you reconsider your air organization affecting
every economy you can, particularly in special units and service
organizations. Special units that you need must be activated in the
theater. If you approve, we will begin sending you trained personnel
above your priority assignments for fillers and replacements but within
the percentage assigned to the overall Air Force shipping allotments.
These you may use to organize provisionally all repair and reclamations
squadrons and other special units for which there is no provision back
here to train by the target date. As these units are provisionally
organized, suggest you request formal constitution and activation. We
will do all possible to send these trained men and grant authority for
your activation within existing policies. Units so activated will be
charge against the Bradley Plan.
```

In accepting this proposal the theater commander indicated a willingness to work on the following basis:

```
The Bradley Plan will be used as the overall guide and organization will
be set up as provided therein. Manpower will be saved wherever possible
in all Echelons of Command and Staff but the overall organizational
framework will be implemented as provided in that plan.

You will advise us what organizations can be dispatched as units. You
will dispatch all other personnel as individuals and we shall first
provisionally organize and activate, and later request formal
constitution and activation authority from you.

The principle which it is urged be followed in this connection is that
whatever personnel cuts are necessary, we be allowed to indicate in
what units the cut will be taken. As the organization progresses it will
be carefully studied and any Headquarters or unit found to be
unnecessary will be promptly inactivated.
```

This basic decision in the carrying out of the build-up plan required the services in the theater of a commission of officers from Washington to explain the personnel situation as it existed in the United States and to discuss War Department and AAF intentions in meeting the program. The work of this commission, headed by an air officer, Col. J. M. Taylor, belongs to the account of the next phase of the bomber offensive.

The third quarter of 1943 saw certain programs made in the organization of the U.S. tactical air force in the United Kingdom and some discussion by U. S. and British leaders of the organizational setup under which that the air forces were to function in support of a Continental invasion. The first commander of that force, Maj. Gen. L. R. Brereton, was selected and approved, the beginnings of a service command organization were made in the activation of the Tactical Air Service Area Command (later Tactical Air Depot area), and General Arnold exchanged views with Air Chief Marshal Portal on the subject of a directive to the commander in chief of Allied Expeditionary Air Forces, who was to have operational control of the U. S. tactical air force.

The U. S. Strategic Air Force also experienced some important command and organizational changes during the third quarter of 1943. On 1 July Brig. Gen. Newton Longfellow was replaced by Brig. Gen. Fred L. Anderson as commanding General of VIII Bomber Command, and VIII Fighter Command received a new commander on 29 August when Maj. Gen. William Kepner succeeded Brig. Gen. Frank Hunter. The Eighth Air Force pressed for and received authorization for the creation of the air divisions and combat wings that had been recommended in the Bradley Plan. The authority was granted by the Adjutant General on 30 August, and formed activation was accomplished shortly thereafter.

This brief account of some of the more significant build-up and organizational problems met by the U. S. air forces based in the United Kingdom has intentionally refrained from detailed discussion of the problems mentioned and had ignored many others that are also quite important but more appropriate to the administrative history of an air force. It is not necessary to examine certain aspects of the operations that constituted the second phase of the combined bomber offensive.

MAGNITUDE AND RATE OF OPERATIONS

In the third quarter of 1043 the Eighth Air Force operated at a rate well above that achieved during the April-May-June period. July, August, and September missions accounted for 20,000 sorties (dispatched aircraft) by all units and more than three-fourths of these were effective sorties – that is, they reached and bombed targets or accomplished other purposes set for them. The numbers of sorties and effective sorties were more than double the corresponding figures recorded for the second quarter, while in the weight of bombs, was more than three times the figure established during the previous quarter.

The increased rate of operations was due in part to somewhat better weather conditions and in part to the expansion of available forces. VIII Bomber Command had 39 daylight operations between 1 July and 30 September. On the latter date there had been but 13 heavy bombardment groups in the command; on 31 July there were 15, and by 30 September there were 20 ¾. Of these 16 ¾ were equipped with B-17 aircraft and four had B-24's.

The Eighth had been required at the close of June 1943 to send its two B-24 equipped groups to the North African theater, while the 369th was diverted temporarily to the Mediterranean. There these units operated from 2 to 19 July in support of the Sicilian campaign. On 1 August they had engaged in the attack on the oil refineries in the Ploesti region, and between 13 and 31 August they took part in certain other operations. One of the most important of these August missions was an attack on a fighter factory in Wiener Neustadt in Austria, further discussed later in this chapter. During the July and August operations these groups flew nearly a thousand sorties.

The North African theater attempted during July to secure additional Eighth Air Force strength – medium bombers, heavy bombers, and fighter – but this was strongly resisted by the commanders of both the European theater and the Eighth Air Force. Then General Eisenhower requested four additional heavy bomb groups, Lt. Gen. Jacob L. Devers so strongly defended the necessity of implementing the CBO from the United Kingdom to the fullest possible extent that the Chief of Staff suggested a compromise — that four medium groups be sent from England to the Mediterranean. General Eisenhower's reaction to this suggestion was that while mediums were no substitute for heavies, the mediums were better than nothing and could be used effectively. General Devers countered with another statement of the significance of operations in his own theater and stressed the important part the mediums could play in the CBO. He said that their diversion would cut down attacks on enemy airfields, increase heavy bomber losses, reduce the pressure that the Eighth was applying to the GAF, and reduce the air support for operation STARKEY (an experimental landing on the French coast). The outcome of this inter-theater contest was that General Marshall in August sided with ETO, and there was no further diversion of air strength to the Mediterranean at that time.

Not only did the ETO strongly resist the diversion of additional strength to the Mediterranean but it pressed for the return of the three groups that it had previously dispatched to that theater. General Eisenhower wanted to keep these as long as possible and made a strong case for their retention. The United Kingdom forces won again, for the Combined Chiefs of Staff directed that the B-24's be returned to ETO because of the critical struggle the Eighth was having with the GAF. The three groups returned in August, and by 8 September the U. S. forces had four B-24 groups (44th, 93d, 369th, plus the 492d) operational.

But this return of the borrowed B-24's did not end the diversion of heavy bomber strength from the United Kingdom. By the middle of September, the American Fifth Army was in serious trouble on the Salerno beachhead and there was not sufficient air power to properly support this operation. On 14 September, General Eisenhower told the CCS that there were possibilities of a serious reverse and that his tactical and strategic air forces were being badly overworked, with each unit attempting to execute two missions daily. On the 15th, he reported that the situation was precarious and urged that long-range bombers from the United Kingdom operate against German lines of communication in North Italy and that the three B-24 groups which had been in his theater be returned without a moment's delay. This plea was not denied. The Joint Chiefs of Staff in Washington told General Devers to approach the British Chiefs of Staff about the dispatch of the groups, and if concurrence were secured, to start the movement at once. General Devers acted with the promptness demanded by the critical situation and by 15 September the 93d, 389th, and 44th groups, with approximately 20 aircraft each were on their way back to Africa. The long-range support from the United Kingdom came on the night of 16 September when five B-17's operated with 340 aircraft of RAF Bomber Command to bomb the marshaling yards at Modane in southeastern France in an effort to close the northern end of the Mont Cenis tunnel to Italy.

All told the Eighth dispatched 80 airplanes, 98 combat crews, and 446 noncombatant personnel to the Mediterranean for the support of the Fifth Army in the Salerno battle. Between 21 September and the first of October this force flew 191 sorties, dropped 406.6 tons of bombs, claimed 50 enemy aircraft destroyed, and lost 11 heavy bombers in combat. General Eisenhower assured the Chief of Staff that the force would be returned as soon as it could be spared; by 24 September General Marshall was told that the crisis had passed, and that it was safe to release the planes. They anticipated in a second raid on Wiener Neustadt on the 1st of October before returning to the United Kingdom bases which they reached on the 4th. Of the 80 heavies sent out, 63 returned to England.

The inter-theater contest for B-24 groups has been recounted to show come of the difficulties experienced by the Eighth in building and keeping its forces. In addition to the heavy groups in VIII Bomber Command, VIII Air Support Command had four groups operational with B-26 mediums during a portion of July and throughout August and September. VIII Fighter Command doubled its operational groups during the third quarter. There had been three P-47 groups at the close of June, but at the end of September there were six.

Aircraft and crew strength are much more important indexes of striking power than the number of groups. Daily average heavy bomber strength in operational aircraft, available crews, and effective strength during the third quarter of 1943 were:

	A/C Fully Opnl. With Tac. Units	Avail. Crews	Effective Strength
July	378	315	279
August	406	341	291
September	461	409	373

The figures make it evident that VIII Bomber Command was better off with respect to operational aircraft than available crews during this period, but it is worthy of note that the effective strength was less than the number of available crews seems to indicate it should have been. The reason for this condition was that the group was the operational unit. Effective strength on a given day was not represented by either the aggregate number of fully operational aircraft or that of available crews in the bomber command, but by the sums of the operational aircraft or available crews assigned to the groups.

Heavy bomber strength was short of the goal that had been set up by the CBO Plan. This had called for 1192 heavy bombers to be in the theater by 30 September. Actually, on the 26th of that month there were 931, and the average figure for the whole of September was only 881.

The CBO Plan had assumed that about three-eighths (37.5) of the heavy bombers assigned to the theater would actually be available at any one time for dispatch on missions. This assumption had been made upon the basis of Eighth Air Force experience prior to April 1943, and second-phase operations were about in line with this experience. In the table below are shown the average number of assigned heavy bombers and the average number dispatched on missions for the three-month period:

	Avg. No. A/C Asgd. To Air Force	Avg. No. Dispd. on Day Opns
July	800	283
August	761	283
September	881	323

The average number of aircraft dispatched on operations was obtained by dividing the total dispatched aircraft on daylight missions for the month by the number of daylight operations. Night operations, involving very few aircraft, were excluded. There were 10 operational days during July, and on each of nine days VIII Bomber Command dispatched more than 200 aircraft. On five out of the nine more than 300 heavy bombers were sent out. The only operational day in July when fewer than 200 heavy bombers were sent out was the 30th, and that was probably due to the fact that the command had been operational six of the seven days ending with the 30th.

August had but eight operational days, and on seven of them more than 200 heavy bombers were dispatched. Four of the seven saw more than 500 sent out, and the well-known 17 August raid on Schweinfurt and Regensburg found 315 attacking aircraft out of the 376 dispatched.

The month of September saw the Eighth attain the figure of 300+ dispatched bombers five times; and on one occasion, 6 September, some 407 were sent out. The top second-phase figure for attacking aircraft was not attained on this date, but came two days later on the 9th, when 330 out of 377 dispatched bombers hit a number of airfields in occupied countries.

In general the VIII Bomber Command was told to utilize its effective strength in excellent fashion. This is evident when figures for effective strength and average number of aircraft dispatched on operations are compared:

	Avg. Daily Effective HB Strength	Avg. No. A/C Dispd. Day Opns.
July	279	283
August	291	283
September	373	323

It has been seen already that the utilization of all heavy bombardment aircraft assigned to the theater was not nearly so satisfactory. This is further emphasized by an examination of the sortie rates for the period under review:

	No. of Sorties per Unit Equipment Aircraft	No. of Sorties per Effective Strength Manned Aircraft
Heavy Bombers		
July	3.9	10.1
August	2.8	7.3
September	3.4	9.2
		27.1

Then it is recalled that there were but 29 operational days during the second phase of the bomber offensive, it is clear that effective strength was quite well used in as much as the heavy bombers ready for operations were used at a rate of about 93% of capacity. However, the sortie rate for unit equipment aircraft (column 1 in above table) shows that VIII Bomber Command was not making such effective use of the planes assigned to units. In no month was the average bomber assigned to a group able to fly as many as four sorties per month. The sortie rate per heavy bomber, considering all aircraft assigned to the theater (that is, including these unassigned to combat units), was naturally even lower.

This unsatisfactory operational rate was recognized in AAF Headquarters and in the theater at the time, and great efforts were expanded to improve the situation. The operational rate for heavy bombers was held down by two factors: (1) Repairs necessitated by battle damage and repairs and overhaul required after a certain amount of flying time; and (2) the replacement rate for crews and equipment. Although it was possible to improve the maintenance and repair situation considerably, the other factor, replacement flow, still operated to keep down rate of operations, for a greater operational rate would have carried losses above replacements and thus resulted in a decrease of theater strength.

PROBLEMS OF DEFENSE AND BOMBING ACCURACY

The examination of the loss and damage figures for first-phase heavy bomber operations led to the conclusion that enemy opposition was becoming more intense during April, May, and June. The effect of that opposition seems to have continued to be very great during July and August, but it lightened perceptibly in September. When this loss due to combat is translated into a percentage of credit sorties, it becomes a measure of the severity of enemy opposition. It has more meaning to calculate loss as a percentage of credit sorties than as a percentage of dispatched planes, for some dispatched planes never were in a position where they could be attacked by the enemy. Losses due to combat computed as a percentage of credit sorties for the three months of the second phase were:

July	5.5
August	6.0
September	3.9

Battle damage to aircraft that returned from operations showed the same trends during the second phase as the combat loss rates. Considering damaged heavy bombers as a percentage of credit sorties, the following is observed:

	No. Damaged	% of Credit Sorties
July	1025	43.9
August	860	42.2
September	745	20.2

July and August rates are high. The reason for the low loss and damage rates in September are probably found in the nature of the operations for this month. Only two of the September operations were over German targets, one on a cloudy day which did not favor German fighter operations, and the other also under cloudy conditions which also employed blind bombing aids for sighting – the first time they were used by the Eighth Air Force. Many of the September operations were made against airfields during the STARKEY exercise and against other targets which required relatively shallow penetrations. Less than half the September sorties were flown against CBO targets. Hence it seems to have been due to the kind of operations conducted rather than to improved bomber defense or lessened enemy effort that loss and damage raids declined in September.

Throughout the three months of the second phase the German Air Force continued to exhibit the same trends that had become evident during the first half of 1943. Fighter aircraft production, particularly of single-engine types, was emphasized at the expense of other craft, and the existing fighter force was so distributed to meet the bomber offensive that the Western Front gained in strength both absolutely (from an estimated 1150 in June to about 1350 in September) and in relation to the Eastern and Mediterranean fronts.

GAF tactical developments during the third quarter saw just one innovation – the flying of captured B-17's in or near the formations of VIII Bomber Command. The use of B-17's by the German was first reported during the early part of July, and the reports caused considerable agitation in AAF Headquarters. The German purposes in using the repaired B-17's that had crashed in enemy territory seem to have been to obtain performance data on Fortress formations, to confuse U. S. crewmen, and perhaps to transmit fire-control data to rocket-carrying and aerial-bombing aircraft. U. S. counter measures included distinctive markings for each mission and orders to train guns on strange craft not properly identified as part of our forces.

German fighters continued to make some use of air-to-air bombing during the second phase of the offensive, but this tactic was never developed to the point where it constituted a real threat to the day bombers. As noted earlier the Germans began the use of fighter-mounted rocket guns in April. Apparently they were used throughout July August, and September but not on a very extensive scale. The mission reports did not begin to identify positively the use of rockets until the latter part of the period under review, but there seems to be little doubt that they were used before Bomber Command was completely aware of this enemy weapon. There were probably a dozen cases of rocket employment against the day combers during the period July-September, and quite certainly there were some losses to this tactic. The first proved success of the weapon occurred on 28 July.

In the heavy bomber battle with the German fighter force there was continued development of defensive techniques. What was perhaps the most important offensive measure adopted by the bombers – the increase in the size of attacking forces – also worked to the advantage of their defense. The Operational Research Section of VIII Bomber Command made a study of loss and damage suffered by heavy bombers during July-September and reached the conclusion that the amount of loss and damage suffered varied directly with the number of enemy fighters that were encountered. The concentration of a certain number of fighters by the enemy on a small force or the spreading out of the same number of his attacks in time and space against a large force resulted in the same amount of damage to bombardment aircraft. The lesson for VIII Bomber Command from this study was clear – increase the size of the attacking force and lower the rate of loss, and at the same time, lessen the probability that any one plane or group would be successfully attacked. It has been seen that the average number of heavy bombers dispatched on daylight missions was 383 during July and August and was increased to 823 for September.

The increased forces of day bombers made possible the use of the diversion and the effective employment of the split target technique. In the course of the 10 daylight operations in July, approximately 25 different targets were hit, or nearly three per mission. The August record was not quite so high: eight operations days saw about 18 targets attacked. September, with 11 daylight operations, and the day bombers attack about four targets per operation. Strangely enough, however, the two best examples of the employment of the "split target" technique during the second phase were days of extremely high losses. On the anniversary mission of 17 August 1943, some 376 bombers were dispatched against the Schweinfurt ball-bearing plants and the Regensburg aircraft factories. At Schweinfurt, 163 actually attacked, while 136 bombed Regensburg. The losses for both raids totaled 60 – 16% of aircraft dispatched and 19.4 of the number attacking. On the 6th of September 47 bombers were dispatched and 323 actually bombed at least 10 different targets. Losses were 47 (45 missing in action and 3 battle salvage) or 11.5% of the number dispatched and 14% of the number attacking. These two operations (17 August and 6 September) were the most costly during the entire third quarter of 1943, both absolutely and in relation to the numbers dispatched. The chief explanations for the losses on the Schweinfurt-Regensburg mission probably were the importance of the targets and the depth of penetration; for the 6 September mission some of the loss seems to have been due to fuel shortage.

The effective strength of the Eighth Air Force was augmented and the German fighter forces were spread still further by the use of B-26 medium bombers during the second phase of the bomber offensive. After a disastrous introduction to the European theater with their low-level tactics in May, the B-26's were removed from operations and transferred to VIII Air Support Command. After a period of training during which the number of aircraft available was increased considerably, the mediums resumed operations on 16 July with an attack on the Abbeville marshaling yards. The two-engine bombers were now employed at medium altitudes (10,000-13,000 feet) and generally had the benefit of fighter escort. They were used to attack near-by industrial targets and airfields and to run diversions for both the heavy and their own missions. There was always the closes coordination between medium and heavy attacks run on the same day in order that the maximum results in harassing enemy fighters might be attained. Operations by medium bombers were on a small scale in July (283sorties) but increased in size and importance in August (1190 sorties) and September (3033 sorties). In the latter month mediums dropped nearly three-fifths as great a weight of bombs as did the heavies.

VIII Bomber Command continued to study and experiment with the problem of the formation. Formation flying was primarily a defensive tactic, but it had very important offensive implications, for the accuracy of bombing was very closely related to the type of formation flown during the bombing run. There was considerable criticism by AAF Headquarters of the Eighth's heavy formations during the second phase because of losses incurred and because of the poor accuracy attained on some missions. General Arnold passed on to the Eighth Air Force an extensive report (including photographs by Hal Roach) from the School of Applied Tactics dealing with heavy formations, in an effort to improve both defense techniques and bombing patterns by the United Kingdom forces. The basic group formation used during the second phase continued to be the 18- to 21 plane combat box. This unit was kept intact during the bombing run and the way in which it was flown determined, in great measure, the bombing pattern achieved. Except on the bombing run, the combat wing, consisting of two or three combat boxes stacked together for mutual fire support, was still the defensive unit. It was the opinion of the Commanding General of the Eighth that the deficiencies in the defensive tactics of the heavy formations lay in the faulty techniques of the pilots rather than in improper planning or false conceptions of the theory of the formation. There was constant emphasis on the fact that pilots arriving in the theater were not properly trained in formation flying and efforts were made to correct this deficiency in the theater before crews were sent into combat.

Although bombing accuracy is definitely an offensive characteristic of operations, it is so closely related to defensive problems, particularly to formation flying, that it is appropriate to discuss it at this point. There are more data available from the missions of the third quarter than from those of the second quarter of 1943, but the assessment of the bombing accuracy for any period in these early stages of the offensive is never entirely satisfactory. Many missions attacked targets of opportunity without pre-assigned aiming point and so often on these, as well as on more successful missions, coverage was not at all satisfactory. All figures on bombing accuracy of VIII Bomber Command have to be considered very cautiously, for they are never based upon the whole effort of the command, but upon a fraction of it – necessarily upon the most successful fraction.

Examination of bombing accuracy by the three-month phases of the bomber offensive is not necessarily the most satisfactory approach. "The Statistical Summary of Eighth Air Force Operations" reports bombing accuracy by quarter years, but the best ORS study on the subject for the 1943 operations ser somewhat different time intervals. "The Statistical Summary" reports the average percent of bombs which fell within 1030 ft. and 2059 ft. of preassigned MPI [Mean Point of Impact] on visual missions of good to fair visibility for the third quarter of 1943 as follows:

Within 1000 feet			Within 3000 feet		
1st Div.	3d Div.	8th AF	1st Div.	3d Div.	8th AF
13	19	16	31	48	38

The expression "preassigned MPI" is meaningless, and that is probably meant is the pre-assigned aiming point. Whatever the reference point, it would seem that day bombing accuracy was on the upgrade during the third quarter. Other evidence from ORS studies also indicates improvement. The accuracy achieved by the entire air force and by divisions for each of the three months in the third quarter was reported as follows:

	Av. % of Bomber Which Fell Within 1000 And 3000 Feet of Aiming Point					
	1000 feet			3000 feet		
	July	Aug.	Sep.	July	Aug.	Sep.
9th Air Force	13.7	21.7	16.2	36.7	47.5	43.1
1st Bomb Div.	8.9	20.9	13.4	29.6	41.3	33.5
3d Bomb Div.	33.9	23.5	18.9	56.0	54.5	51.0
2nd Bomb Div.	-	-	8.3	-	-	21.5

The reason for no report on the 2d Division in both July and August was the absence of most of the aircraft of that organization from the United

Kingdom during these two months. The reason for the smaller figures in the September column for 1st and 3d Divisions and for the entire air force is probably to be found in the nature of the operations for that month – during the first nine days many sorties were flown in connection with STARKEY (presently to be discussed), several missions were carried out in heavy cloud conditions, and several missions were devoted to targets at the request of the Admiralty. Despite limited data it seems reasonable to conclude that Eighth Air Force accuracy, while improving during the second phase of the bomber offensive, was not outstanding. As a matter of fact, according to General Arnold's grading standards, Eighth Air Force bombing was poor. During August Headquarters AAF sent a grading system to all air force commanders for the purpose of standardizing reporting of bombing results. Certain adjectives were designated to go with certain percentages of bombs within 1000 feet of assigned aiming points:

50 % or more	excellent
40 %	good
30 %	fair
20 %	poor
15%	unsatisfactory

General Eaker thought that such a scale might be satisfactory for peace-time training, but not good for wartime measurement because it did not take into account the destruction of the target, the amount of enemy opposition, or the prevailing weather conditions.

Loss and damage figures already examined have indicated something about the severity of enemy opposition to the daylight attack. The other side of the picture, seen in claims of enemy aircraft destroyed and damaged, is a measure of the ability of the bombardment aircraft to defend themselves. The heavy bombers claimed the destruction of 543 enemy aircraft in July, 440 in August, and 273 in September. Medium bomber claims for the same months were 3, 4, and 13 respectively. Thus the total number of enemy aircraft destroyed by day bombers during the second phase was 1375 if the claims represented the true results of the air battle. An additional 236 were reported as probably destroyed and even more damaged during the three months of operations. It is very difficult to assess these claims accurately. They were recorded only after very rigid examination which attempted to eliminate all duplications. There is no fault to find with the standards set up for the various categories of combat claims, yet it seems that the toll of enemy aircraft claimed by the bombers might have been greater than the actual wastage experienced by the German Air Force.

One of the difficulties involved in accepting claims of the Eighth's heavy bombers is the constant criticism of the combat-crew gunnery. One example, typical of many, is worth citing. The Commanding General of the European Theater of Operations on 3 July 1943, reported to General Arnold: "Your bombardiers can do their job with a high degree of proficiency, but your gunners need training and more training, particularly at high altitudes. It is the most important existing deficiency."

Air British Air Ministry estimate of German losses (total combat and noncombat losses) were generally considerably short of Eighth Air Force claims of enemy aircraft destroyed. A complete and accurate account of the matter will probably have to wait for a careful analysis of GAF operational records.

The defensive power of the heavy bombers was great, but the opposition of the fighter forces of the enemy was so determined and his rocket guns were so menacing that it was well known that the only solution of the defensive problem lay in the development of fighter escort all the way to the target. The urgency of the matter was great during the second phase of the bomber offensive, and it can be understood even more easily from the words of air force leaders than from the statistics of operations. A memorandum drawn up on 1 July by Maj. Gen. B. M. Giles for General Arnold said, "The 8th Air Force now has insufficient fighters to conduct escort for the strategic bombers and counter-antiaircraft artillery operations. A minimum of one fighter group to two heavy bomber groups for escort must be established at the earliest possible date." At that time the ratio of fighter groups to heavy groups was less than 1 to 4. After inspecting the bases in England, the AAF Proving Ground Command reported in August to the Assistant Chief of Air Staff, Operations, Commitments, and Requirements: "The only real answer to protection against enemy air-to-air bombing and rockets is fighter protection. The fighters must be able to accompany our

bomber formations on the entire mission if they are to render efficient protection." The same idea was stated by General Anderson, the commander of
VIII Bomber Command "It is obvious that the ideal fighter protection is
time which can accompany the bombers from enemy territory to target.
Failing that, the greater the escorted penetration the better." Again in September General Anderson said: " ... the most likely solution for the
problem of long-range, high caliber gun fire, as well s rocket projectiles from
enemy fighters, is the extension ad improvement of fighter escort.

Toward the end of September the need became so strong that General
Arnold wrote to Air Chief Marshal Portal, "The increasingly strong enemy
fighter opposition to the Army Air Forces bomber offensive over continental Europe requires an immediate strengthening of our fighter escort
forces." The Commanding General of the AAF thought the need was so
great that he requested that the RAF place certain P-51 squadrons under
the control of the Eighth Air Force and release some of the same type to
AAF fighter squadrons.

Other evidence of the desperate need for solution of the escort problem
is to be found in a suggestion from AAF Headquarters at the beginning of
the second phase that some of the B-26's be used as escort destroyers for
the heavy bombers, and by the continued efforts to make something of the
YP-40 after its disappointing showing during the second quarter of 1943.

The account of the development of the fighter escort during the first
phase has called attention to the facts that VIII Fighter Command had successfully introduced the P-4? Thunderbolt into the European theater, that it
had begun the escort of heavy bombers within very limited ranges, and that
it had made progress in solving the problem of range extension by experimentation with various kinds of expendable tanks. The work on the drop
tanks was probably the most important development in the history of VIII
Fighter Command during the third quarter of 1943, and was one of the
most important single developments in the history of the whole Eighth Air
Force.

It has been noted that the first droppable tanks to be used with the
Thunderbolt were paper ferry tanks of 25 gallon capacity. These were
employed on the 28 and 29 July escort operations and on some missions in
August. Since the supply in the theater was limited it did not last long. No

effort was made to procure more of these tanks, for they were not capable of pressurization.. These tanks would give the P-47 a range of about a little above 360 miles if the climb to altitude were delayed until the fuel capacity of the tank had been fully utilized.

A 103-gallon paper bomb was designed by the British for VIII Fighter Command and initial small scale deliveries were made in July. This tank was capable of pressurization and promised to be quite satisfactory in extending the radius of action of the P-47 to about 350Miles. British agencies at first promised to take care of all Fighter Command requirements for expendable tanks after the end of September, but this proved to be impossible, and the problem was solved only by depending in considerable measure on U. S. production. An effort to expand the capacity of the 108-gallon paper tank to 150 gallons proved unsatisfactory from an aerodynamic standpoint.

Besides the limited number of paper tanks and tanks of British manufacture, Fighter Command used regular 75 and 150-gallon ferry tanks. These required a considerable quantity of expandable plumbing in order to make possible the withdrawal of fuel during flight, and supplies for this purpose were obtained from the United States. The small tanks were suspended from both fuselage and wings. This and the whole droppable tank problem was not worked out until the last quarter of 1943. However, by the end of the year there were between 2000 and 3000 jettisonable tanks were available at each of the Eighth's fighter stations.

While the P-47 was an excellent airplane for escorting heavies to the extent of its limited range, it had certain other deficiencies for work in the European theater. Its acceleration and rate of climb were poor, and it could not compete on even terms with the best enemy fighters below 20,000 feet. To improve acceleration and rate of climb considerable experimental work was performed during the second phase on a new paddle propeller and a water injection system designed to give the Thunderbolt more emergency power. Even with these improvements it was felt that the European theater demanded more than one type fighter for the varied tasks that had to be performed. Even with droppable tanks the P-47 did not have the range desired for the deepest penetrations. To supplement the Republic fighter the Eighth Air Force wanted both the P-38 and P-51, especially the latter— because of both its range and its performance characteristics at medium altitudes. But the state of aircraft production did not permit the Eighth any fighters except the P-47 for second-phase operations. There were, it is true, two P-38-equipped groups in the United Kingdom by 13 September (20th and 55th), but it was 15 October before one of them (the 55th) was placed on operations. VIII Fighter Command had only six operational groups by the end of the second phase. The ratio of fighter groups to heavy bombardment groups was about 1:3.3 at the time.

VIII Fighter Command became independent of RAF operational control on 30 June 1943, at which time all groups were placed under the operational control of the 65th Fighter Wing. VIII Fighter Command grew considerably during the third quarter of 1943 but in contrast to VIII Bomber Command, it found its effective strength limited by aircraft rather than crews.

Although some of the heavy-bomber escort work was performed by the RAF (support for medium bombers was practically all furnished by the RAF), the U. S. P-47's took over the lion's share of this task. Thunderbolts executed several independent forays into the Continent, but most of their second-phase work was in heavy bomber support.

The testimony of VIII Bomber Command leaders was very clear in that they felt the escorts furnished allowed more planes to get to the target, it allowed greater accuracy on the bombing run, and it brought more heavies back. An ORG study of second-phase operations showed that loss and damage from enemy aircraft was about four times as great on unescorted missions as when escort went all the way to the target. During July, August, and September Eighth fighters flew some 7701 sorties on 41 operational days, claimed 138 enemy aircraft destroyed, 13 probably destroyed, and 61 damaged, at a cost of 35 P-47's missing in action.

PATTERN OF DAY-BOMBING OPERATIONS

The major portion (75%) of the bomb tonnage dropped during the second three months of the CBO fell on targets in occupied countries. During July, Germany received slightly more than half (51%) of Eighth Air Force bases, in August less than one-third, but in September only 14.7. The heavy weight of bombs falling in France during the second phase is accounted for by the large number of raids made on airfields, especially by the medium bombers.

Although the weight of bombs droped during the second phase of the bomber offensive was considerably greater than that of the first phase, the second-phase effort showed less tendency to keep to the target pattern that had been prescribed by the CBO Plan. As facilities supporting the German fighter force still constituted first priority for the Eighth, 53% of the tonnage dropped by the heavies was used against aircraft targets. Only 7.5 fell on aircraft construction facilities, while German repair and storage depots received slightly more than 10% and airfields received about 28% of heavy bomber tonnage. A major fraction of the medium bomber effort was directed against the latter type of target. Submarine yards, port facilities, ball-bearings, coastal defenses and other military installations were bombed as were 4, light metals transportation targets.

The Eighth began to employ fragmentation bombs on airfields in August, dropping about 81 tons in that month and 333 tons in September.

The German Air Force utilized a number of facilities in occupied countries for repair of damaged aircraft and for storage of reserves. There were about eight such major facilities in France and Belgium and a very large number of secondary importance located in these two countries and in Holland. Several of these, as the following table indicates, were second-phase targets for the Eighth Air Force is its war on the GAF:

Date	Place	Target	A/C Attacking	Tons
4 July	LeMans	Gnome and Rhone Aero engine Works	103 B-17	254.5
4 July	Nantes	SNCA de L'Quest	58 B-17	145.00
14 July	Paris	Le Bourget	52 B-17	122.85
14 July	Villacoublay	SNCA du Nord	96 B-17	202.5
16 Aug.	Paris	Le Bourget	168 B-17	397.35
24 Aug.	Villacoublay	SNOA da Sud Quest	86 B-17	257.20
24 Aug.	Bordeaux	SNCA du Sud	57 B-17	141.75
3 Sep.	Romilly	sur-Seine	100 B-17	294.25
3 Sep.	Neulan	les-Mureaux	38 B-17	113.5
3 Sep.	Paris	Soc. Caudron Renault	20 B-17	60.0
7 Sep.	Brussels	Evere Repair Depot	104 B-17	310.75
9 Sep.	Paris	Soc. Caudron Renault	20 B-17	58.0
15 Sep.	Paris	Soc. Cadron Renault	40 B-17	118.75
15 Sep.	Paris	Hispane-Siza Bois Colombes	78 B-17	229.0
15 Sep.	Romilly	sur-Seine	87 B-17	235.5

Of the facilities listed as targets in the above table, Romilly-sur-Seine, Villacoublay, Le Bourget, and Brussels-Evere were rated as major repair depots. Of the attacks, two are particularly worthy of attention: the 16 August raid on Le Bourget in Paris because of its size and because it was escorted all the way to target by P-47's using drop tanks; and the 24 August attack on Bordeaux because it was a shuttle mission performed by bombers on the way from North Africa to English bases.

It is not possible to state quantitatively the effect on the GAF of the bombing of storage and repair facilities. Such raids destroyed stored aircraft, lengthened the repair time, and lessened enemy air force mobility. Repair facilities constituted reasonably profitable targets at relatively short distances from United Kingdom bases.

In the attack on the German Air Force the VIII Bomber Command and VIII Air Support Command (medium bombers) made a great many raids on the airfields in occupied countries. It had already been noticed a large portion of the tonnage dropped by the heavy bombers was directed at airfields. A much greater fraction of the medium effort was delivered to like targets. The reasons for the heavy attention to airfields were that such targets were frequently open when weather did not permit the heavy bombers to go to Germany. They were also within reach of the medium bombers, and airdrome attacks increased the attrition of the German fighter force and reduced its mobility.

Ball-bearings.

The only significant attack on the German ball bearing industry during the second phase was the now-famous deep penetration (450 miles from bases) to Schweinfurt on 17 August 1943, the date of the first anniversary of Eighth Air Force operations. The 17th of August also saw the equally well-known Regensburg attack on the single-engine fighter industry. At Schweinfurt there were three plants responsible for nearly half of all Western Axis production of ball and roller bearings and for approximately three-fourths of all those bearings used by the German military.

The Bomber Command Narrative of Operations reported the Schweinfurt bombing results as "very good"

Opertation STARKEY

Operation STARKEY the enemy and to give Allied forces experience for later operations. Troops and vehicles were actually loaded into assault craft and naval vessels were maneuvered to simulate a landing on the French coast in the Palais region. The air aims of the operation were to compel the GAF to fight battles of attrition at times and places advantageous to Allied air forces with the objects of destroying the maximum number of enemy aircraft both in the air and on the ground and of building up sufficient air superiority over the Luftwaffe to facilitate subsequent operation against the Continent.

The air targets for STARKEY were in two main classes: prearranged targets much as airfields, marshalling yards, industrial targets, ammunition dumps, oil stores, bench defenses, gun emplacements, and roads; and second, targets of opportunity such as troop concentrations, mobile headquarters, shipping and emergency airfields.

The operation was executed in three phases: a preliminary phase from 16 to 24 August, a preparatory phase from 26 August to 8 September, and a culmination phase on 8 and 9 September. D-day was originally scheduled for September, but had to be postponed to the 9th because of weather. During the preliminary phase air operations were directed almost entirely against enemy airfields. During the first part of the preparatory phase (to 3 September) intensive attacks on airfields were continued; and from 4 to 8 September the attack was shifted to marshaling yards. In the final days there were heavy attacks on the beach defenses, large gun experiments, and airfields.

The attacks on the bench defenses and special construction sites in the coastal region during this exercise were forerunners of man such raids which aircraft based in the United Kingdom were to make in an attempt to neutralize enemy preparations for launching new weapons against the British Isles. The principal STARKY missions against both defenses and construction sites were:

27 Aug.	Watten	186 B-17	369 tons
30 Aug.	Watten	34 B-26	49
7 Sep.	Watten	58 B-17	116
8 Sep.	Boulogne	68 B-26	100
9 Sep.	Boulogne	202 B-26	336

Eighth Air Force participation in STARKEY involved the Bomber Command, Fighter Command, and Air Support Command.

		Sorties			
		Preliminary	Preparatory	Final	Total
VIII Air Support					
Command	Bombers	554	1196	231	2031
	Fighters	---	16	21	37
VIII Fighter Command		513	975	308	1796
VIII Bomber Command		505	1001	335	1841

All participating forces claimed 341 enemy aircraft destroyed, 69 probably destroyed, and 163 damaged.

The anticipated large-scale air battle with the GAF did not materialize. Operations were greatly impeded by weather, but the Germans did not react as if they thought a Channel landing was imminent. Some air reinforcements were sent into the area, but the enemy air activity was quite reserved. Aerial reconnaissance was neglected. The chief concern of the German fighters seemed to be the prevention of deep penetrations by the heavy bombers. It was quite evident that the enemy was at no time deceived into thinking that a serious invasion landing was intended.

Night Operations of the Eighth Air Force

Six times during September small numbers of specially equipped heavy bombers belonging to the 422d Squadron of the 305th Bombardment Group (11) participated in night operations with RAF aircraft. The first of these was on the night of 8 September, just prior to D-day in the STARKEY exercise.

RAF Bomber Command Operations

RAF Bomber Command dispatched 1,903 night bombing sorties and dropped 54,751 tons of bombs during the third quarter of 1943. Without doubt most of the RAF efforts was devoted to German targets, and the remainder was divided between Italy and France. Slightly more than half (51.6) of the night bomber tonnage was dropped on light industry, nearly one-fifth (13.7) on ports and submarine yards, and approximately 4% each on heavy industry, railroads, chemicals, and various miscellaneous targets absorbed the balance.

The destruction of the great port of Hamburg was quickly accomplished by four large-scale RAF missions, assisted by the two much smaller ones run by the Eighth Air Force. The night attacks occurred during the last week in July and the first week of August.

The RAF attacks on Ruhr and Rhineland industry begun during the second quarter of 1943 were continued throughout July, August, and September. The aims were to complete the destruction of industry in this region, to prevent the removal of defenses to other threatened areas, and to discourage attempts at reconstruction.

Outside Germany, the RAF attacked targets at Turin, Leghorn, Milan, and Gesso in Italy during July and August. Great damage was done to the transportation system in Milan.

Three small-scale raids were made on French targets during July and August.

4

THE THIRD PHASE OF THE COMBINED BOMBER OFFENSIVE, OCTOBER – DECEMBER 1943

ORGANIZATIONAL DEVELOPMENTS

The third phase of the combined bomber offensive was coincident with the fourth quarter of 1943. This three-month period saw some very important decisions affecting not only strategic bombing but the whole course of the war in the European theater. The build-up plan for the United States air forces in England was completed and approved by the War Department, and the Ninth Air Force assumed its separate role in the United Kingdom. A new strategic air force was set up in the Mediterranean theater, a directive was issued for the Allied Expeditionary Air Forces' support of the planned Continental invasion, and a whole new slate of commanders was selected for many important roles in the European air drama.

The preceding chapter gave some attention to the difficulties experienced in working out the build-up and organizational problems in the most economical manner possible. The inability of the Army Air Forces to train on time the variety of special units required by the Eighth Air Force had been the cause of the basic decision to send a considerable portion of the air force troop strength to the theater as fillers rather than as units. It has been seen that this important decision necessitated the sending of a new commission from Washington to the theater to rework the organizational setup, the flow schedule for units and fillers, and the troop basis. This Baylor Commission finished its work by 17 October and succeeded in effecting a considerable saving in manpower. The revised build-up plan was to take care of both the strategic and tactical air forces in the United Kingdom, the latter having by that time assumed an existence separate and distinct from the Eighth. The War Department formally approved the revised plan on 8 November 1943, and the Bradley Plan tag which had identified the air force build-up plan for six months was formally dropped.

During the second and third quarters of 1943 the Eighth Air Force had undertaken to perform two principal tasks. One was to bomb CB) targets and the other to build up a tactical air force. The later task was at least partially completed on 15 October 1943 when the Ninth Air Force was established in the United Kingdom. The Ninth had, of course, quite a long record before 15 October, for it had been activated in the Middle East and had fought Rommel across the African desert. By the time the Germans had been expelled from North Africa and Sicily most of the Ninth's men and equipment had been absorbed by the Northwest African Air Forces, and in September 1943 Commanding General Lois H. Brereton took a skeleton organization to England to be reconstructed and to fight the Axis in a new theater.

What happened in England on 1 October was that the Ninth Air Force assumed command over most of what had been the VIII Air Support Command and the Tactical Air Service Area Command. The organizational work in the Ninth progressed rapidly in October and November, and medium bombers and fighters of that air force were active in support of the CBO and in preparation for combined operations to come.

Thus the Ninth Air Force became the tactical force that had been contemplated in the build-up plans for U. S. air power in the British Isles. Now that there were two air forces in the United Kingdom, a higher headquarters was necessary to exercise supervision and to provide coordination. This need was met by the creation of the United States Army Air Forces in the United Kingdom (USAAFUX), which was established the same day (15

October) as the Ninth. This superior headquarters was commanded by Lt. Gen. Ira C. Eaker, the commander of the Eighth; its general staff was identical with that of the Eighth, and its special staff practically the same as the special staff of VIII Air Force Services Command.

The medium bombers that had belonged to VIII Air Support Command came under the jurisdiction of IX Bomber Command, and Generals Eaker and Brereton worked out an allocation of fighter strength between the strategic and tactical air forces about the middle of November. According to this agreement, the Eighth kept 10 groups of P-47s and five groups of P-38s. All other groups and types, including the P-51's, went to the Ninth but with the understanding that Ninth's fighters were to be used to support the heavy bombers until the invasion of the Continent was imminent. Operational control of the Ninth remained with USAAFUX until 15 December 1943, when it passed to the Allied Expeditionary Air Forces.

A week after the Ninth was set up, the Combined Chiefs of Staff approved a directive for the establishment of a second United States strategic air force to take part in the combined bomber offensive against the Western Axis. On 23 October General Eisenhower, in the Mediterranean theater, was informed that the Fifteenth Air Force was to be established under his command effective 1 November 1943. This force was initially to consist of the six heavy bombardment groups and two long-range fighter groups that were assigned to the Twelfth Air Force at the time. The scheduled growth of the Fifteenth in combat groups was forecast as follows:

	Heavy Bomb Groups	Long-Range Ftr. Groups
By 31 December 1943	12	4
By 31 March 1944	21	7

General Eisenhower was directed to use the Fifteenth primarily against targets of the CBO, and to insure the close coordination between the Eighth Air Force and the Fifteenth against such targets.

For the Eighth this development meant another diversion of its strength to the Mediterranean. The same message that announced the directive to

General Eisenhower forecast the augmentation of Eighth Air Force heavy groups to the end of June 1944 as follows:

	Heavy Bomb Groups
By 31 December 1943	28
By 31 March 1944	34
By 30 June 1944	41

This ultimate strength of 41 heavy bombardment groups was 13 or 15 short of the goal established before the constitution of the Fifteenth. Preparations had been made by U. S. and British leaders in the United Kingdom to accommodate 54 or 55 heavy groups by the summer of 1944. The reduction in planned strength consequently necessitated some revision and curtailment of the airdrome construction program.

To the commander of the Eighth the new Mediterranean diversion was not pleasing. Such diversions had been resisted by him throughout his connection with the Eighth, and this latest was no exception. General Eaker felt that the bomber offensive would be weakened and that Continental invasion would be jeopardized by the new deployment of heavy bomb groups. He made strong efforts to show General Arnold that the move was unwise, and to convince him that heavy bombers could operate at a satisfactory rate during the winter months from bases in the United Kingdom.

Air Chief Marshal Portal criticized the directive creating the Fifteenth Air Force on the grounds that it meant a reduction of the total number of heavy groups to be used against Germany, that bases available in Italy during the winter of 1943-44 could accommodate very little more than the six heavy groups that were already in the Mediterranean, that the Eighth would lose during the last six months of 1943 six groups for which preparations had already been made, and that weather in Italy gave no promise of great advantage over that in the British Isles. General Arnold reported to Eisenhower that the British Chiefs of Staff challenged the wisdom of sending additional heavy groups to Italy and that they contended the groups could not be based, maintained, and operated there as efficiently as in the United Kingdom.

The decision to create the second U. S. strategic air force in Europe seems to have been made by the U. S. Chiefs of Staff, and in this decision General Arnold's influence was evidently very great. He informed Eisenhower that the reasons for the move were two. The bases in Italy provided a better point of take-off for (1) reduction of German ability to continue to wage war and (2) forcing the dispersion of German fighter and other defense agencies.

To comply with the Combined Chiefs of Staff directive for coordinating the two strategic forces, a conference was held on 8 and 9 November at Gibraltar with Marshal Tedder and Generals Spaatz, Eaker, and Doolittle (the last named of whom had been given command of the Fifteenth at its activation on 1 November) in attendance. The conference arranged for: (1) allocation of targets to the two forces, (2) procedure for combined operations, and (3) liaison officers at each headquarters to insure rapid interchange of operational experience and intelligence data. Radio communications between the two headquarters were pronounced satisfactory. It was stated that full exploitation of the bomber effort was dependent upon an adequate supply of blind-bombing equipment for both forces. Organizational experience, operational technique, and technical data were discussed and agreement was reached for prompt and continuous interchange of ideas and experience.

A further step in the coordination of the efforts of the U. S. forces engaged in the strategic bombardment of Europe was the creation of the United States Strategic Air Forces (USSTAF) in January 1944 with Spaatz commanding. This over-all air command was to function under the Supreme Allied Commander in Europe and was to be concerned exclusively with the combined bomber offensive. Its history falls, however, outside the period covered by this study.

Tactical air coordination for operation OVERLORD (Continental invasion) was to be secured through still another headquarters, the Allied Expeditionary Air Forces (AEAF). The directive for this organization was approved on 5 November by the Combined Chiefs of Staff and announced to the Commanding General of the European Theater on the 18th. The directive, which was to be issued through the Chief of Staff, Supreme Allied Command, provided: (1) under the Supreme Allied Commander, a British air officer with the title Air Commander, AEAF, was designated to exercise command: (2) the Allied Expeditionary Air Forces would comprise the RAF Tactical Air Force, the Ninth Air Force, and such formations as were allotted to the air defense of Great Britain; and (3) the Ninth Air Force was to pass to the operational control of the Air Commander, AEAF on 15 December 1943.

All these organizational changes necessarily involved a shifting of air officers in preparation for the year 1944. On 18 December 1943, General Arnold sent to Air Chief Marshal Portal a cable which gave the American slate of air officers for top commands in Europe:

Allied Air Forces in Mediterranean theater	Lt. Gen. Ira C. Eaker
Twelfth Air Force	Maj. Gen. J. K. Cannon
Fifteenth Air Force	Maj. Gen. N. F. Twining
U. S. Strategic Air Forces	Lt. Gen. Carl A. Spaatz
Eighth Air Force	Maj. Gen. James H. Doolittle
Ninth Air Force	Maj. Gen. L. H. Brereton

It was General Arnold's opinion that this American setup was the most satisfactory that could be secured.

After this brief review of changes in organization and command, it is appropriate to examine certain characteristics of third-phase strategic operations.

MAGNITUDE AND RATE OF THIRD-PHASE OPERATIONS FROM THE UNITED KINGDOM

In the account of second-phase operations given above in Chapter III it was noted that VIII Bomber Command ended the month of September with 20 ¾ heavy bombardment groups operational. That number was not changed during nearly two-thirds of the third phase, for throughout October and practically all of November the operational heavy group status remained at 20 3/4. On the 25th of the latter month the 401st Group became operational with B-17s. On the 14th of December three B-24 groups (445th, 446th, and 448th) were declared operational, and on the 24th another

B-17 group (447th) reached operational status. VIII Bomber Command therefore ended 1943 with 25 ¾ heavy groups operational.

The Combined Bomber Offensive Plan had contemplated a heavy bomber strength of 1746 in the theater by 31 December 1943, assuming that this number of aircraft would provide a striking force of 655 at the end of the period and that there would be a third-phase average striking force of 550. The last weekly status report for Eighth Air Force in December (as of the 28th) indicated that there were 1636 heavy bombers assigned (1309 B-17's and 327 B24's), and that 908 were operational with tactical commands. At the same time there were 1937 heavy bomber crews assigned to the Eighth. Therefore, the Eighth had attained about 93% of the assigned heavy bomber strength called for by the CBO Plan.

Even the figures for the average number of assigned heavy bombers and crews are quite formidable for the entire fourth quarter of 1943:

Daily Average by Month	Heavy Bombers	
	Assigned	Crews
October 1943	1000	820
November	1254	1085
December	1503	1556

The position of the Eighth Air Force in regard to effective strength for combat was actually better than the planning of April and May had anticipated. It was in December that for the first time the number of available heavy bomber crews was greater than the number of fully operational aircraft.

VIII Bomber Command was able to perform 7 daylight missions in October, 11 in November, and 10 in December, a total of 28 during the last quarter of 1943, only one less than for the third quarter. In October, the average number of heavy bombers dispatched on daylight missions was 346; the largest number sent out during this month was 399 (on the 8 October Bremen mission); and on only one daylight mission during the month (20 October) were there fewer than 300 bombers dispatched. The October average for attacking bombers, 273, was pulled down considerably by the failure of blind-bombing equipment to function on the 20 October

operation against Duren. Bad weather reduce the average attacking force on
November missions to 225, and a number of small operations pulled down
the average dispatched per daylight operation to 349, about the same as
October. There were, however, three occasions in November when VIII
Bomber Command was able to send out more than 500 bombers and once
(3 November, Wilhelmshaven) 539 actually bombed on a single day. In
December the 10 daylight missions dispatched 5898 sorties for an average
of practically 590. The bombing average for the month (469) was spoiled
on 5 December when only three out of 546 taking off were able to bomb
targets in occupied France because of the weather. Three times in
December the Eighth was able to dispatch more than 700 heavy bombers,
and on six other days more than 500. The record mission for the quarter
and for the year was on 24 December, when 722 B-17's and B-24's were dispatched and 670 actually bombed special construction sites for launching
rocket weapons (CROSSBOW of NOBALL targets) in the Calais region.
This Christmas Eve mission became even more impressive because it was
conducted without the loss of a single heavy bomber.

During the fourth quarter there were 34 night operations by the heavy
bombers of the Eighth. These were small missions involving from one to
seven aircraft each and were run chiefly for the purpose of dropping leaflets.
Six of the night operations took place in October, 14 in November, and a
like number in December.

The rate of VIII Bomber Command's operations was never satisfactory
to AAF Headquarters. Just before the start of the third phase, General
Arnold sent a cable to General Eaker in which he said that since German air
power appeared to be at a critical stage, it was necessary to send the maximum number of planes against the enemy. "We are under constant pressure," he added, "to explain why we do not use massive flights of aircraft
against a target now that we have planes and pilots to put over 500 planes in
the air." Some days later, near the middle of October, in a letter to Sir
Charles Portal he said, "... we are not employing our forces in adequate
numbers against the German Air Force in being, as well as its facilities and
sources. On my part, I am pressing Eaker to get a much higher proportion of
his force off the ground and put them where they will hurt the enemy."

The explanation of what AAF Headquarters considered as unsatisfactory rate of operations was to be found partly in weather conditions and partly in the fact that the bomber forces were organized by groups for operations. As was noted above, during most of the third phase there were only 30 ¾ heavy groups operational and each group had an authorized establishment of but 35 aircraft (not counting reserve). Nevertheless, a comparison of effective bomber strength and average number of aircraft dispatched on missions makes it appear that some of the criticism of the operational rate was justified.

	Avg. Effective Heavy Bomber Strength	Avg. No. Heavy Bombers Dispd. On Daylight Missions
October 1943	417	346
November	578	349
December	723	590

Despite a somewhat unsatisfactory scale of operations, the third phase of the bomber offensive saw all units of the Eighth Air Force complete 27,283 sorties (about half of these were heavy bomber sorties) and drop 23,470.4 tons of bombs on targets. This was a 41% greater tonnage than in the previous phase and was more than 47% of the total weight dropped during the entire year 1943.

Defensive Side of Third-Phase Operations

Third-phase United States operations from British bases cost 431 heavy bombers missing in action, 44.4% of the total such losses in 1943. Enemy aircraft alone accounted for 115, flak and enemy aircraft together for 44, accidents for 15, and other causes for 258. October was the most costly month of the fourth quarter with 176 lost in combat; November had 93; and December, 153. The heavy battle loss in October is explained by that month's deep penetrations into Germany, including the famous Schweinfurt raid on the 14th which cost 60 planes. That loss represented nearly one-fifth of the number dispatched and more than one-fourth (26.2 %) of the number actually dropping bombs on that mission. Three other October missions (on the 8th to Bremen and Weser, the 9th to Anklam and Marienburg, and the 10th the Munster and other targets) were also very costly, with 88 bombers lost in combat. These three plus the Schweinfurt operation cost more heavy bombers than were lost in any other entire month during 1943 save December.

Total heavy bomber loss during the third phase, counting both combat and nonoperational salvage as well as missing in action, was 550, or the equivalent of the initial equipment of nearly 16 heavy groups at 35 aircraft per group. When this loss is translated into an attrition rate calculated on the basis of unit equipment, the following is observed:

	Losses	Aircraft	Loss as %
October 1943	214	996	21.4%
November	119	1044	11.9
December	217	1236	17.5

October had the highest heavy bomber attrition rate for the quarter and for the whole of 1943 as well, due principally to the four extremely costly missions already mentioned.

Heavy bomber battle damage during the third phase showed 2825 damaged in all categories, distributed by months as follows:

	Number Damaged	Credit Sorties	Damaged as % of Credit Sorties
October 1943	900	2159	41.7 %
November	649	2916	22.2
December	1276	5618	22.7
Third Phase	2825	10,593	26.4

The damage rate for the last quarter was not so high as for the entire year 1943 (30.9%), but October's 41.7% was well above the annual figure and was surpassed only by January, July, and August.

Heavy bomber claims of enemy aircraft destroyed for the last quarter were 1181 probably destroyed 266, and damaged 562. Nearly one-third (32.6%) of all claims of aircraft destroyed by bombers during 1943 were made during the third phase; October alone accounted for 68.6% of the claims for this phase and 22.4% of these for all of 1943. The four October missions noticed in connection with high loss rates were also responsible for great numbers of the enemy destroyed:

Date	Targets	Claims
8 October	Bremen and Vegenack	167–33–85
9 October	Anklam, Marienburg, and Polish targets	123–29–51
10 October	Munster	183–21–51
14 October	Schweinfurt	186–27–89
Total for four Oct. Missions		658–99–286

The loss of 60 bombers in combat and the bomber claims of 185 enemy aircraft destroyed marked the Schweinfurt mission in October as the year's outstanding air battle. The cabled report of the battle by the Commanding General of the Eighth to General Arnold contains a graphic description of the fight and proceeds to analyze the third-phase defensive program. The report begins: "Yesterday the Hun sprang his trap. He fully revealed his final counter measures to our daylight bombing." General Eaker's account declared, however, that these countermeasures were not unexpected, for many of them had been exhibited in previous air battles as the enemy experimented and trained with them. The Schweinfurt battle was but the culmination of these previously tried tactics executed with perfect timing.

The report stated that the first enemy maneuver was to attack from the front at very close range with a screen of single-engine fighters firing 20-mm. cannon and machine guns. Following this screen were numbers of twin-engine fighters in formation, firing rockets from projectors suspended under the wings. The rocket-firing craft began their attacks at a distance and did not come in nearly so close as the single-engine fighters. The Fortress formations were subjected to great numbers of the rocket projectiles.

After the single-engine fighters had made their initial assault, they refueled and returned to the battle, this time attacking from all directions in an attempt to confuse the gunners in the heavy bombers. Then followed the second effort of the enemy twin-engine fighters, which attacked principally from the front and rear.

The rocket-firing craft seemed to concentrate upon a single combat wing until their ammunition was exhausted. After these maneuvers, all enemy fighters centered their attention on the bombers that had been crippled by the organized attacks. All told, more than 300 enemy aircraft participated in the battle and these made above 700 separate attacks on the bombers during the principal fight.

General Eaker's report did not minimize the losses at Schweinfurt. He said that one combat wing was practically wiped out and that the total loss amounted to 60 bombers. It was his opinion that all the losses had been to enemy fighters rather than to flak. He believed, also, that the effect of the rockets had been to damage rather than to immediately destroy the bombers. The rocket-damaged heavies were forced to fall out of formation where they were finished off by single-engine fighters.

After an excellent description of the air battle over Schweinfurt, the Eighth's commander continued his report with an appraisal and a program. "This does not constitute disaster," he declared; "it does indicate that the air battle has reached its climax." The measures which the air force was to take in its future campaigns were stated in clear and positive terms. They were four in number:

1. It was proposed to use more fighter cover at longer range. General Eaker was satisfied with the Thunderbolt to the limit of its range, which was 350 miles with a 110-gallon droppable tank. But for longer ranges, he intended to use the P-38 and the P-51 as rapidly as these types became available.

2. In the second place, it was planned to use an expanding force to saturate the enemy defenses with multiple attacks. The employment of seven or eight combat wings against widely dispersed targets might result in heavy damage to one or two formations, but the others would escape with minor damage.

3. The third measure involved an emphasis on operations directed against the facilities supporting the German Air Force. All possible airfields were to be attacked with mediums and the heavies were to strike hard at repair and storage establishments.

4. Full advantage would be taken of blind-bombing equipment which would permit strikes on cloudy days when enemy fighters would find it difficult to operate.

After stating his operational program, General Eaker in this report presented a plan for the help he needed from the United States. He asked for replacement bombers and crews to be sent as rapidly as possible. He wanted the number of replacements to be larger than his losses in order that the air force might grow in striking power. In the second place, he asked for every available fighter, and he emphasized his need for Lightnings and Mustangs. Finally, he asked for large numbers of 110- and 150-gallon expendable tanks and a monthly shipping schedule for this equipment that would keep up with his rate of operations.

The Schweinfurt battle report concluded with a note of optimism. "We must show the enemy we can replace our losses ... . We must continue the battle with unrelenting fury. There is no discouragement here."

The lower loss and damage rates for heavy bombers experienced during the last two months of 1943 were no doubt due considerably to the way in which the measures proposed in General Eaker's report were carried out. The number of fighters for escort was increased, the range of escort was lengthened by a better supply of droppable tanks, the greater size of the bomber forces dispersed the enemy defenses, and blind-bombing techniques were frequently employed.

There was one defensive measure not mentioned in the Schweinfurt battle report. That development, the use of radio-countermeasures, became important during the last quarter of 1943. The two most important devices in this category were generally known by the names "Window" and "Carpet," and were first employed in October after RAF experiences and U. S. tests had demonstrated their effectiveness. During the fourth quarter the Eighth made much greater use of Carpet (airborne jamming transmitter) than of Window (metal foil discharged from aircraft to upset German radar). An ORS study of 18 operations conducted between 8 October and 30 December indicated that Carpet was a definite protection against flak, for the average losses of unprotected groups attacking the same targets were 83% higher on the first 14 missions and 31% higher over the entire 18 missions that formed the basis for the study. There was not sufficient fourth-quarter use made of Window to determine its protective value.

At the beginning of December, Eighth Air Force representatives held a conference with interested British agencies for the discussion of radio countermeasures and for the constitution of a special organization to be called Radio Counter Measure Unit. Both United States and British forces were to contribute 12 specially equipped B-17 airplanes and crews each to this unit, which was to operate in support of night bombers and day bombers without discrimination. Authority was received from Washington for this project and on 28 December the VIII Bomber Command was charged with the building and training of the organization.

BLIND BOMBING INITIATED BY THE EIGHTH AIR FORCE

Blind or overcast bombing by daylight is an important offensive technique in that it allows operations on days that would otherwise see the force grounded or, at best, unable to strike the most desirable target. According to an ORS report, weather studies in the European theater stretching back over eight years prior to 1943 showed a need for some device which would allow bombing through heavy cloud; for, throughout the year, there were on the average fewer than six days per month suitable for high-level visual bombing of typical European targets. During the months from November to February suitable weather was to be anticipated only two or these days per month.

Overcast bombing is also a defensive technique, for it allows bombardment forces to operate under conditions much less advantageous to the enemy than those found in visual bombing.

The need for blind-bombing devices was recognized quite early in the war, and in the first part of 1943 experimentation was under way with several types of equipment. Two of these showed more promise than any others and were given special attention. Both employed the "phenomenon of pulse radiation giving highly directional radio waves." They are best known by their code names – OBOE and H2S. Both were largely British developments, but an American version of H2S, called H2X, was a considerable improvement of the British model OBOE employed ground-sending stations and a receiver in an aircraft. The aircraft was guided to the target by a technical expert at one of the stations and told when to drop bombs. OBOE, dependent as it was upon airborne reception of radiation emanating from the ground stations, had a very limited range. H2S and H2X were completely airborne units involving no ground stations and consequently had at least the same range as the aircraft in which they were carried. They had the property of making a representation of the terrain over which the aircraft was passing by reception of reflected microwaves. In the early stages of development H2S was useful only for area bombing. The American H2X made possible a representation of landmarks in much sharper outline.

Ideal conditions would have allowed blind-bombing equipment for several aircraft in each group, but because the sets were so scarce and production and training facilities so limited, it was determined to place all equipment and trained crews into a single unit known s a "pathfinder force." This force was modeled after a similar unit in the Royal Air Force which began to use the blind-bombing devices some months ahead of the Eighth Air Force.

General Eaker presented the plan for the organization of a pathfinder force to General Bradley in May 1943, when the latter was in the United Kingdom working on air force build-up problems. At that time there was a small force of about one squadron set aside for radar work. General Eaker had drawn up a manning table for his proposed organization and he asked that it be approved. On 1 June, a special request for the approval of the pathfinder force manning table was sent to the Commanding General of the Army Air Forces through Headquarters, ETOUSA. It was explained that the force would be made up of highly trained personnel and would be put in possession of the latest target-finding devices. The hope was expressed that the pathfinder unit would be ready to function about the first of October.

The pathfinder force manning table was approved by General Arnold by 11 July, and by the War Department on 19 July. The 482d Bomb Group (H), which contained the radar equipment and crews, was activated on 20 August and became operational 10 days later. This pathfinder group contained three squadrons and furnished the overcast bombing leaders throughout 1943. It continued operations until March of 1944, when it became essentially a training unit.

One squadron of the 482d Group was formed in the theater and fitted out with British equipment – OBOE and H2S. The other two were formed in the United States from replacement crews destined for the Eighth Air Force. Their planes were equipped with H2X. One of these American-trained squadrons arrived in the theater about 1 October, and the other some months later.

The first use of pathfinder (PFF) planes to lead daylight bombers was on 27 September, in a mission to Emden. This operation was guided by the squadron that had been outfitted in the theater with British equipment. H2S-fitted planes were used on this Emden raid and on most of the other blind-bombing missions of the third quarter. OBOE was first used by the Eighth Air Force on 20 October in an operation against Duren. The path-finder force might have participated in combat operations earlier in the year but Air Chief Marshal Sir Charles Portal objected to the possibility of the compromise of radar target-finding equipment. The RAF used H2S on night missions during the summer of 1943, but on very fast Mosquito bombers which ran such less chance of being shot down than United States pathfinders, which necessarily had to occupy the dangerous lead positions.

Pathfinders were used on about 18 missions from 27 September to the end of the year. Many of these were run against port cities because places on the seacoast were much easier to identify than inland targets. Without the pathfinders November would have been a very poor month for VIII Bomber Command, as eight of the 10 daylight missions made were of planes equipped for blind bombing. Altogether, the first PFF operation in September and these of the last quarter of 1943 dropped 13,781 tons of bombs.

The PFF experience during the third phase definitely demonstrated the defensive advantage of blind bombing. Losses to enemy aircraft on blind-bombing missions were about one-third the figure for visual missions against similar targets. Flak damage was considerably less on the blind-bombing missions, and damage to bombers by enemy fighters occurred three to four times as often on visual as on blind-bombing raids. The lower rates of loss in November and December, mentioned earlier in this chapter, were due in considerable measure to the fact that most of the bombing was done with PFF. An ORS study on losses and battle damages lists three fac-tors in explanation of the November-December rates: "Our loss rates are primarily attributable to the use of fighter escort, to our failure to get near enough to targets to come within flak range, and especially in December, to the advantage derived from the dispatch of a total force large enough to begin to saturate enemy fighter defenses in the zones penetrated." The phrase "failure to get near enough to targets to come within flak range" does not, however, give blind-bombing credit for much offensive value. In this connection, another statement from the above-quoted ORS report is in point: "However, our offensive record to date [the report covered the period from 17 August 1943 through 31 December 1943] indicates that blind-bombing results have been far from as accurate as visual bombing, with many targets missed altogether. Accordingly, even tough losses seem to be out to approximately 1/3, a balance in favor of blind-bombing technique requires that this offensive effectiveness be more than 1/3 as great as visual bombing." The implication seems to be that third-phase bombing experience left the offensive balance in favor of visual sighting, but it must be remembered that the operations of this period were beginning efforts with a new and complicated technique. These initial efforts aided the daylight bombers to much more effective use of radar target-finding devices in subsequent months of the offensive.

The first mission on which PFF aircraft led has been discussed in its proper chronological order in the account of the second phase (Chapter III). Third-phase blind-bombing missions are now to be considered along with visual missions in an examination of operations from the standpoint of target systems.

PATTER OF THIRD-PHASE DAYLIGHT OPERATIONS

The major portion (78%) of third-phase bomb tonnage dropped by the Eighth Air Force fell on German targets. Objectives in occupied countries – France (14%), Norway (4%), Holland, and Poland – received proportionately less attention than in preceding phases of the offensive. The Fifteenth Air Force hit targets in Italy, the Balkans, Austria, and southern France, with Italian targets getting most attention.

The Combined Bomber Offensive Plan had anticipated that third-phase attacks should include all the principal target systems on the priority list and that repeat operations would be performed against installations still had top priority in the fourth quarter of 1943, but submarine targets were of less consequence than they had been when the CBO Plan was drawn. Nevertheless, the Eighth Air Force hit German port cities where submarines construction yards were located with greater tonnage than was allocated any other target category. Attention has been given to the fact that much of the Eighth's third-phase bombing was done with pathfinders and that these found coastal points much easier to locate than objectives in the interior. Both the Eighth and the Fifteenth gave some attention to aircraft construction, airfields, ball bearings, synthetic oil, and railroad transportation. There were no attacks on production of rubber or rubber tires and none of consequence on production facilities for motor transport vehicles. The Eighth made one big attack on German construction sites where preparations were being made to launch new weapons, out much of its effort was directed to miscellaneous industrial targets of opportunity, because of failure of pathfinder equipment and difficult weather conditions. The performance of both of the U. S. strategic air forces during the fourth quarter of 1943 presented, in general, a disappointing demonstration of strategic bombardment.

It is scarcely possible to make a valid general statement about the accuracy of third-phase bombardment because of the small proportion of attacks made by visual sighting. It does not appear to be worthwhile to examine statistically the accuracy achieved on blind-bombing missions, for in many cases there is no assurance that bombs fell even close to the target. What data there is on Eighth Air Force visual accuracy shows an improvement over the first and second phases, but the fourth quarter compilations are made on returns from very few missions.

Several missions during the period achieved outstanding accuracy and deserve special consideration. The most remarkable job of precision bombing in 1943 was the attack on the fighter factory at Marienburg òn 9 October. On that mission 58% of the bombs fell within 1000 feet of the aiming point and 83% within 2000 feet. The photographs taken after the raid show what seems to be almost perfect coverage with scarcely any bursts outside the target area. The raid on the factory at Anklam the same day achieved 28% within 1000 feet and 52.5% within 2000 feet of the aiming point. The relatively low bombing altitudes at Marienburg (from 11,000 to 13,500 feet) and at Anklam (from 12,200 to 14,500 feet) probably explain the better-than-average accuracy on 9 October.

The famous 14 October-Schweinfurt raid under very strong opposition got 85% of the bombs within 1000 feet and 51% within 2000 feet of the aiming points.

Aircraft Facilities

The Eighth Air Force made several important attacks on German fighter and components factories in October. B-24 aircraft sent in September to the Mediterranean from the Eighth Air Force participated shortly before their return to British bases in a raid at Wiener Neustadt on 1 October which saw 157 tons of bombs dropped on one of the Me-109 plants at that place. The Fifteenth Air Force dispatched 139 B-17's and B-24's against Wiener Neustadt on 2 November, and 112 of the heavies dropped 327 tons of bombs with excellent results reported.

All these attacks on manufacturing facilities were accomplished by visual sighting, and except for the first Wiener Neustadt mission, achieved good success considering the small size of the attacking forces. As noted above, the Mariensburg raid was outstanding.

The Assistant Chief of Air Staff, Intelligence made an assessment of the results of strategic bombardment as of 15 November 1943. It was estimated in this assessment that the attacks on aircraft construction by that date had cut into German single-engine fighter production by about 21.5% for the period which would extend from August 1943 through April 1944:

Production anticipated without bomb damage	8940
Estimated production after bombing	7015
Production loss due to bombing	1925

The results of the attacks do not seem to have been exaggerated, for the estimates of production loss were somewhat more conservative than those of the British Air Ministry.

Eighth Air Force B-24's made a medium-sized raid (302 tons) on two engine-repair factories and an airframe-repair installation at Oslo, Norway, on 18 November, and B-24's of the Fifteenth dropped 86 tons on an Me-109 plant at Augsburg on 19 December. Other attacks on GAF facilities during the third phase were confined chiefly to airfields. The Eighth made at least three such attacks in October and seven in December. The mediums of the Ninth Air Force contributed more than a score of airfield attacks during the fourth quarter of 1943.

Port Cities, Submarine and Ship Building

Emden and Bremen were favored targets of VIII Bomber Command during the October-December portion of the strategic offensive. Emden was attacked twice: There is no certainty about what portion of the city was hit on the blind-bombing 2 October raid; the December attack did some damage to port and harbor facilities, but the operation probably should be classified as a general industrial area attack, for a railway station, a meat packing plant, and built-up areas of the city were hit.

The city of Bremen was a target seven times. On 8 October a small portion of the force (44 B-17's) hit one of the submarine and warship building yards, and the balance of the force (197 B-17's) bombed the city of Bremen and its ort facilities. The 13 November mission was ruined by failure of all PFF equipment; the raid of 26 November was really an area raid of the city and not a precision attack; and the operation of the 29th was of the same type. Somewhat better success attended the December raids on oft-bombed Bremen, largely because of the better functioning of PFF aircraft.

The mission to the Baltic ports on 9 October was noteworthy at the time for the distance covered, and the Wilhelmshaven raid on 3 November for the size of the attacking force, but the accomplishments of these operations do not appear to have been great.

The submarine base at Toulon was hit by 108 Fifteenth Air Force B-17's on 24 November, the Marseilles pens were bombed by Fifteenth formations (118 planes attacked) on 2 December, and on the 5th of the latter month, two Eighth Air Force B-17's bombed St. Nazaire.

Antifriction Bearings

The third-phase daylight assault on the Western Axis ball-bearing industry was distributed over the three months and engaged both U. S. strategic air forces. The Eighth contributed one raid in October and one in December, and the Fifteenth struck four times in November and once in December.

The Schweinfurt mission of 14 October by the 1st and 3d Heavy Bombardment Divisions of the Eighth Air Force was the most important and the most damaging to the German war effort.

The Kugelfischer Werke, which was thought to employ about 12,000 workers at the time and to turn out about one-quarter of Germany's ball and roller bearings, was apparently heavily damaged by hits on assembly and machine shops. The VKF plants, estimated to employ about the same number of laborers as Kugelfischer, were likewise heavily damaged.

The Schweinfurt raid damaged a motorcycle factory, a bearing-cage plant, a malt factory, railroad buildings and rolling stock, and barracks buildings in addition to the three main bearing plants. Despite the heavy loss of bombers (60 missing in action, 26.5% of the number attacking), the operation called forth hearty congratulations to the Eighth from the Secretary of War, the Chief of Staff, the Commanding General of the Army Air Forces, Air Chief Marshal Portal, the British Air Staff, and the Royal Air Force.

It was thought that the destruction wrought at Schweinfurt had occasioned great concern to the Germans and caused efforts to increase output and to bolster the defenses at Turin in Italy. The Fifteenth Air Force operation against the latter plant on 8 November achieved good concentration and caused considerable damage, and the 1 December mission was thought to have produced good results. The raids on the Villar Perosa and Annecy plants seem to have had very slight effect.

The Eighth Air Force attack on the last day of 1943 wrought damage to the CAH bearing plants at Bois Colombes and Ivry (Paris) and seems to have hurt the Hispano-Suiza aero-engine works as well.

Oil

The German oil industry was not much damaged by United States strategic air forces during the last three months of 1943. Two Eighth Air Force raids may have affected this target category slightly. On 5 November 328 B-17's, including 5 pathfinders equipped with "OBOE," dropped bombs on Gelsenkirchen. Despite the presence of PFF, the sighting seems to have been visual on this raid, for the weather was reported clear with some industrial haze present. The majority of the Fortresses apparently attacked marshaling yards, but 96 of the bombers dropped about 238 tons on the Hydrier Werke

Scholven A. G. and Galsenkirchener Bergwerks synthetic oil plants. The first plant was damaged but the second seems to have been missed. On 19 November Gelsenkirchen was a first-priority objective for a pathfinder mission, but the equipment functioned imperfectly and other targets were hit. A large-scale raid on Ludwigshafen (653 attacking bombers), aimed at the I. G. Farbenindustrie chemical works and other installations, on 30 December may have caused some damage to synthetic oil production. The target was completely cloud covered and bombing was done with the aid of pathfinders.

Miscellaneous Operations

A relatively large number of the fourth-quarter operations were completed against targets that were not on the POINTBLANK priority list. Railroad marshaling yards were Eighth Air Force objectives on four days for fairly large forces and on a number of other days for smaller numbers of bombers.

The Fifteenth Air Force conducted nearly half of its November and December missions against railroads, bridges, and marshaling yards in Italy and the Balkans.

An Eighth Air Force mission to Norway on 16 November hit a molybdenum flotation plant at Knaben and power and hydrogen plants at Rjukan, two days before the aircraft repair facilities were attacked at Oslo. The electrolysis hydrogen plant, reported the largest of its kind in the world, was a subsidiary of I. G. Farben. The Norway operation was a fine demonstration of airmanship and navigation against a very distant target.

Many of the operations performed by the United Kingdom-based U. S. strategic bombers are best classified as area raids of industrial towns. These missions were frequently performed under adverse weather conditions with the aid of pathfinder aircraft. On both PFF and visual operations targets of opportunity were hit when the primary objectives were not located.

Special construction sites which the Germans were preparing for the purpose of launching pilotless aircraft against England became targets of great importance in the last quarter of 1943. The British Chief of the Air Staff asked that medium bombers of the Ninth Air Force be used to attack these objectives, and after it became apparent that the number of sites was large and the enemy was pushing their completion with maximum effort, it was decided to use heavy bombers on them when the weather was suitable in coastal areas and unsuitable for attack on fighter factories. The B-26's completed many raids against such targets and on 24 December, VIII Bomber Command dropped 1745 tons of bombs on 23 sites from 478 B-17's and 192 B-24's. The bombing on this occasion was done by squadrons using individual sightings. By the end of December 83 construction sites had been discovered and photographed, and at 70 of them the work was believed to be 50% complete. There were at the same time 82 other locations where suspicious activity had been reported. Since it was believed that if the Germans were left unmolested they would be able to launch the equivalent of a 1000-ton raid on England by February, the "Ski" sites, as they were called, had become high-priority targets.

Eight Missions by the Eighth Air Force

The Eighth Air Force engaged in 34 night operations during October, November, and December. These missions involved three kinds of activity – participating in RAF Bomber Command attacks, dropping of propaganda leaflets, and the testing of special equipment. In October there were two bombing and four leaflets, and the testing of special equipment. In October there were two bombing and four leaflet missions. Seven and one-half tons of bombs were dropped over Munich and Frankfurt and 2,293,548 leaflets were dropped in France and Germany. In November there were 12 leaflet and two special photographic and instrument-testing missions. The 12 propaganda missions dropped 15,167,500 leaflets in France, Belgium, Holland, and German. The 14 night missions in December beat this record slightly with 17,886,300 leaflets on targets in these countries.

RAF Operations, Fourth Quarter 1943

During the last quarter of 1943 the RAF Bomber Command carried out a series of very difficult operations against distant German targets, including eight attacks on the Reich's capital city. These operations were made successful by the use of new tactics and countermeasures designed to reduce losses and by improvements in navigation and night target-marking designed to secure better bombing concentrations. Nearly all (94.7%) of the 40,070 long tons of bombs dropped by the RAF during the last three months of 1943 fell on German targets. This fourth-quarter tonnage was slightly more than one-fourth (25.3%) of the total effort of Bomber Command for 1943, which saw 157,434 long tons dropped.

The German capital had been attacked three times in force during the third quarter of 1943, but the month of November marked the real beginning of the Battle of Berlin. Fourth-quarter major raids on Berlin involved more than 3600 attacking aircraft and dropped 14,000 long tons of bombs.

The Berlin operations of November and December did very heavy damage to the industry of that great city. Electrical concerns, plants making aero and other type engines, machine tool factories, and a variety of other plants were heavily damaged. Commercial concerns and railway services were also seriously affected. Public utilities and public buildings in great number were destroyed or damaged, and certain military installations were badly hurt. The Berlin raids accounted for more than one-third of the entire fourth-quarter effort expended by Bomber Command.

Hannover was attacked twice in October by fairly large forces: The first attack seemed to have been more important than the second and did effective damage to business and residential property and to public buildings around the central portion of the city.

One raid was made in October and one in December against the important commercial city of Leipzig in southern Germany. The December raid was the more successful and caused tremendous damage to the most important business districts of the city. Railroads, aircraft engine manufacturing concerns, and other industrial plants were also hurt badly.

Two of the most successful RAF attacks were made on the important manufacturing city of Kassel. These October raids damaged the three great Henschel locomotive factories at Kassel which were reported responsible for approximately one-third of the total German output.

Germany's third largest inland ort, Dusseldorf, was the objective for a very successful mission on the night of 3 – 4 November when 527 aircraft dropped 2193 tons of bombs at a cost of 16 planes missing. Some 21 identified factories were damaged and the devastation was so great that the city was no longer regarded a first-priority target.

One medium and three small raids were made against the Mannheim-Ludwigshafen area in western Germany largely for the purpose of preventing recovery from damage caused on previous missions. The great city of Frankfurt was attacked three times during the fourth quarter, once in each month. The October raid was quite damaging to the east side of the city. The subsequent raids, while larger, were less successful; out they did considerable damage to business and industrial property.

Other major RAF Bomber Command fourth-quarter attacks included two raids on Stuttgart in southwestern Germany and one each against Hagen in the Ruhr, Munchen in south Germany, and Modane in southern France. Hagen in the Ruhr, important in the manufacture of submarine components, was damaged quite heavily. Scattered damage was done to an I. G. Farbe Iindustrie instrument factory, other industrial plants, and military installations in Munich. Business and residential property and about 40 concerns in Stuttgart suffered in the two fourth-quarter attacks, and the November mission to Modane in France produced an excellent concentration on transportation facilities.

The major RAF attacks during the last quarter of 1943 were well calculated to serve the aims of the bomber offensive. The heavy weight of explosives dropped on Berlin contributed to both the destruction of German industry and the undermining of German morale. Hannover had been designated as a third-phase RAF objective and was the seat of important rubber-tire plants and other industries. Kassel and Stuttgart had also been assigned in the CBO Plan as third-phase targets and both possessed important production facilities in the aircraft industry. One of the outstanding features of 1943 RAF operations war the campaign against the Ruhr-Rhine industrial region. The missions to Dusseldorf and Hagen were a continuation of that campaign. The strike on Modane in France was designed to cripple transportation facilities supplying the German forces in Italy. Frankfurt, Mannheim, and Munich were important transportation targets in Germany.

Besides the major attacks of Bomber Command, well over 100 minor raids were made on a variety of targets. These operations were important in themselves and in many cases were of great assistance to the conduct of major raids. In addition to the dropping of explosives and incendiaries the RAF distributed 143 million propaganda leaflets during the quarter.

CONCLUSION

The first three phases of the combined bomber offensive were, for the United States Army Air Forces, more important in the preparations they made for future action than for the operations they witnessed. Developments during the last three quarters of 1943 – the organizational changes, the material and personnel build-up attained, the plans made for future growth of forces, and the tactical and technical improvements achieved — all made possible the tremendous assault on the Western Axis in 1944 and after.

Of the preparations made for future strategic aerial warfare, three developments of 1943 seem to be of outstanding importance.

1. The build-up of the Eighth Air Force to formidable striking proportions and the organization of the Fifteenth Strategic Air Force for the utilization of Italian bases appear as achievements of first magnitude in the European air war.
2. The need for fighter and radio defenses to aid the heavy bomber in the accomplishment of its task was recognized, and progress was made in the build-up of the fighter forces with a variety of types, in the extension of the fighter range with expendable tanks, and in the use of countermeasures against German radar.
3. The offensive capabilities of the strategic air force were augmented by the experimentation with blind-bombing techniques during the fourth quarter of 1943.

On the operational side, the 1943 effort of the United States strategic air forces seems to have had telling consequences on two chief target categories.

1. The German aircraft industry, or specifically the planned single-engine fighter production program, was delayed by approximately three months by strategic attacks on FW-190 and Me-109 assembly plants in July, August, and October. Acceptances of the Me-109 single-engine fighter were cut from 725 in July to a low of 357 in December. Acceptances of FW-190's were reduced from 325 in July to 203 in December 1943. Some of the reduction for both types was due, in part, to the fact

that bad weather hindered acceptance flights; furthermore, aircraft acceptances were not necessarily the same as production figures. Nevertheless, the results of the 1943 air attacks on fighter production facilities had an important bearing on the defeat of the GAF in 1944.

2. The center of the German antifriction bearing industry was very badly damaged by the important August and October missions of the Eighth Air Force to Schweinfurt. The heavy losses incurred on these raids strongly reinforced the lesson that other deep penetrations had taught – the heavy bomber had to have fighter help on long missions over Germany if it was to accomplish its purpose. The intervals between raids may have hindered the accomplishment of the strategical aim for this target category because of the time given the enemy to effect dispersal.

The relatively large proportion of Eighth Air Force 1943 effort devoted to submarine yards and bases and port cities, reinforced as it was by RAF area raids, particularly those on Kiel and Hamburg, seems to have had slight effect on Germany's U-boat output. It has been pointed out elsewhere that the battle against the submarine was won at sea and not in the yards and bases.

Operations against other CBO target categories during 1943 now seem of relatively small importance. The August raid against the Ploesti oil refineries apparently had only a temporary effect; other attacks on this category gave only slight results. Of the U. S. attacks on the rubber industry, the 22 June Eighth Air Force mission to Huls was the only one of real significance. This one raid apparently closed the entire plant for a month and caused such damage that full production was not regained for seven months. The output of motor vehicles does not seem to have been seriously affected by the raids on plants in occupied countries.

The enemy's efforts to develop new aerial weapons and his determined construction of sites for launching them gave the USAAF a new target category that did not exist when the CBO Plan was drawn, but one that was to become of great importance in 1944.

Of the 1943 accomplishments of the RAF, the Ruhr campaign aimed especially at the German steel industry seems most significant. Loss in enemy steel production because of the direct and indirect effects of bombing during all of 1943 was something above 13% of actual output. So great was the impact of the air attack on Ruhr industry that the section was never able, after the middle of 1943, to match the steel output that had been achieved at the beginning of the year. RAF area raids did tremendous damage to a number of German cities during 1943; the outstanding example here was the terrible destruction wrought on Hamburg in July and August. So great was the havoc that this city never recovered its productive capacity. The same thing can be said, however, of Dusseldorf, Bochum, and other cities in the Ruhr.

The total loss of German armament production from air raids has been estimated by the United States Strategic Bombing Survey at from 3 to 5% for 1943. It appears that the indirect effects of the 1943 attack may have been greater than the direct. That is to say, the enemy lost more production because of shifts and dispersal than he did from bomb damage.

In a sense, this 1943 preparatory, experimental period made the subsequent phases of the bomber offensive more difficult because of this dispersal and because of the time given to the enemy to improve his serial defenses. That was unavoidable, however, for strategic air power in Europe could not, like Pallas Athens on Lake Triton, spring into being fully armed and ready for tremendous action. It had to grow slowly and learn operational lessons as it grew.

5

STRATEGIC BOMBING

One of the principles involved in strategic bombing- the destruction of the enemy's ability to wage war by attacking his home front—is not a new one. Before the advent of the airplane, attempts to accomplish this purpose were usually in the form of sabotage, formation of strikes and general unrest, blockade and certain military operations. The Northern blockade at Southern ports in our own Civil War, Sherman's march to the sea, and Sheridan's devastation of the rich Shenandoah Valley had as their ultimate goal, at least in part, the denial to the Confederate government of the ability to maintain an efficient army in the field. In World War I the beginnings of strategic bombardment were made, but results were inconclusive and possibilities limited by the still crude development of the airplane; and the combatants continued to depend upon sabotage, blockade, and ground operations in their attack on the enemy's war potential.

In the years intervening between the two World Wars the idea of strategic bombing grew in spite of opposition. There were two schools of thought as to how the air arm should be employed. One was that the Air Forces should serve as a support for ground armies—in other words, act as a purely tactical organization. The other school believed not only that the Air Forces had value from a tactical standpoint but that they could also function as strategic forces hitting far beyond the immediate battle lines and strangling those elements which made it possible for a ground army to fight successfully. The Luftwaffe was primarily designed as a supporting unit and even the Russians seemed to place their faith more in their troops and artillery than in the heavy bomber. In the United States and England, on the other hand, the possibilities of strategic bombardment were kept alive by determined airmen, although not without creating some bitterness and unpleasant situations.

There were numerous and difficult problems to be solved if strategic bombardment were to be successful. There were problems of plane design, types and fusing of bomb loads, protection of bombers against enemy action, supply and maintenance, training, target system and target intelligence, and numerous other questions. Very few, if any, were completely solved before 1939, and even during the progress of the war constant experimentation resulted in changes of plans, ideas, and programs. There were also differences in opinion among proponents of strategic bombardment, and numerous were the arguments, pro and com, on the relative merits of methods and target systems. For example, the British held to night area bombing while the United States operated daylight precision operations. There were disputes over target priorities, a case in point being the relative value of political or morale targets over industrial ones, or of transportation over oil. Fortunately, these divergences of opinion were ironed out and satisfactory compromises reached.

Even after the acceptance of the principles of strategic bombing by the military leaders in the United States and England it was necessary to educate the public to it. It was hard for the people at home to realize that the war was being won when the communications told only of air attacks on this or that city. The average individual was accustomed to measuring the success of his country in terms of territorial advances. As long as troops were massed and held in England he wondered if after all we were not just playing soldier. It was hard to understand that a thousand- plane strategic attack could have more significance than a ground battle involving a whole division of infantry and artillery. It was equally hard to realize that the aerial destruction of an industry might have the same results as capture by ground forces. Concern for the education of the public was evidenced by the American air staff in its attempts to get the proper perspective before the people.

General Arnold felt, for example, that a better presentation of the effectiveness of our air war would result from publishing low-altitude oblique photographs of destroyed objectives. These would thus give the American people a clear, graphic picture of the damage inflicted. At other times war correspondents were directed to explain more fully in their dispatches the importance of targets attacked. Failure to understand the necessity of hitting German installations, wherever they might be, often led to protests by certain specialized groups. People of foreign extraction, for example, often felt that attacks on their homeland, although it might be German-occupied, was in effect an attack against their nation. To counteract this impression war correspondents were again advised to highlight these operations as being directed only against the Germans and their military installations.

Despite all the problems inherent in strategic bombing and those which arose during the course of the program, the United States and England launched a combined air offensive in 1942 and ruthlessly continued it to the end of the war. After the failure of the Luftwaffe to win the Battle of Britain in 1940-41, Hitler gave up the idea of immediate invasion and conquest of England and turned his attention eastward toward Russia. He planned to keep England isolated by a submarine blockade and await a more opportune time to bring the English people to their knees. At this time England, unable to stage an invasion of the Continent, was left with no alternative except to continue the war with her sea and air forces. The only ground fighting was in North Africa. Except for cooperating with the Royal Navy in the war against the U-boats at sea, the RAF operating out of the United Kingdom was left only with strategic targets. These it struck on a loose priority system, putting most of its weight of bombs on submarine construction and repair and other coastal targets

Early plans of the United States envisioned a strategic bombing force stationed in England and cooperating with the RAF in the event that this country became involved in war. These plans were activated by the organization of the Eighth Air Force and its arrival in England in June 1942. The first bombing directives under which it operated were issued by the Commanding General of the U.S. Army in European Theater of Operations and in accordance with a bombing policy established by the British Air Ministry. The objectives were transportation, German Air Force (GAF) installations, and other military targets in the occupied countries of western Europe. This arrangement was not too satisfactory, however, because under it there was no clear-cut definition of the duties of the Eighth Bomber Command, and there developed a movement to have the heavy bombers join with the RAF in night bombing. If this should occur the American bombers would be diverted from their original purpose – that of daylight precision bombing. It was evident to the United States, therefore, that a more definite plan for strategic bombardment would have to be developed in order to utilize the full capabilities of the USAAF and the RAF.

This problem was debated at the Casablanca Conference, and after full consideration there was issued on 21 January 1943, the so-called "Casablanca Directive" of the Combined Chiefs of Staff (CCS) which was to govern the operations of the Eighth and RAF Bomber Commands. The primary object to be accomplished by these two forces was "the progressive destruction and dislocation of the German military, industrial and economic system, and the undermining of the morale of the German people to a point where their capacity for armed resistance is fatally weakened."

In December 1942, prior to the Casablanca Conference, Arnold, who was anxious to have a precise plan and program of action for strategic bombing, directed that the group of operations analysts prepare for him a study on the "rate of progressive deterioration that should be anticipated in the German war effort as a result of the increasing air operations" and give as accurate an estimate as possible as to the date when this deterioration would have progressed to a point permitting a successful invasion of western Europe.

In compliance with this directive, the Committee of Operations Analysts submitted on 8 March 1943 a comprehensive report on air industry. No attempt was made to give priority ratings to the targets, but the committee did conclude that it was better to bring about a high degree of destruction in a few really essential industries than to dissipate bombing efforts over a large number of targets which would result only in small damage to many industries. In the selection of target priorities, the committee recommended the following factors for consideration: (1) essentialness of the product to German war economy (2) current and capacity production and stocks on hand; (3) enemy requirements for various degrees of activity; (4) possible substitutes; (5) recuperative powers of the industry; (6) time lag until destruction of the industry would be felt. Information concerning the above factors could, of course, be obtained only through careful intelligence. It was also impossible for the committee to prophesy when enemy strength would be so reduced through aerial bombardment that an invasion of the Continent could be successfully undertaken.

Nineteen vital industries were selected, however, which if destroyed would, in the opinion of the analysts, stagnate the German war machine. These industries and the number of targets involved in each were:

Industry	Number of Targets
Single-engine fighter aircraft	22
Ball bearings	10
Petroleum products	39
Grinding wheels and crude abrasives	10
Nonferrous metals	13
Synthetic rubber and rubber tires	12
Submarine construction plants and bases	27
Military transport vehicles	7
Transportation	No specific number
Coking plants	89

Industry	No. of Targets
Iron and steel works	14
Machine tools	12
Electric power	55
Electrical equipment	16
Optical precision instruments	3
Chemicals	Not vulnerable to air attack
Food	21
Nitrogen	21

Antiaircraft and antitank artillery were not vulnerable to air attack. The effects of destruction would vary, of course, and in some cases the total number of targets indicated would not have to be destroyed in order to disable the enemy. The destruction of the 22 single-engine fighter aircraft factories would, it was estimated, virtually eliminate single-engine fighter operations after three months, and recuperation would be slow. Effective attacks on only three of the 10 ball-bearing plants, those at Schweinfurt, would reduce Axis production 42 per cent with a time lag of only one month before affecting the war effort. Likewise, the destruction of 13 hydrogenation plants would eliminate the most vital 25 percent of German petroleum resources, and with the knocking out of 12 Ploesti refineries this figure would be raised to 90 per cent. The effect would be feltwithinthree to four months.

It mustbe remembered that the importance of the afore-mentioned targets and the estimated effects of bombardment were based on conjectures and that later developments proved some of them ill-founded. It is interesting to note that twin-engine fighters and bombers were not included inthe list, although before D-day arrived it was found necessary to attack these industries as well as the single-engine ones. Nor were aero-engines included (although they were later added to the target lists) and recent surveys show their heavy attacks on these planes might have been highly profitable. It was also discovered that destruction of more than 30 per cent of ball bearing production did not produce the results expected. A similar discovery was made regarding the attacks on submarine bases. For a variety of reasons the campaign against U-boats was more successful at sea than at their pens. Bomb damage to machine tools was later found to be negligible. The statement that the chemical industry was not vulnerable to air bombardment because of its dispersal was also proved false, and the U.S. Strategic Bombing survey has indicated that more thorough bombing of such plants would have paid dividends. In general, the committee misjudged German ability to recuperate, and it did not take into consideration the overall development of plant dispersal or the strategy of moving plants underground. Nevertheless, at the time the report was made the findings were probably were based on the best information available, and very few men are blessed with the ability to foresee the future accurately.

Regardless of its faults this report formed the basis for selecting target systems in the European Theater. In May 1943, the Combined Chiefs of Staff (CCS) selected six systems with a total of 70 precision targets from those proposed by the Committee of Operations analysis. The six target systems were: (1) submarine construction yards and bases; (2) aircraft industry; (3) ball bearings; (4) oil; (5) synthetic rubber; and (6) military transport vehicles. With the acceptance of these systems there was also an attempt to integrate the efforts of the U.S. Army Air Force (USAAF) and the Royal Air Force (RAF). The striking power of the latter was designed to destroy material facilities and at the same time undermine the German working man's morale through area bombing. The American Air Forces were tasked with the destruction of specific targets essential to maintaining the war economy. The two programs were complementary and the most effective results could be obtained by coordinating their efforts. The method to be employed was simply to follow up USAAF daylight precision bombing with RAF night area attacks on cities associated with these targets. This amounted to a round-the-clock bombing program. It required practically no change in RAF plans, since the American targets were located in most cases in regions already marked for mass bombing by the English. So, in general, the directives for the Combined Bomber Offensive (CBO) assigned specific key industries to the USAAF, and the task of destroying German cities, dispossessing the working population, and breaking morale to the RAF.

6

COMBINED BOMBER OFFENSIVE PLANS JANUARY – JUNE 1944

The pre-invasion operation for the strategic Air Forces under the combined bomber offensive was given the code name of POINTBLANK, and it was intended to prepare the way for OVERLOAD, code name for the cross channel invasion of France. In order to assure the success of OVERLOAD it was first necessary to eliminate the threat offered by the GAF The Germans, realizing at the outset of the Allied bombing offensive that their entire war economy was threatened, began an expanded fighter-production program in 1942 to ward off the Allied bombers and protect their industries. They had succeeded so well by the spring of 1943 that the CCS was led to state in May that "if the growth of German fighter strength is not arrested quickly, it may become literally impossible to carry out the destruction planned and thus to create the conditions necessary for ultimate decisive action by our combined forces on the continent." Thus it became necessary to revise the target priorities and make the destruction of the GAF the first, or intermediate, objective of the CBO. The counter air program of the Allies mounted in fury in the last half of 1943 and ended in a blaze of Glory for in February in what was known as the "big week." Thereafter campaign tapered off and became largely a policing job which left the strategic forces free to turn their attention to other POINTBLANK target systems.

There was, however, no specific definition of subsequent operations after this primary objective had been attained, and therefore General Carl A. "Tooey" Spaatz, commanding general of the United States Strategic Air Forces in Europe (USSTAF), felt that further planning was necessary. Accordingly on 12 February 1944, Major General F. L. Anderson, deputy commander for operations, USSTAF, appointed a special planning committee composed of Cols. C. G. Williamson, R. D. Hughes, C. P. Cabell, and J. J. Nazarro and lieutenant colonels F. P. Bender and W. J. Wrigglesworth "to prepare plans in supporting studies for operations to follow after accomplishment own primary objective of the combined bomber offensive ... and for operations of the strategic Air Forces in the direct support of OVERLORD." The final report, due headquarters, USSTAF on 1 March 1944, was to include the following subjects: (1) summary on the status on the CBO; (2) possible target systems and operational policies; (3) possibilities of all the heavy bomber participation in direct support of OVERLORD; and (4) plans supplementing the CBO plan.

The report, entitled "plan for the completion of the combined bomber offensive," agreed that the GAF fighter production and ball-bearing industry had been reduced to a satisfactory degree and that subsequent attacks on them could be ancillary to other operations. It would not be necessary, therefore, to give these industries the same high priority as before. The only factors then remaining which could prevent the successful accomplishment of the CBO were adverse weather, misapplication of effort by selecting unprofitable target systems, and the continuance of attacks on targets beyond the point where the law of diminishing returns might set in. Even adverse weather could be, and was in time, circumventing the development of blind bombing and improved navigational aids.

In the light of the new conditions the committee recommended five target systems for future attack. In order of priority they were:

1. Petroleum industry, with special emphasis on gasoline production
2. Fighter aircraft and ball-bearing industries
3. Rubber production

4. Bomber production
5. Transportation centers in Germany as substitute targets when weather prohibited precision attacks on the first four priorities

These efforts would give maximum support to the invasion by: (1) assuring air supremacy on D-Day; (2) confronting the German army with a growing scarcity of fuel on all fronts and thus affecting adversely for redistribution of strategic ground reserves at the time of the invasion and afterwards; (3) further restricting essential military production; and (4) providing required direct support.

To determine these suggested target priorities, the committee studied the essentiality of each industry to the overall enemy war economy in the sense of the specific effect its destruction would have on Germany's armed might. Bombing for moral purposes in order to bring about a collapse from home front was not considered profitable for the American Air forces. "Neither fear, war weariness, nor the prospect of impoverishment," said the committee, "is likely to be sufficient to enable impotent political and social groups to overthrow the efficient, terroristic NAZI social controls."

This view was shared in USSTAF by the planners on the American side of the Atlantic. Major General W. S. .Fairchild, said the war must be over in the minds of the German high command and not in the minds of the German people, since the latter could not take effective action. The objective, said General Fairchild, still must be to defeat the enemy forces. For this reason, therefore, the committee concluded that the morale bombing on German towns should be resorted to only if periods of bad weather prohibited precision attacks on the objectives of direct military importance. In such conditions did occur, industrial cities were to be preferred, it was possible to manufacturing areas of such places should be considered as more advantageous for goods and residential zones. Likewise, if not the administrative or commercial sections of cities like Berlin, Munich, or Vienna should be treated as exceptions to this principle.

In addition to the target priorities, the geographical revision of the effort of the Eighth and 15th Air Forces was suggested. The targets for the Eighth Air Force would consist of most of Northern Germany, while the 15th was assigned Southern Germany along the one from Munich to Vienna, the remainder of Austria, Czechoslovakia, Hungary, and the Balkans.

According to the committee the target system which would offer the most effective immediate results was oil, with emphasis on gasoline. The defeat of the GAF by the Allied Air arm was linked to oil in a 1 March 1944 report that spoke to the very profitable effect attacks on this industry would have in both the military terms and the German High Command. "No other target system," read the report, "hold such great promise for bolstering German defeat." It was estimated that 90% of the synthetic oil refinery output was accounted for by 23 synthetic plants and 31 refineries, with a total production of approximately seven million tons annually. These installations also supplied about 30% of the gasoline fuel. Air opposition by the GAF to the USAF and RAF would cease when the already small stocks were used up. The will to resist for the German high command, or industrial leaders, was also be affected. Nevertheless, the denial of things other than battle for purpose, such as industry and agriculture, would have additional value by imposing severe restriction on general economy.

In case of extreme necessity, the Germans could resort to the additional capacity of plants in France, Holland, and Italy, although these were inconveniently located and many of them were coastal refineries and within easy reach of Allied bombers. In addition, there were coastal refineries in the Balkans, Poland, Austria, and Germany. After considerable study the committee recommended immediate attack on the 23 plants producing 90% of the synthetic output and 13 of the 31 crude oil refineries.

In second priority were placed the fighter aircraft and ball-bearing industries, although there were some men who believe they should have been retained in first place. It was believed in USSTAF, however, that by continuing attacks on fighter factories on the same scale as previously there was danger of wasted efforts since the point of diminishing returns had been reached. It was possible now to maintain air supremacy by a policy of policing, and for the most part future attacks on fighter planes could be incidental to attacks on other systems of German industry which permitted the enemy to wage war. The attrition of the remaining GAF could be accomplished by attacking such vital targets that the Germans would be forced to protect them with every flyable airplane.

The remaining targets for the aircraft industry consisted of 19 fighter and seven bomber factories. For the fighter aircraft they were divided into three categories: (1) prime targets, as yet undamaged; (2) secondary targets, as yet undamaged; and (3) prime targets, partially or wholly out of action but in need of policing. The first category was selected for early attack and comprised the Focke-Wulf factories at Krzesinki, Posen, Tutow, Marienburg, and Sorau; the Wiener Neustadt complex Bad Voslau and Fischamend Markt; and Duna Repulogepgyar at Budapest/Szigetszentmiklos. The second category targets, located at Schkeuditz, Halle, Gyor, and Brasov were to be attacked in the course of missions having other primary objectives. The third consisted of the Focke-Wulf plant at Oschersleben; the Erla at Leipzig/Mockau and Leipzig/Abtnaundorf; the Junkers at Bernburg and Halberstadt; and the Fieseler at Kassel/Bettenhausen and Kassel/Waldau. Responsibility for the destruction and policing of these targets was divided between the Eighth and Fifteenth Air Forces. The latter was assigned Bad Voslau, Fischamend, Gyor, and Brasov, and the Eighth took all the remaining places. It was estimated that the successful completion of this program would limit the monthly production of fighters to less than 200 single-engine and 120 engine aircraft, and with this level of production Allied Air supremacy would not be challenged. The GAF would be incapable of offering serious opposition to the strategic operations for giving close support to the German army from D-day onward.

Ball bearings, to which the committee gave equal priority with fighter aircraft, were also divided into three categories. The prime targets (those yet undamaged and selected for early attack) were VKF (Versinigte Kugellager Fabrik) at Berlin and DKF (Deutsche Kugellager Fabrik) at Leipzig. The undamaged secondary targets were the Jaeger and Muller plants at Wuppertal and Nuremberg. The prime targets which were partially or wholly out of action but which needed to be closely watched for resumption of activity were the factories at Schweinfurt, Steyr, and Stuttgart. The last two cities were the responsibility of the Fifteenth Air Force, and all other targets were assigned to the Eighth. It was estimated that this cleanup of the antifriction bearing industry would reduce production to the 35 percent of the November 1943 level, and this reduction, it was believed, would produce a

major crisis in the aircraft and finished garments industries and in the GAF
and ground army maintenance compounds.

In the field of rubber, which had third priority, there were five targets
which were selected for immediate attack. It was believed that within three
months after the attacks began the German army would begin to feel the
pinch and that a crisis would be reached in 6 to 8 months.

The fourth priority went to bomber aircraft production. There were
seven assembly plants which still remained undamaged: Henschel (Ju-86)
at Schoenfeld; Siglel (Ju-86) at Schkeuditz; Dornier (Do-217 and Me-410)
at Oberpfeffen; the Me-177 plants of Heinkel and Arado at Oranienburg
and Brandenburg respectively; and Junkers (Ju-220) at Bessau. All of these
factories and the associated airfields, however, were considered as secondary targets. Assembly plants were chosen rather than components factories
because of the slow turnover of bombers in first line strength. Attacks on
components would allow too long a delay between attack and effect on first-
line strength. The estimated effects of this program would be the reduction
of bomber production to less than 150 a month. At this level the German
bomber force would be incapable of sustained operations in close support,
but it could still carry on sporadic attacks of a limited nature.

Transportation, which had fifth place, was regarded as a sort of last resort
target to be attacked only when it was impossible to get any plant included
in the first four priorities. Certain other industries were left off the list
because it was believed they would be affected through the bombing of an
allied system. The influence on one phase of manufacture by the destruction of another phase is well illustrated by the committee's suggestions on
the value of hitting aero-engine factories. The conclusion reached was that
since the attacks on airframes and assemblies had created a surplus of
engines such that the bombing of plants producing the latter was unwar-
ranted. Because of an excess of engines over requirements a dispropor-
tionate amount of damage would have to be inflicted before any strategic
effect would be gained. This task would be further complicated by the com-
parative ease with which engine manufacture could be dispersed. The
wisdom of this decision, of course, can be debated, and the U. S. Strategic
Bombing Survey itself said that after the war was over it was difficult to

decide even then whether attacks on engines would have been more profitable than those against airframes.

In his conference with General Anderson early in March 1944, General Fairchild urged that grinding wheels be placed among the top priorities when the aircraft industry was disposed of. The Plan for the Completion of the Combined Bomber Offensive noted that a concerted series of attacks on seven grinding wheel factories, although not accorded high priority by the committee, would affect productivity of a wide, but unpredictable, range of armament and engineering industries. The military would probably begin to feel the pinch within 5 to 7 months after completion of the attacks.

Submarine construction was also discarded as a profitable target. Antisubmarine techniques had proved more effective than attacks on construction yards. As a rule U-boats were built under covered slips which were practically invulnerable to anything but a direct hit. The complete destruction of yard facilities, such as power plants and metalworking shops, had also proved impracticable, and, therefore, further attacks would yield very little strategic benefit.

Two other industries which if attacked long enough would affect the German war effort were motor vehicle and tank factories, but under the circumstances at that time, the committee felt that the attacks would pay dividends too late to justify the amount of effort that would be expended on them. It would take at least a year for the Wehrmacht to feel the effects of heavy bombing on the motor vehicle industry and furthermore it was capable of rather rapid recuperation because of the ease of replacement of the conventional machines which were employed. In the case of tanks, even if the chief plants of Maybach, Nordau, and Zahnradfabrik were severely damaged, the stocks of engines and gear boxes were sufficient to prevent a decline in final assembly for two months. In any event attacks on the tank industry would not affect early enemy resistance to OVERLORD.

A similar situation existed in the matter of tire, but not necessarily rubber, production. The destruction of tire factories and stocks would not prevent or hinder resistance to the invasion. If the six largest manufacturers were successfully attacked, only about one-fifth of a month's supply would be cut off. The six factories, however, were of value in secondary targets and for filling out missions against more significance systems.

The completed proposed target systems was forwarded home 5 March to General Eisenhower, Supreme Allied commander, and to Air Marshall Portal, British Chief of Air Staff, for coordination and final clearance through the CCS. In this letter of transmittal, General Spaatz stated that the "intermediate objectives" of the CBO, that is, the gaining of air superiority, had been achieved, and therefore the target systems of POINTBLANK had been re-examined in the light of that fact and of the necessity for giving maximum support to OVERLORD. The calculation of possible results to be achieved by the plan were considered conservative, but the plan itself had been "pitched in terms of so lowering the German fighting efficiency on existing fronts that the German ability to safely move strategic reserves will be despaired; and in the months following D-Day, the capacity of the German ground forces effectively to continue resistance must inevitable be low."

Eisenhower did not accept the plan submitted by USSAF. Another plan, which provided for the direct support of OVERLORD, was proposed by the office of the Supreme Allied Commander This called for transportation target as the top priority.

If the GAF were to the obliterated and at the same time the other factors which influenced the German Army's ability to resist were to be destroyed, then the targets to be selected should be of such importance to the enemy that the GAF would be forced to fight to protect them. Spaatz did not believe that such strength would be expected by the Luftwaffe to defend marshaling yards since the Germans had a rail transportation cushion sufficient for military needs. With oil, however, the situation was different. If he were denied oil the capability of his ground armies to wage a successful war could collapse. The target areas of both systems were approximately of equal size and the weight of attack would be similar. Oil had the advantage, though, in that 80 per cent of the production of synthetic fuel the lubricants was concentrated in 14 plants which could easily be put out of operation for several months. Comparable attacks on the same number of marshaling yards, which would be only a fraction of the German rail potential, would not seriously disrupt enemy military operations, particularly in the light of the fact that rail tracks could be more quickly and easily repaired than an oil plant. Spaatz therefore suggested that the strategic air forces (USAAF and

RAF): (1) continue with the destruction of the GAF and aircraft and ball-bearing industries; (2) initiate immediate attacks on axis oil production; and (3) join with SHAEF, AEAF, and the Air Staff in planning for direct tactical support of OVERLORD so as to provide for attacks in great strength upon communications and military installations of all kinds and thus give maximum assistance to the initial phases of OVERLORD.

From the end of March 2 plans had been reconciled for the final formal endorsement of Eisenhower and Portal. Under the compromise, USSTAF and RAF bomber command, priorities for POINTBLANK were: (1) destruction of the GAF, its factories and supporting installations, and ball-bearing clients; and (2) destruction of transportation facilities. Eisenhower felt transportation attacks were most necessary for insuring the initial success of overlord. From the time Allied soldiers arrived, the most important thing was full coordination of air effort in support of this operation.

B-24s form up during a practice mission before deployment to England.

The combat box was the strongest mutually defensive combat formation. Developed by General Curtis LeMay, this tight clustering allowed for the maximum number of guns pointed out towards the German fighters.

These B-17s are likely to be returning from a mission. Normal departure practices would require the bombers to climb quickly thus large formations were not usually evident from the ground on the way over to a target.

"Idiot's Delight" spins up its engines on the way off the hardstand and out
to the runway. Its ground crew stand by. The Combined Bomber Offensive
required maximum effort missions as often as planes and crews were available.

The one variable over which the Pointblank crews had little control was
the bleak British weather. The winter of 1943-1944 was one of the worst
winters on record.

Engine crates and drop tanks boxes were converted into makeshift homes by industrious ground crewmen. These belly tanks boxes were put out on the flight line and were used to get out of the wind and cold. A B-17 is in the background.

This B-17 from the 100th Bomb Group is covered in snow giving in a slim appearance.

The departure interval between aircraft was reduced to less than a minute.
B-17s move into position for takeoff.

P-47 Thunderbolts. One of the most important decisions made by Spaatz
and Doolittle was freeing the fighter pilots to roam ahead and attack the
Germans before they reached the bomber formations. Before that, fighters
were more or less pinned to the sides of the bombers which sharply reduced
their effectiveness.

An section of four P-51 Mustangs form this element as they escort a bomber into Germany. Note the alternating black-and-white "invasion stripes." These markings readily identified them as Allied aircraft.

52585

The mainstay fighters of the United States Army Air Forces – top to
bottom, the P-38 Lightening, the P-51 Mustang and the P-47 Thunderbolt.
The Ninth Air Force turned their fighters pilots into deadly ground interdiction experts who attacked any German ground forces.

Returning B-17s peel off to land. Most USAAF missions under the Combined Bomber Offensive launched before daylight and returned in the late afternoon.

Wedges of B-17s make for a perfect picture behind an American flag snapping in the breeze.

It didn't take much to tear open a hole in the paper thin aluminum skin of a bomber. Here a pilot examines the hole caused by a flak burst.

One can only imagine the howling wind rushing into this B-17 after its nose assembly was shot off by the Germans. Bullet or flak holes are clearly visible behind the nose.

The fighter pilots ready room. Coffee in hand, map in the flight suit.

More than 20 B-17s are lined up to go. This scene might be repeated at thirty of forty air bases as more than 1,000 bombers took to the sky in a single mission.

This aerial view shows the layout of a typical American air base in
England.

General Jimmy Doolittle, commanding general of the Eighth Air Force, left , talks to General Hap Arnold, the Commanding General of the United States Army Air Forces. Arnold was one of the first American military aviators earning his wings from the Wright Brothers themselves.

General Dwight D. Eisenhower and General Carl A. "Tooey" Spaatz,
behind him.

7

TARGET SELECTION UNDER PRIORITY SYSTEMS

At that time of the entrance of the United States into the war it was belatedly realized that they were sadly lacking in combat intelligence techniques and requirements. Therefore it was necessary to rely heavily on the British. Shortly after the arrival of American forces liaison was established with the British Air ministry, and American representatives would assist the British committees in planning air operations. The air ministry set policy and the directives under which the Eighth Air Force operated were issued by the commanding general, European Theater of operations, United States Army.

Until the Casablanca Conference, however, there was no clear-cut directive defining the tasks of the working bomber forces, and considerable pressure was put on the Americans to work their heavy bombers in with the RAF night bombing program. The Americans were opposed on the ground that this would defeat the purpose for which the Eighth Air Force was developed – daylight precision bombing. In Casablanca the CCS stated that the primary goal of the British and American bomber commands was "the progressive destruction and dislocation of the German military, industrial and economic system, and the undermining the morale of the German people who would rather passive the form resistance is fatally weakened," and it also set the priority objective for destruction according to the following priorities: (1) submarine construction yards, (2) aircraft industry, (3) transportation, (4) oil, and (5) other targets in the enemy war industry. These priorities, said the CCS, would probably vary from time to time to meet certain contingencies of the moment. In attacking the above-named objectives, the American and British commanders were directed to conform to such instruction as might be issued through the British Chiefs of Staff.

In the meantime the committee of operations analysts completed its report to General Arnold, and after being reviewed by headquarters, the Joint Chiefs of Staff, the British authorities, and other interested persons, the report formed the basis for the plan for the combined bomber offensive adopted by the CCS as in May 1943. This plan was incorporated in the CCS directive on 10 June 1943. The determination of detailed targets within this framework was still left up to the British chief of staff, who was the CCS deputy in the United Kingdom.

In order to aid the British in determining targets, a 30 June directive established the combined operational planning committee for coordinating the efforts of all forces involved, and had representatives of the VIII Bomber and Fighter Commands, the Ninth Air Force (later in 1943), the RAF fighter and Bomber Commands. The committee not only recommended the specific targets to be hit each week but also studied all intelligence reports and planned the operations against major objectives. Code names were assigned and plans filed at all operating headquarters. Once the commanding general of the Eighth bomber command received his weekly priority list, a code name was immediately forwarded to all related commanders and the previously prepared operational plan was put into effect.

There was much work to be done by the various intelligence sections and squadrons.

Once the target was selected for a mission, they were, however, still some matters to be determined at the lower echelons. Daily operation conferences were held to settle all last minute problems, such as the proper selection of bombs into uses for particular targets.

In the determination of what target should be their first there were a number of questions to be considered. Since the primary goal from the beginning was to destroy the enemy's ability to wage war the most important questions stressed how the bombing of an industry would affect front line strength. Except on the eastern front, were the reserves of army fighting equipment was small, and in most items would be negligible until after the Allied ground forces had joined battle with the Germans in France, bombing there was put aside. With the German Air Forces it was different, of course, because here the expenditure was considerable, due to the determined policy of the Allies to destroy the GAF wherever it was – on the ground, in the air, or in production.

It was estimated that an attack on steel production would not affect the military situation for six months, and the effects of an attack on coal will not be felt for even longer. Pair this with the ability of the industry to recover the flow would soon be reestablished in the form of new production and the overall results were unaffected.

It was generally agreed, therefore, those industries which were the most direct and had quickest effect on the German military should be disposed of first. Priority was given to bomb aircraft assembly airframe components for this reason and also because these factories will frequently in the same target area and a large portion of the core production capacity was centered in a few areas. On the same basis friction bearings industry, also offered a concentrated target. Furthermore, it was believed the destruction of this industry affected German capabilities across all lines — army equipment as well as airplanes. Thus in January 1944, the British and the U.S. unanimously agreed that strategic bombers should concentrate on fighter production and the ball-bearing industry. The conditions should arise, however, which would prevent precision attacks, and in such conditions the Eighth Air Force was to supplement the RAF bombing of Berlin when weather and tactical conditions were adequate. Next to the aircraft industry other POINTBLANK targets that took precedence for all precision attacks were the CROSSBOW (V-1 and V-2 bomb sites) objectives.

In the meantime the RAF was to maintain steady pressure on the denser concentrations of German heavy industry and supplementing the daylight bombing of individual factories with night assaults on industrial centers associated with aircraft and ball-bearing manufacture. The same directive which established January targets for the Eighth Air Force assigned the following cities to the RAF in order of priority: Schweinfurt, Leipzig, Brunswick, Regensburg, Augsburg, and Gotha. In any OBOE or GEE-H (types of blind bombing) attacks the Jaeger ball-bearing factory at Wuppertal was to have priority. As in the case of the Eighth Air Force, the RAF was to attack Berlin when conditions prohibited raids on the above-mentioned places.

The stepped-up offensive against the GAF continued through January and February with other targets relegated to second place. Air Marshal Portal, as CCS Deputy in the United Kingdom, again in February emphasized the need for destroying the GAF, and his orders for that month retained fighter airframe and components factories and ball bearings at the top of the priorities. The secondary priority was accorded to installations supporting the GAF and to aircraft not forming a part of the German fighter force. Other objectives were: continued attacks on CROSSBOW targets in order to neutralize the threats developing under the rocket-bombing project; attacks from Berlin and other industrial areas by both RAF and USSTAF, the latter to hit these places when unable to perform precision bombing and to use bombing-through-overcast (BTO) methods; and lastly, attacks on targets in southeastern Europe, such as cities and transportation. Attacks in the Balkans would be delivered by the Fifteenth Air Force when weather or tactical conditions prevented POINTBLANK operations or support of the Italian land campaign.

Sufficient progress had been made against enemy aircraft production by March to allow the daylight bombers to turn a greater share of their attention to other POINTBLANK objectives which would impose maximum injury on the German ground forces and pave the way for a successful OVERLORD. The controversy over whether are not transportation authority over the oil industry has been discussed in the preceding chapter. Despite the fact that one did not renew over transportation, its importance was recognized and give them a place on this. Actual full-fledged bombing of oil installations did not begin until April and May, however, when the 15th Air Force started concerted action against Balkan refining facilities. The Eighth Air Force launched its first attacks against synthetic plants in May.

When target lists were drawn up, there was also a division of effort between the Eighth and 15th Air Forces and the RAF. In general, this RAF bomber command was instructed to conduct area night bombing in support of daylight precision assaults. The Eighth Air Force had as its chief primary targets during the first half 1944 the fighter aircraft airframe and components and ball-bearing factories. To these were added marshaling yards, airfields, and airdromes as the time for invasion drew nearer. Considerable bomb tonnage also was to be dropped on CROSSBOW and other military installations in the Pas de Calais and Cherbourg Peninsula regions. One month before D-day, the priorities for this Air Force were set as: (1) POINTBLANK targets, which had aircraft factories first, and then other industries, such as oil; (2) railroad centers in occupied countries; and (3) airdromes in occupied countries. CROSSBOW also was to have overriding priority in France for one satisfactory mission. Although POINTBLANK carried top priority it can be clearly seen that the requirements for OVERLORD were the main factors determining targets for the forces operating out of the United Kingdom.

It was in the Mediterranean Theater of Operations (MTO), however, that the greatest number of changes in priority occurred. This was due in part to the multitude of tasks allocated to that theater. In addition to this Italian campaign the CCS also assigned to the Commander-in-Chief of the Allied Forces the responsibility for operations in Greece, Albania, Yugoslavia, Bulgaria, Rumania, Hungary, Crete, the Aegean Islands, and Turkey. This, of course, involved the Fifteenth Air Force as well ifs other air units in the MTO. In addition to heading the Balkan program, the Allied Commander-in-Chief was also allowed to use the strategic Air Forces under his command (the Fifteenth Air Force and the 205 Group, RAF) for operations not a part of POINTBLANK when a tactical or strategic emergency arose in the Italian campaign. This resulted at times in a confused state of priorities, but the wonder is that under these circumstances the system worked as well as it did.

At that time of the organization of the Mediterranean Allied Air Forces in December 1943 the project which had top priority in the MTO was Anvil — the landing in Southern France to coincide with OVERLORD. The uncertainty as to whether anvil (later called Dragoon) would ever be mounted after its downgrading following the Anzio stalemate made air planning in the MTO difficult. By May, however, it had been decided that

ANVIL would be staged in the near future, and in preparation for it railroad centers in southern France were given a priority immediately below those for the Italian campaign and POINTBLANK. The disruption of communications in this region was intended not only to prepare for an invasion on the southern coast of France but also to help OVERLORD by making it difficult for the enemy to shift reserves to the Normandy beachhead.

Aside from ANVIL other MTO projects for foreign aid the Strategic Air Forces were the Italian Land campaign and the bombing of the Balkans for political or tactical reasons. In February, the Italian campaign was given overriding priority for all operations in the MTO and had first call on all land, sea, and air resources in the theater. Balkan bombing was given last priority, although in the spring and early summer it was given temporary precedence, from time to time, to meet certain political exigencies and to aid the Russian advance. For the month prior to the date, the priority target systems for the 15th Air Forces were, therefore: (1) support of the Italian campaign; (2) POINTBLANK; (3) railroad centers in Southern France in preparation for overlord and dragoon; and (4) Balkan targets.

Early in January 1944, forces in the Mediterranean were given a five-fold mission: (1) destruction of POINTBLANK targets; (2) support for the Italian Land campaign; (3) bombardment of important rail centers outside of Italy; (4) bombardment of special industrial targets of strategic importance; and (5) bombardment of specially named objectives for political reasons. The night bombers were to attack marshaling yards and such targets as the Wiener Neustadt complex and other airframe factories, but only when conditions were such that they could be located and bombed effectively.

The top of the list for POINTBLANK targets were, of course, the German fighter factories and ball-bearing industries. These remained in first priority, and some specific targets were withdrawn and others added as conditions warranted, until after D-day. . Airdromes and similar installations gained importance, however, as the noose was tightened about the GAF neck and the time for OVERLORD and ANVIL drew nearer. In May oil was given recognition as possessing more than a last- resort or target-of-opportunity status, although it was not yet accorded a top or secondary priority. OVERLORD requirements were still uppermost. On the May list, 18 refineries and storage facilities were recommended as non-POINTBLANK filler targets to be used where tactical considerations required supplementary targets in the same general area as POINTBLANK objectives.

The 205 group, RAF in the MTO, like the RAF Bomber Command in England, was primarily interested in night area or semi-area bombing as supplementary to the precision work of the U.S. heavies. With the introduction of bombing-through-overcast techniques for use by the day bombers it became possible for these forces to fly missions hitherto considered impossible or unprofitable. Since this meant that the 15th Air Force would now engage in some daylight area bombing, priorities for this type of operation had to be set up. First priority was given to those cities which complemented first priority POINTBLANK targets, such as Regensburg, Schweinfurt, Steyr, Augsburg, and Stuttgart. Second priority was assigned to cities not necessarily connected with first priority POINTBLANK targets but which if bombed would contribute to the mission of the strategic air forces. These places were in order of precedence: Budapest, Sofia, Bucharest, Vienna.

Perhaps the most troublesome problem which confronted the planners on the selection of targets within specified systems was that of the Balkans. This region, as such, was not a part of POINTBLANK, but with the assumption of responsibility for operations there by the Allied Commander-in-Chief of MTO, this area fell within the sphere of the Strategic Air Forces in the Mediterranean. It was necessary, therefore, to fit a political and tactical target system into the scheme without interrupting the CBO. The adjustment was made after a fashion, but not without some misgivings on part of the Americans and some confusion in the bombing schedules.

In February 1944 the CCS notified both General Spaatz and General Wilson that when it was impossible to stage POINTBLANK attacks OR support the Italian campaign, the Balkan priorities would be first Bulgaria, then Budapest, and lastly Bucharest. The following month the Balkan forties became: (1) Sofia, Varna, and Burgas for political reasons; (2) Bucharest; and (3) Budapest. The tottering position of Bulgaria made this country seemingly ripe for bombing out of the war, and the CCS informed Wilson that there was no prohibition against using the 15th Air Force to hit this target whenever such operations might be a prime factor in deciding the course of Bulgarian affairs.

The wisdom of trying to take Balkan satellites and work at this time in using the 15th Air Force for this purpose at the expense of POINTBLANK was questioned by General Eaker, commanding general of MAAF. He wondered if, rather than aiding OVERLORD, it might not release more German divisions to oppose that operation. If the British insisted on using the 15th Air Force for political bombing, he told Air Marshal Slessor, it was possible that the American chiefs of staff might regard this as sabotage of POINTBLANK and remove that Air Force from under his control. If this were done the Balkan program would be crippled, whereas if the present arrangements and authorizations were not disturbed, bombings could be carried on to the satisfaction of both the CBO and the Balkan situation. In the belief that the Germans in southeastern Europe needed only a little prodding to force them to lay down their arms, the CCS in late March authorized Portal to instruct Spaatz and Wilson to depart from the order of priorities currently in force and make one or two heavy attacks on the Balkans whenever important results could be expected. The matter of reducing to a minimum the diversion from the Italian campaign and POINTBLANK was left to Portal's discretion. Under this authority Portal directed that when favorable opportunities offered themselves, Wilson would order one or more of the following places attacked: Bucharest; Budapest; Sofia and other Bulgarian towns. Wilson was requested to keep Portal informed of his intentions after consulting with either Eaker or Twining, as the case might be, as to possible conflict with coordinated operations of the Eighth and 15th air forces. Twining was responsible for keeping USSTAF informed of these Balkan operations, and Spaatz was to issue the necessary orders for the attacks.

Spaatz objected, however, to allowing theater commanders to authorize attacks by strategic Air Forces against political targets. Such a policy, he felt, would nullify single control established over POINTBLANK, and it might disrupt attacks on vital war industries at critical times. Furthermore, it would let theater commanders judge according to their own standards for relative merits of precision and area bombing populations and this might in turn change the whole CBO program. He recommended that the CCS had confidence in precision strategic bombing and that they adopt a firm policy of resisting unnecessary diversions. There would always be time to submit factual data from political bombing to the CCS for their consideration, instead of letting the theater commanders make the decision. Portal explained that theater commanders had always been empowered to use strategic Air Forces for nonstrategic operations when in their opinion a tactical emergency required it, and in giving first priority to the Italian campaign in the MTO, the CCS had recognized the necessity of occasional diversion from POINTBLANK. In Portal's opinion, and also in that of the British chiefs of staff, from the precarious position of the Germans in the Balkans constituted an emergency although, to be sure, it was the Germans and not the Allies who were threatened. Any increase in any difficulties in that area would "yield incalculable benefit" to the Allied position and to the prospects of OVERLORD. Furthermore, because the weather seldom allowed operations in more than one section at a time, a few heavy attacks on Bucharest and other cities of southeastern Europe would not interfere with through POINTBLANK.

Arnold, on his part, also believed that attacks on certain Balkan targets would aid OVERLORD and do more damage to the Germans than certain other targets on the priority lists, but that such attacks should be tied in with the general bombing program. Complete coordination and a minimum of diversion were necessary to secure maximum effectiveness. Since the USAAF had built an extremely powerful bombing force which must be used efficiently, he requested that Portal coordinate all strategic bombing efforts and keep Spaatz informed at all times of what was expected of his air fleet. Portal answered that he was in agreement on all points and that he would keep in closest touch with Spaatz. He also assured Arnold that there would be no diversion from POINTBLANK unless really important results could be expected.

This, with the exception of some differences of opinion between nine states and Russia for one bomb line (which will be discussed in chapter eight), ended the Balkan controversy for the most part. Each week Portal sent through channels the targets to be attacked in Southeast Europe. These varied from time to time as the political and military situation changed. At that time of the day the priorities were: (1) oil refineries at Ploesti, in Hungary, and in Austria; (2) mining of the Danube River, fifth and attacks on

Giurgiu and the Iron Gate Canal; (3) chrome plants at Radusa and Hanrijevo, and the Tung ram Works at Budapest. Because of the lull in fighting on
the Eastern Front and the calls for the strategic bombing force to aid in the
Italian battle, Balkan transportation, hitherto holding a high rating, was
given a low priority, and it was provided that if attacks were made on railroad centers they should be confined to centers such as Bucharest or Budapest which were the main outlets for the Germans.

8

ORGANIZATION OF THE UNITED STATES STRATEGIC AIR FORCES

The means for carrying out the American portion of the Combined Bomber Offensive were the Eighth and Fifteenth Air Forces. Together these formed the bulk of the United States Strategic Air Forces in Europe.

The Eighth had a long and varied career. It had been the first of the American Air Forces to arrive in Europe and it initiated the United States daylight precision bombing program. Its development had been hindered at times by lack of personnel and supplies, lack of long-range fighter escort, and by the loss of planes and men transferred to form the Twelfth Air Force when TORCH (invasion of North Africa) was mounted. Despite all its troubles, however, it continued to be the nucleus of the striking force which was to carry out the American policy of strategic bombing.

The Eighth was organized into three bombardment divisions, each composed of four or more combat wings. The latter, however, were purely operational in function, although toward the end of the war they began to assume certain administrative duties. Each combat wing was, in turn, composed of groups and squadrons. In addition to the bombardment divisions the Eighth Air Force also included the VIII Fighter Command, VIII Air

Force Service Command, VIII Air Force Composite Command, and the Reconnaissance Wing. The bombardment divisions carried out the heavy bombing missions; the Fighter Command furnished escort and executed certain strafing, dive, and low-level bombing operations of their own; the Composite Command was charged with training as its chief responsibility; and the Reconnaissance Wing performed the necessary photo work.

After the acquisition of suitable bases in Italy, the Fifteenth Air Force was formed out of the XII Bomber Command of the Twelfth Air Force in late 1943. The Fifteenth was planned to supplement the work of the Eighth by attacking from the Mediterranean those targets beyond the range of the latter air force. The Fifteenth, however, was not organized along lines of bomb divisions and combat wings like the Eighth. Instead, the major subdivisions were the bomb wings, which were both administrative and operational, and each of which was composed of three to six groups. At first the fighter groups were included as a component part of each bomb wing, but ultimately they were withdrawn to make up a separate fighter command, consisting of two wings. Other units composing the Fifteenth Air Force were the XV Air Service Command and a reconnaissance squadron (later a group). Also included in the Air Force was the 885th Heavy Bombardment Squadron (S) (which formerly was the 122d Liaison Squadron and which later with the 859th Heavy Bombardment Squadron made up the 2641st Special Group (Prov). The 885th was engaged in supplying the Balkan Partisans.

A matter which complicated the relations between the Eighth and Fifteenth Air Forces was the fact that they were in different theaters of operation and therefore under separate commanders in chief. The Eighth, operating in the European theater (ETO), was a part not only of USSTAF after that organization was formed but also of ETOUSA, and still later, in April 1944, it came under General Eisenhower and SHAEF (Supreme Headquarters, Allied Expeditionary Forces). There was not too much difficulty in coordinating for the first six months of the year was designed to aid OVERLORD, a theater project. The Fifteenth, however, was involved not only in POINTBLANK but in MTO programs as well, such as the Italian campaign, Balkan bombings, and ANVIL (later DRAGOON). Its operations, therefore, were subject to numerous influences. In late 1943 when the

MTO was set up as an Allied theater, an over-all air command (MAAF) was established and placed under the Allied Commander-in-Chief of the theater. Under the Air Commander-in-Chief of MAAF there was an American deputy who had administrative control over the Twelfth and Fifteenth Air Forces. There were likewise a British deputy who had similar jurisdiction over the RAF, and an Air Officer Commander-in-Chief of the Middle East. A combined staff had operational control over the strategic, tactical, and coastal air forces.

The strategic Air Force of MAAF was composed of the Fifteenth Air Force and the 20 Group, RAF. In large part, however, the operations conducted were an American show. The 205 Group at the most consisted of six to eight squadrons, and while their night attacks were valuable they were small in comparison with the huge onslaughts of the Fifteenth. The latter organization in turn lacked the polish of the Eighth. It took considerable time, patience, and training to make the Fifteenth as smooth and efficient as its elder brother. In March, General Eaker reported that it was a "pretty disorganized mob," but he had some very good men and they were "perfecting the reorganization and training of their groups pretty rapidly." Nevertheless, both he and Spaatz were discouraged. The problems of inadequate training, lowered morale, lack of airdromes, poor living conditions, and general ineffectiveness seemed almost insurmountable obstacles. Furthermore, it had been necessary to build within a few months an Air Force of more than 20 groups from an original strength of only three.

By the next month, however, Eaker was considerably encouraged and reported that the Fifteenth looked like a different organization. The benefit of lessons learned by the Eighth Air Force, insistence on high standards, new and better qualified wing and group commanders, and lack of intense enemy opposition had all played their part in developing the Fifteenth into a good strategic force. In this same month of April, General Eaker was able to report that out of over 10,000 heavy-bomber sorties, 72 per cent had been effective and nearly 500 enemy aircraft had been destroyed by the heavies. The fighters flew over 6,000 sorties, of which 77 per cent were effective, and for each fighter lost the enemy had paid with 2.4 of his own aircraft. In May the Fifteenth launched its first 1,000-plane attack. The Mediterranean strategic Air Forces had come of age.

In late 1943 it had been realized that if two strategic Air Forces were to operate from separate theaters in an efficient and economical manner against POINTBLANK targets there must be closer coordination than had previously existed. As early as November 1943, Washington was concerned over this problem. It felt that during this month neither Air Force had flown successful missions against what Headquarters, AAF considered priority targets of POINTBLANK, and it believed that the Eighth and Fifteenth Air Forces should furnish Washington with their latest pans for strategic bombing so that theater and AAF Headquarters planning would be in consonance. Not only was there a need for coordination between the Eighth and Fifteenth, but it was also necessary to harmonize the efforts of the British and American heavy-bomber forces which were operating practically independently of each other. As early as September 1943, on the suggestion of Air Marshal M. H. Bottomley, this matter had been discussed among Generals Arnold, Eaker, and Devers, and it had been concluded that the current system of coordination through the British Chief of Air Staff was satisfactory and should be continued. It was felt, however, that there was need of some agency to integrate the efforts of the American forces operating out of the MTO and ETC.

The solution as finally reached was the establishment in January 1944 of an over-all coordinating organization for the American side known as the United States Strategic Air Forces in Europe (USSTAF). The purpose was twofold. Not only would this new organization serve as a coordinating agency for the Eighth and Fifteenth but it would offer the GAF the difficult choice either of splitting its Air Force to meet attacks from two different directions or of concentrating on raids from one direction and letting the others go unresisted.

When the first plans for the unified control were submitted to the British Chiefs of Staff for consideration they objected to it on the grounds that such an organization might tend to disrupt coordination between the USAAF and RAF, and that the provision for transfer of aircraft and crews from one theater to another would be a waste of manpower and effort. The United States Joint Chiefs of Staff, however, answered that they felt that the advantages of the proposal far outweighed the disadvantages. Since the headquarters of the new organization would remain in the United Kingdom and there would be no alteration in intelligence and other services performed by the British, coordination between the United States strategic Air Forces and the RAF would be strengthened. Furthermore, the plan would have the advantage of bringing the Fifteenth Air Force into closer control. The JCS did not consider the occasional transfer of aircraft from one theater to another as wastage of manpower or facilities since each AAF group was organized to handle the need of two groups for brief periods.

After disposing of the British objections the JCS proposed to the CCS that: (1) control of all U.S. strategic Air Forces in the ETO and MTO be vested in a single command and be employed against POINTBLANK objectives or such others as the CCS might from time to time direct; (2) such over-all command coordinate its operations with the RAF Bomber Command; (3) the commanders of the U.S. Army Forces in both the United Kingdom and Mediterranean retain responsibility for over-all base services and administrative control of the strategic air forces; (4) provision be made to assure adequate support to POINTBLANK as the air operation of first priority;(5) the headquarters of the U .S. strategic Air Forces be established in the United Kingdom; (6) the Commanding General of the U.S. Army Air Forces have direct channels of approach to the Commanding General of USSTAF.

On the basis of the above points the CCS established USSTAF, effective 1 January 1944. Under the terms of the directive USSTAF was to come under the command of the Supreme Allied Commander (SAC) at a later date, and in the meantime the British Chief of Air Staff would continue as deputy for the CCS and be responsible for coordinating all POINTBLANK operations. The Commanding General, USSTAF was charged with determining the priorities of POINTBLANK targets to be attacked by the Eighth and Fifteenth and with coordination of the efforts of these two air forces. He was also authorized to move the units of the Eighth and Fifteenth between the ETO and MTO within the limits of base area facilities and available for his forces. USSTAF was also to keep the Allied Commander-in-Chief. The U.S. commanding generals in ETO and MTO would continue to be responsible for the administrative control of the AAF in their areas of command, including the base services. Whenever a strategic or tactical emergency arose, however, theater commanders could, at their discretion, employ the strategic Air Forces based in their theater for purposes other than POINTBLANK, but they must inform the CCS and Commanding General, USSTAF of their action.

Lt. Gen. Carl Spaatz was designated Commanding General of USSTAF and immediately began organizing his new command. The headquarters of the Eighth Air Force became the headquarters of USSTAF under the new setup. The VIII Bomber Command was inactivated and its headquarters became that of the Eight Air Force. The POINTBLANK operations of the Fifteenth Air Force were controlled by Spaatz's Deputy Commanding General Operations who also coordinated efforts of the Ninth Air Force and the RAF. Personnel and logistic requirements of the Eighth and Ninth Air Forces were coordinated by the Deputy Commanding General for Administration, who also had under his jurisdiction the over-all air service command.

On 20 January, Spaatz assumed responsibility for all United States Air Forces in England; and the old office of Commanding General of USAAF in the United Kingdom, which had been held by Eaker along with his job as Commanding General of the Eighth Air Force, was abolished. The question arose, however, as to the wisdom of this move, and after the return of Maj. Gen. B.M. Giles from a visit to England it was suggested to Arnold that Spaatz be officially given such command as an additional duty. Arnold was cold to this recommendation, although Spaatz was willing to assume the added responsibility. Arnold pointed out that in forming USSTAF he not only had had in mind the unification of the two strategic United States Air Forces but also the building up of an American air commander to the same level as Harris, The RAF commander, and parallel to General Eisenhower. "If you do not remain in a position parallel with Harris," he wrote Spaatz, "the air war will certainly be won by the RAF if anybody. Already the spectacular effectiveness f their devastation of cities has placed their contribution in the popular mind at so high a plane that I am having the greatest difficulty in keeping your achievement (far less spectacular to the public) in its proper role not only in publications, but unfortunately in military and naval circles and, in fact, with the President himself." Arnold was likewise afraid that Eisenhower would not be SAC after the cross-Channel invasion had been achieved, and therefore if Spaatz were not on an equal basis he would be subordinate to Eisenhower who as Commanding General of the American Army Forces, would, in turn, be subordinate to SAC. Spaatz then would have limited responsibilities. If a common administrative authority over the USAAF in England was necessary, he recommended that Spaatz's deputy commander be given the job as additional duty. This would not give Spaatz any lawful authority over administrative matters; but Arnold said he could not imagine one of Spaatz's deputies going contrary to Spaatz's wishes merely because he had the legal right to do so.

Spaatz replied that both the progress of USSTAF in coordinating the efforts of the Eighth and Fifteenth and the accepted channels of communications were satisfactory and should give Arnold no cause for alarm. Eisenhower, he said, planned to make Air Marshal Tedder the SHAF executive in over-all control of air operations when USSTAF went under control of SAC in accordance with the original directive. Leigh-Mallory would command the Allied Expeditionary Air Forces, which would include only those units assigned to it. There was no danger of USSTAF becoming subordinate to or a part of AEAF. Harris and Spaatz would be coequal and would receive orders from SAC through Tedder in accordance with a basic plan which would be developed by equal representation from the RAF, AEAF and USSTAF. Furthermore, both Tedder and Spaatz were agreed on the vital necessity of POINTBLANK. If Eisenhower's plan of organization was not accepted, however, then Spaatz recommended Arnold's suggestion of appointing the Deputy Commanding General (Administration) of USSTAF as Commanding General of USAAF in England as an additional duty. But until a decision was made on Eisenhower's plan, Spaatz recommended a status quo on the situation.

At this same time the discussion over target priorities for the completion of the CBO was being carried on the AEAF, USSTAF, and SHAEF. With the acceptance of the AEAF proposal that transportation be given priority over oil in preparation for OVERLORD, the CCS passed the responsibility to SAC for directing all air operations out of England, including USSTAF and the RAF Bomber Command. This change of responsibility became effective on 14 April, and Spaatz was instructed to look to Tedder for direction on all operations concerned with POINTBLANK and OVERLORD. In regard to the Balkan operations of the Fifteenth Air Force, however,

Portal would continue to determine the weekly priorities. Once OVER-
LORD was established the CCS would review the future method of direction and employment of the strategic air forces. This, then, was the situation
that existed through D-day.

Although in early March Spaatz had expressed satisfaction with the
operational setup, the divided lines of authority and the provision that the
theater commanders could declare emergencies and divert the strategic
forces from POINTBLANK objectives created at times confusion and mis-
understandings. Again it was the Balkans which provoked the most trouble.
During the period of debate over the USSTAF and AEAF plans for the completion of the CBO, Spaatz continued to assign target priorities for his
forces under the authority granted him by the CCS when USSTAF was
established. The USSTAF plan under consideration gave oil the high priority, and Spaatz had placed the Ploesti refineries on the list of primary targets for the Fifteenth Air Force. Portal, after conferring with the CCS and
His Majesty's Government, decided against oil and substituted the Ploesti
marshaling yards. This he did under his authority to determine Balkan targets for the Fifteenth and under the authority of the Allied Commander-in-
Chief, MTO to use the strategic Air Forces under him for targets other than
POINTBLANK hen an emergency existed. This decision brought from
Spaatz a complaint that too many people were giving orders to the Fifteenth. As he understood it, this organization operated under his instructions except when a tactical situation of the ground forces in Italy
demanded otherwise, and he declared that if this confused state of affairs
continued he could not accept the responsibility for the Fifteenth Air Force.
Unless the CCS took definite action on command channels, he said, the
power of USSTAF would be emasculated. Arnold backed up Spaatz and
emphasized the purpose of the Fifteenth in the POINTBLANK program to
Portal. The latter replied that he regretted the trouble which had arisen and
assured Arnold that any by-passing of Spaatz in giving orders to the Fifteenth was wholly unintentional. He did insist, however, that he had the
right to divert the strategic Air Forces in the Mediterranean when a strategic
or tactical emergency arose, and because of the political situation and status
of the Russian advance he considered that an emergency existed in the
MTO.

Another area where diversion from POINTBLANK targets occurred was the Italian peninsula. This was understandable since the CCS had given highest priority in the MTO to the Italian campaign. It must also be remembered that the Allied Commander-in-Chief, MTO had the authority to requisition the strategic Air Forces under him whenever he considered a tactical emergency was uppermost in importance. The three Italian campaigns which called for specific aid from the Mediterranean Allied Strategic Air Force (MASAF) were: Anzio (SHINGLE); Cassino break-through; and DIADEM (interdiction of north Italian railroads) which included the final push against Rome. Not all bombing in support of these projects, however, called for diversion, and often support to both the Italian campaign and POINTBLANK could be given simultaneously.

Since USSTAF was organized for the purpose of coordinating the efforts of the Eighth and Fifteenth Air Forces and bringing about uniformity in POINTBLANK, the question naturally arises as to how successfully the objective was achieved in actual operations. The numerous changes in command that took place in early 1944 because of the reorganization in the MTO and ETO delayed coordinated action for the Eighth and Fifteenth Air Forces for several weeks. On 3 February General Spaatz issued his first directive outlining the methods by which these attacks would be carried out. There were three possible types of coordination. The first method was coordination initiated by either air force. The commanding generals concerned would notify each other daily of their bombing intentions in order that either one could take advantage of any diversionary effect or give support to the other's mission. Direct communication between the Eighth and Fifteenth Air Forces for this purpose was authorized, but Headquarters, USSTAF and Headquarters MAAF also had to be notified simultaneously of the daily bombing plans and any changes therein. The second method was coordination by previously prepared plans worked out by the Combined Operational Planning Committee. Either Air Force could initiate any such already planned operation, with necessary modifications to meet conditions of the moment, upon proper notification to the other headquarters. The third method was coordination by special direction of the Commanding General of USSTAF. This method would be employed when

USSTAF decided the necessity for direct execution of a coordinated attack, and it might be ordered on very short notice.

Early difficulties encountered in successfully executing this directive led Spaatz to revise it on 22 February. The three types of coordination remained the same but direct communication between the Eighth and Fifteenth Air Forces was prohibited and all notices of bombing intentions or changes would be reported to the other Air Force by relay through USSTAF and MAAF. If one Air Force wished to put in operation one of the CCPC's previously planned attacks the request would be made through normal channels. In the case of the Fifteenth the request would go through MAAF and, if approved by Eaker, would be forwarded to USSTAF, which would accomplish all necessary coordination. When the third type of coordination was employed there could be no cancellation without authority from the Commanding General of USSTAF. If an emergency which would interfere with the proposed mission existed in the Italian battle, it was left to the discretion of the Commanding General of MAAF as to whether all or a part of the Fifteenth Air Force would be withdrawn. USSTAF, however, was to be promptly notified of any changes in the plans in order that the operations of the Eighth could be amended. Notification also had to be given when weather prohibited participation in a planned mission.

In the period covered by this study, however, only three coordinated attacks were completed, but the results of these three fully paid for the effort expended in setting up an over-all control agency. Numerous other benefits also were derived from having USSTAF. It harmonized the work of two Air Forces operating in different theaters and planned and executed other important operations such as the shuttle bombing to and from Russian bases (FRANTIC) which began in June 1944.

9

WEAPONS AND DEFENSE

In addition to operational and administrative planning and organization there were numerous other problems to be solved in order to make the Combined Bomber Offensive a success. Well-trained combat crews were necessary to insure maximum usefulness of the air forces. Adequate supplies had to be available. New and modified weapons needed to be developed to meet ever-changing battle conditions. If the enemy were to be subjected to round-the-clock bombing, techniques for defeating the weather had to be evolved. Self-defense measures and methods of penetrating the enemy defenses had to be worked out.

Although the Training Command and the four domestic Air Forces provided the great bulk of training, supplementary training and indoctrination in combat techniques were necessary in the theaters of operation. After the reorganization of the Eighth Air Force and the establishment of USSTAF in January 1944, this work became the chief function of the Composite Command. In addition to combat training the Eighth gave instruction in a number of miscellaneous subjects, such as the use of personal equipment and air-sea rescue procedures. Provision was also made for keeping up to date on engineering advancements. A Boeing aircraft school for engineering personnel of B-17 units had to be provided because of the number of modifications made on the Flying Fortress since the first groups had arrived in the theater. The Eighth also made use of schools not under its jurisdiction, but to which it sent personnel on temporary duty at various times. Some of these gave instruction in B-17 armament, Cyclone engines, Wasp engines, sheet metal, and Link trainer maintenance.

In the Mediterranean theater, training was at first under the Training and Equipment Section of MAAF Combat Operations Division, but in April 1944 this was transferred to A-3 of AAF/MTO. The latter was now charged with formulating training policies of all USAAF units in the theater. Although much of the necessary instruction was given by the individual wings and group in accordance with A-3 directives, arrangements were made with several RAF schools in the Middle East to give specialized training to U.S. personnel. The courses so arranged provided instructions for gunnery leaders, filterers and plotters, pilot gunnery instructors, fighter controllers, and bombing leaders. The best course, however, did not prove satisfactory since the instructors dealt entirely with RAF tactics and equipment which differed considerably from those of the Americans.

One of the biggest problems faced by the Air Forces was the training of aircrews for combat after arrival in the theaters. It was impractical to dispatch green crews to combat without some training and indoctrination in actual battle conditions as opposed to the theoretical conditions learned in the Zone of the Interior. In the Eighth Air Force this job was undertaken by the Composite Command and new crews were assigned to one of its combat crew replacement centers (CCRC) for the necessary training. When the Composite Command assumed this increased responsibility in early January it was possible to accept only 20 crews at a time, but by the end of this same month the program was revised, and with enlarged accommodations 40 crews could be trained in each course. A shortage of B-24 crews in early April led to orders to speed up the program. This was done by assigning new crews to combat units as soon as they finished their ground school, in which case flying training was accomplished at an operational airdrome. Here, by performing practice missions before going into combat, crews did not fly alone or in a lead position until they had the required experience. It was also in April that the Composite Command established its peak record when it graduated 467 heavy bomber crews and 581 fighter pilots from its CCRC's.

The Fifteenth Air Force lacked an organization similar to the Composite Command and its training of combat crews was carried out largely by the groups and squadrons to which they were assigned. The burden on both the MTO and ETO was lightened somewhat in the late spring of 1944 when the four domestic Air Forces were required to specialize in the type of training they gave. All the heavy bombardment crews of the First, Second, and Third Air Forces were scheduled thereafter to go to the European and Mediterranean theaters, and they were given as much theater indoctrination as time allowed before their departure.

Another plan for combat crew training was evolved in late January 1944. This concerned crews which were already battle-wise, however, and not new replacements. When USSTAF was established, its commanding general was authorized to move units from one theater to another when the occasion demanded; but varying theater conditions did not make this feasible unless the crews were familiar with each other's problems. Therefore a mutual exchange of combat crews between the Eighth and Fifteenth Air Forces was contemplated. Eighth Air Force commanders did not look with favor on the scheme. They argued that the crews they would lose would be more experienced in leadership under ETO conditions than the ones they received. Thus, the effectiveness of the operating force would be reduced, at least temporarily. Headquarters, AAF and the War Department, however, believed the idea an excellent one for equalizing experiences and losses, and Spaatz was authorized to proceed without further authority, but to keep Washington advised as to timing and methods to be employed. The first exchange of crews took place in February. Eighth Air Force crews to be exchanged were to have completed 12 to 15 missions and those of the Fifteenth 23 to 27 missions. In the new theater the crews from the Eighth would complete 23 to 27 missions and the Fifteenth from 12 to 15, but once rotated the crews would not be again interchanged.

While plans for the interchange of crews were being discussed, an alternative scheme was proposed by Brig. Gen. Robert B. Williams, Commanding General of the 1st Bombardment Division. He suggested sending 15 of his crews and 10 airplanes to North Africa for a short period of training, all to be returned to him upon completion of it. It was decided to study this proposal and if feasible carry it into execution. In April, arrangements were completed for sending 10 airplanes and crews of the 1st Bombardment Division for training at Fifteenth Air Force bases in Italy. Each aircraft was to bring three maintenance men, but all other facilities would be provided by the Fifteenth.

Pilots, as well as crews, needed a certain amount of training during their combat tour of duty. In February, the Eighth Air Force initiated two pilot-training courses. The first course was in the use of SCS-51 blind-landing equipment, which was new and considered superior to all other such equipment. Each bombardment group furnished one pilot to attend this school. Upon completing his training, he returned to instruct the other pilots in his group. The second course taught pilots how to operate airplane engines more efficiently. This instruction had a two-fold purpose: (1) to reduce fuel consumption, particularly on long-range missions; and (2) to reduce general wear and tear on aircraft power units. The curriculum was drawn up by the A-3 Training Section and the Operational Research Section, and instruction was carried out in each group.

In the Fifteenth Air Force, the inexperience of pilots was a source of concern to Headquarters, AAF as well as to the commanding generals in MTO. Arnold cabled Eaker that he was aware of the lack of leadership in airplane commanders (not only in the 15th, but all in all the air forces) and that an attempt was being made in the Zone of the Interior to improve the quality by placing more emphasis on knowledge of equipment and military discipline for replacements. The training period could not be lengthened, said Arnold, but he would welcome any suggestions from the theater. Major General Nathan F. Twining, Commanding General of the 15th Air Force, recommended, therefore, that during the training period pilots should be drilled in the responsibilities of airplane commanders; personal discipline of all crew members; preservation of command channels; dangers of undue familiarity between commander and crew members; technical knowledge and responsibility for proper operation of all airplane equipment; ability to give orders with assurance; and careful and precise execution of commands. In the theater, training was continued by using nonoperational days to keep the men proficient. Long periods of sustained operations had tended to lower efficiency and bring about deterioration in both formation flying and bombing. It was for this reason that nonoperational days were utilized for training. Instruction, though, was carried on in the group and not at a centralized location.

Fighter pilots also came in for their share of training. In the Eighth Air Force the VIII Composite Command handled this instruction in the 495th and 496th Fighter Training Groups. Fighter pilots for the 15th Air Force that first received their theater precombat training in the Fighter Training Center of the XII Allied Air Force Training and Replacement Command (Prov.). This training for P-38 pilot was later transferred to the 15th Air Force because of a lack of serviceable planes in the Training Center. P-38 replacements were sent, therefore, directly to the air force's fighter bases and there given the necessary training. In April the same policy was put into effect for P-47 and P-51 replacements. The introduction of the P-51 into the 15th posed a new training problem. With no centralized training center and no experienced P-51 personnel to give instruction, the 15th was obliged to request the Eighth to lend the needed instructors, including at least one squadron or flight leader. The same procedure had also been followed earlier for P-47 training.

Since the chief function of heavy bombers was to drop bombs directly on a target considerable attention was given to achieving a high degree of accuracy. In the United States crews and bombardier had been trained under more favorable conditions, and this resulted in the belief that American flyers could hit fish in a pickle barrel. In the theater, however, weather and enemy defenses such as smoke screens, flak, and fighter opposition limited the degree of accuracy obtainable and made necessary many adjustments in technique. Many lessons had to be learned the hard way in actual battle, but it was possible to pass on the experience so gained to green crews before they began to fly combat missions.

Although the VIII Composite Command trained the Eighth Air Force replacements, there was constant need for continuous training in the operational groups. In January, the Eighth Air Force training director urged greater use of synthetic equipment by those groups possessing it, and those without these aids were told to requisition them immediately. The problem was further aggravated by a scarcity of practice bombing ranges, but this situation was considerably alleviated by March. A new problem complicated Eighth Air Force training as the time for the invasion of the Continent drew nearer. It was realized that the heavy bombers would be assigned a number of tactical targets on D-day and in the weeks following, and since this work required different techniques than those employed in strategic bombing, studies of such methods were made, and training on the new procedures began in May.

The need for training in the Fifteenth Air Force is illustrated by a complaint of Eaker to Twining in March that studies of accuracy, particularly of B-24s, in attacks on marshaling yards and airdromes were disappointing, and he stressed the necessity for improved accuracy, formation flying, and leadership. Twining replied that he fully concurred with Eaker and he hoped to show a marked improvement in the near future, especially when the Fifteenth got back to more frequent strategic bombing and when blisters for navigator and bombardier were installed in the B-24 airplane. In order to improve the accuracy, Headquarters, 15th Air Force had established a full-time school for bombardiers and by June was turning out approximately 20 potential leaders a week. The Operations Analysis Section made exhaustive studies on bombing problems and error and in collaboration with the training section published a weekly "dope sheet" called "straight and level," which listed all bombing results and helped stimulate competition between groups. One practice bombing range for each wing was also provided and it was hoped that by summer two would be available for each. Training was given on these ranges on all nonoperational days and at any time when individual planes were not being used in combat.

In general the Eighth showed better results than the 15th, although the latter indicated an improvement of 5% on the basis of Circular Probable Error (CEP) in the first four months of 1944. In May the average CEP for Eighth Air Force B-17's at a 15,000 foot altitude was 900 feet and for the B-24s it was 1100 feet. The CEP in the Fifteenth for B-17s at 15000 feet was 1050 feet and for B-24s it was 1250 feet. At a 20,000-foot altitude the Eighth Air Force CEP was 1100 and 1300 feet for B-17s and B-24s respectively; and in the Fifteenth, 1470 feet for B-17s and 1600 feet for B-24s. It was expected that accuracy of the Eighth would be better than that of the Fifteenth, which was a newer and less well integrated air force. Despite the striving, a high degree of accuracy was not achieved in this period. A survey of over-all bombing results for the entire war shows that only 20% of bombs aimed at precision targets fell within a circle having a radius of 1000 feet. This low percentage of accuracy made it necessary, of course, to send larger tonnages of bombs against targets than would have been required if accuracy had been greater. One of the most persistent training problems in the theaters of operation was that of aerial gunners in heavy bombardment units. A high degree of efficiency was needed even after the increase of long-range fighter escort reduced the danger from the GAF, because there was always a group or two upon which the enemy concentrated with ferocity and determination. The blame for the poor showing of gunners lay in large part in the training they received in the Zone of the Interior. The chief deficiencies complained of in the combat zones were (1) inability of many gunners to perform their basic mission; (2) little or no knowledge of the .50 caliber machine gun; (3) inability to load turrets; (4) lack of information on sighting.

During January 1944 in conjunction with its combat crew training, the VIII Composite Command established a ground school for serial bombers at Greencastle, Holland. The gunnery school at Snettisham was also reorganized to give flexible and turret gunnery instruction to 4000 men a month, and all gunnery replacements in the ETO were sent here prior to being assigned to a tactical organization. An exchange of Eighth Air Force gunners with instructors from the Zone of the Interior was worked out. Those from the United States were assigned to the three bombardment divisions where they participated in a minimum of three missions, and then were placed in a CCRC or bomb group as gunnery instructors. Training turrets were set up in some groups, and it all, practice missions were flown in which fighters made mock attacks while the gunners practiced tracking and aiming. Training films and pamphlets were widely used and instruction was given in aircraft recognition.

In the 15th Air Force arrangements were also made with the Zone of the Interior to provide instructor training for flexible gunnery. Devices such as the Poorman trainer and training turrets were employed in the groups, and practice ranges were set up. Fixed gunnery training was carried on in the fighter units in addition to sending two pursuit pilots a month to the RAF school at Ballah, Egypt.

Supply was another persistent problem of both the strategic air forces. Foremost interest in this matter was, perhaps, in maintaining a constant flow of planes and crews from the United States to the theaters in enough volume to allow both for build-up to authorized strength and for adequate replacements. Next in importance was the problem of keeping the planes on hand operational, because regardless of how much equipment was assigned, it was useless unless it was ready for combat. During the first five months of 1944, the percentage of heavy bombers operational in either one of the strategic air forces ranged from 65 per cent to 86 per cent, with the monthly average for both being somewhat over 70 per cent. One of the chief reasons for the nonoperational state of aircraft was the lack of spare parts for repair. In February, it was stated that 10 per cent of the B-17's in the Eighth Air Force were grounded for this reason. In other cases maintenance men were handicapped by shortages of tools and such raw stock as sheet metal, cable, wire, and hose. The Fifteenth Air Force had the same experience. It was estimated that 9 per cent of the non-operational bombers in that organization in March were grounded because of spare-part shortages. In most cases these were small items which could be brought from Patterson Field to Italy in one transport plane. Maj. Gen. Walter H. Frank, Commanding General of the Air Service Command, recommended that a plane or two be sent to the United States to procure the necessary items and bring them back to the theater. This would be sufficient to put 60 aircraft in commission. Accordingly, Twining was directed to dispatch to Patterson Field one Fortress and one Fortress and one Liberator from his force to pick up the needed supplies. The planes used were to be those least likely to be needed for tactical operations, and their crews would be those with great experience and most deserving of a trip home.

Another factor in determining the number of planes that could be put into the air at any one time was the number of crews available. The attrition rate rose steadily as the bomber offensive was stepped up. For the first three months of 1944 the Eighth Air Force lost a total of 857 bombers, of which 723 were missing in action. The crew casualties were 430 killed, 656 wounded, and 7160 missing; and, with losses due to other causes, the Eighth lost a total of 1094 combat crews during this same period. More than half this number, or 552 bomber crews, was lost in May alone. The Fifteenth lost a total of 229 heavy bombers in the first quarter of 1944, with approximately the same number of crews. In May alone the loss amounted to 168. The flow of replacements did not always keep pace with the needs. At one time Eaker complained that although the Fifteenth lost 114 heavy bomber crews in February, he was told to expect only 57 replacements in March and 51 in April. Even though the Eighth Air Force fared somewhat better than the Fifteenth, its available craw strength dwindled from a surplus over operational aircraft in January to a reverse situation in May. The relationship of operational aircraft to operational combat crews determined the combined effective operational strength of both air forces.

One of the theories upon which heavy bombers had been developed was that they would be able to furnish their own protection. The practical application of this theory early in the war proved, however, very costly. Numerous modifications in armament and armor were made, mostly in 1943, o correct the faults discovered by actual battle experience. Satisfactory modifications in armament of the B-17 had been completed by late summer of 1943 and it was not until a year later that further major changes were made. On the B-24 several gun changes were tried in the early months of 1943. In the fall of that year several more occurred. The waist gun position, for example, was relocated farther outboard to increase the azimuth of fire. A nose turret also superseded the twin .50-cal. Nose gun so as to give more frontal protection. The retractable ball turret, installed in production aircraft in the fall of 1943, was removed on some of the Liberators in June 1944. This turret had lost much of its value since the enemy ceased attacking in the field covered by it, and its removal gave increased performance to the airplane. Several changes in armor also were instituted in both the B-17 and B-24. In order to reduce the weight of the aircraft, flak curtains were substituted for armor plate to protect the crew, and the results appeared to be satisfactory. One of the most vital points in an airplane is its engine. The number of planes which were lost when the enemy was successful in hitting the engines led to experimentation in 1944 with heavily armored power units. The changes proved unsuitable in operation, however, because the added weight of the protective equipment reduced the speed of the plane too much.

Excluding outside help, the best defense for the heavy bombers seemed
to be in the type of formation they flew. When the Eighth began to operate
in August 1942 it used a squadron formation of six aircraft each, but the
squadrons were so widely separated that they were unable to give mutual
fire support. This small formation had, however, an advantage in flexibility
and permitted greater bombing accuracy. In September, the 18-aircraft
group composed of two squadron combat boxes of nine planes each was
used. Each squadron, made up of three elements, flew a V formation, and
each element was a V of three aircraft. This gave greater compactness to the
group at the expense of flexibility. Then came the 36-plane group and the
javelin and wedge formation. The increasing enemy opposition and lack of
long-range fighters to escort the bombers all the way to the target and back
demanded still more fire power and minimum exposure. To provide this the
54-plane group was devised in the spring of 1943, and remained the
standard formation throughout the rest of the year. Despite its protective
advantages, it was unwieldy and inflexible, it failed to take care of stragglers,
and pin-point bombing accuracy was reduced. In January 1944 the increase
of fighter escort and its longer range allowed the return to a 36-plane formation. The introduction of pathfinder force (PFF) equipment also necessitated a smaller and more compact organization. The effectiveness of the 36-
plane type of formation was proven in the attacks of February in which the
Luftwaffe suffered its worst setback. This became standard operating procedure until the spring of 1945 when a 27-plane formation was inaugurated.

By the spring of 1944 the danger from the GAF had decreased and
danger from flak had increased, so that there was need for a revision in the
internal organization of the 36-plane formation. There were more damages
than losses from flak, but in both categories there was a constant increase. In
order to offset the hazards of flak, Lt. Gen. James H. Doolittle, Commanding General of the Eighth, requested his division commanders in
March to study types of formations best suited for defense against flak. In
the coming months increasing attention would be focused on such installations as marshaling yards, roads, railroads, and bridges, all of which would
be heavily defended by antiaircraft fire. In May the 12-ship stagger which
gave the necessary protection to each group of 36 planes and allowed safer
bomb dropping was perfected.

The best defense against enemy air opposition, however, was in the use of fighter escort. It was realized very early in the war that regardless of the armor and formations of heavy bombers the losses were great unless they were adequately protected by fighters. In general, therefore, the range of the fighters limited the depth of penetration which could be economically effected by the heavies. This did not mean, however, that the experiment of self-protection ceased. Formations of B-17's and B-24's continued to fly beyond the fighter range, but usually at great cost. This continued until the fall of 1943 when operations were more or less restricted to the fighter ranges. The peak for average monthly losses in the Eighth Air Force was reached in October with 28 bombers lost per mission. Thereafter, when bomber missions were held down to or not far beyond the capabilities of the escort, the average monthly losses were cut to half and less than half.

In May 1943 when P-47's began to join the Spitfires in escort duties their range was only about 175 miles from their base. This meant of course, that the bombers had the benefit of their protection for only a short distance across the English Channel. In August of that year the addition of a belly tank increased the range to about 375 miles. Two 108-gallon wing tanks attached in February 1944 extended the P-47's radius another 100 miles. With the wing tanks this airplane could fly still farther when not escorting. In fact, it was possible to reach beyond Berlin on a sweep. The first group of P-38's became operational in October 1943 and was used to provide escort beyond the range of the P-47's. In November, P-3's with two wing tanks of 75 gallons each were able to fly escort for 520 miles. Increasing the size of wing tanks to 108 gallons each in February 1944 extended the range to 585 miles. One of the most satisfactory of the fighters for escort purposes was the P-51. Without any additional fuel tanks this airplane could range as far as the P-47 with its wing tanks. The addition of two 75-gallon wing tanks in March 1944 allowed the P-51 to escort for 650 miles, and with two 108-gallon wing tanks, added the same month, its potential range was 850 miles from base. The high point in escort for this plane was on 29 May 1944 when it furnished escort all the way to and from Poznan (Posen) – a distance of over 700 miles. From that time on fighters escorted the bombers to every target.

The range of the fighters and the number available to accompany the bombers demanded that various methods of escort tactics be developed to meet varying conditions. Three basic types of escort were finally evolved: (1) close or direct support, (2) area support, and (3) combination area and close support. In the first, the fighters flew with the bombers protecting them from the enemy. Since there was considerable weaving back and forth to ward off attacks and cover the slower bombers, the potential range was greatly reduced. In order to overcome this deficiency, a system of relays was worked out, whereby the bombers would be met at various rendezvous points by fighters flying directly from their bases to relieve the old escort. The new group would give escort for another specified distance, and then in turn be relieved by another group, and so on until the target was reached. A similar plan was followed on the return.

The second basic type, area support, was used when continuous direct support was too difficult because of the splitting of the bomber stream into small units to attack a number of targets. In this case, fighters would precede the bombers and patrol the area through which they would pass to clear it of enemy planes. This third type was used when there was a deep penetration into enemy territory before division into smaller units. In this case, continuous support was given until time for dividing and area support was given in the target areas. Continuous protection was again resorted to on the return trip after the bombers had re-formed into a single force.

Despite the need for adequate numbers of long-range fighters, it was not until the spring and summer of 1944 that the supply began to meet the demand. Adding to the difficulty resulting from the shortage was the fact that the planes had to be divided between two strategic air forces, each operating in a separate theater. The Eighth Air Force, being the older and larger of the two and considered the leader in POINTBLANK, naturally had first call on personnel and equipment. General Eaker by dint of argument and hard work, however, was able over a period of six months to build up the fighter force of the Fifteenth to its authorized strength. In January he convinced General Spaatz that P-38 groups scheduled for transfer to the ETO should remain in the Mediterranean. At that time Eaker's P-38 groups were down to an average of less than 36 operational planes, and he maintained it would be absurd to take away the only long-distance escort for the heavy bombers at the very time that deep raids into Germany on an extensive scale were in the offing. Gain in February the question arose as to the advisability of transferring certain pursuit units to England for the build-up of OVERLORD, and once more it was decided to let the Mediterranean forces alone. The heavy bombers of the Fifteenth were desperately in need of these escorting planes. The P-47's could not range farther than the Alps, and for this reason could be used only to escort bombers to targets in the Po valley and parts of the Balkans. There were only three P-38 groups at half strength, and since they were of the old type their range did not much exceed the Alps. The shortage of planes also prevented the use of relays to and from the target, which meant that the bombers were needlessly exposed to enemy attacks. But as soon as sufficient and properly equipped P-38's and P-51's, able to escort the bombers all the way to and from the target, were available the hazards of POINTBLAN missions would be greatly reduced. The presence of just one fighter group in the target area, Eaker maintained, would cut bomber losses 75 per cent.

The build-up in the Fifteenth Air Force continued, however, at a slow pace. Devers explained that the greater losses sustained by the Fifteenth in February than by the Eighth were due to the shortage of long-range escorts. In February and March plans were developed to have three groups of P-38's and four of P-51's eventually assigned to the Fifteenth with one P-47 group being retained until full strength of the P-51's was reached. Some of the P-47 groups already in the Fifteenth, such as the 325th, would be converted to P-51's to accomplish this. It was also decided to transfer three fighter groups from the Twelfth to the Fifteenth Air Force and equip them with P-51's for long-range escort purposes. The groups selected were the 31st, 52d, and 332d. The first transfer, that of the 31st Fighter Group, became effective on 1 April, and the last, that of the 332d, in late May. This latter group, composed of Negroes, presented several problems. Experience, particularly at Anzio, showed this group was more efficient at aerial fighting than in giving ground support. At first it was planned to equip the 332d with P-63's, but since these planes were not yet free of "bugs" the idea was dropped. It was finally decided to put the 332d Fighter Group into P-47's. The equipping and transfer of the group was dependent, however, upon the re-equipping of other P-47 units with P-51's. The transition was finally accomplished, and on 31 May the 332d Group was transferred to the Fifteenth Air Force for duty.

Slowly but steadily the work of equipping and transitioning proceeded. In the latter part of March Eaker informed Arnold that he could cease worrying about the Fifteenth since there was now "the means and the will to bring it to a high level of efficiency." The 31st Fighter Group, the first P-51 unit of the Fifteenth, was fully equipped and started operations in April. For the first time the Italy-based strategic bombers had full support to and from targets beyond the Alps. By June, the long-range fighter program was practically complete and it was possible to provide increased protection to the 21 heavy bomber groups in the Fifteenth Air Force.

Although the Eighth Air Force did not have so much trouble as the Fifteenth in regard to long-range escorts, it was faced with similar problems. When it was decided in January not to transfer the pursuit units from MTO to VIII Fighter Command, plans were formulated to bring a P-38 squadron from Iceland to the Eighth to help meet the requirements of that air force. In spite of shortages, however, the Eighth was able to reach a new high in the use of fighter escort in January when full sport was given on all major attacks except two. Work had also been started on equipping all fighters with extra fuel tanks and/or bomb shackles. Though the VIII Air Force Service Command did not hold out much hope that these installations could be fully completed before 1 September, by pushing the job practically all the aircraft in the VIII Fighter Command were equipped with the additional tanks by the end of April.

The Eighth like the Fifteenth used the same process of converting and transferring in order to get an adequate number of groups capable of long-distance escort. In February the 358th Group, equipped with P-4's, was transferred to the Ninth Air Force for a P-51's, and by 31 May seven such groups were operational. By this time the Eighth Air Force had 522 P-51's on hand of which 383 were fully operational, 634 crews assigned with 459 available, and an effective strength of 382. This meant that practically 100 per cent of the serviceable P-51's cold be flown at any time. In addition to the P-51's the Eighth also had four groups of P-47's and four of P-38's by the end of May. Altogether there were 870 fully operational fighter aircraft, 1039 available crews, and the effective strength was 856.

In general the P-51 was the preferred plans for long-range escort, and during the transition period these airplanes and their pilots were borrowed from the Ninth to participate in critical missions. The P-47 was considered very dependable, but its usefulness was limited by its range. Cold cockpits, low carburetor air temperatures, and poor functioning of the turbo-regulator affected the efficiency of the P-38. New flying suits, electric gloves and spats, however, solved the cold problem, and a modification program of Lockheed promised to remedy the mechanical defects. Brig. Gen. Francis H. Griswold, Chief of Staff of the VIII Fighter Command, believed that despite these corrections the P-38 had reached its zenith of potentialities for escort at high altitudes, but he also believed that it would be extremely valuable in other operations at lower altitudes.

The effectiveness of the fighters in reducing bomber losses was cited by Spaatz in April while the fighter program was still incomplete. On 17 April 1943, 115 bombers were dispatched without escort to attack the Focke-Wulf plant at Bremen. They flew 40 miles over the sea in order to lessen the danger from enemy attack, but 16 bombers were lost that day. On 18 April 1944, nearly 1000 bombers took off to attack several targets in the Berlin area. Protected by almost 700 fighters they flew straight through enemy territory in broad daylight with a resulting loss of only 19 bombers and 6 fighters. The Germans were hoarding their fighter force by this time, however, and despite efforts to provoke the GAF to combat only one of the three bomb divisions encountered formidable opposition. One of the most telling arguments for strong long-range fighter escort was given by the German Reichsmarshal himself. When he was asked at the close of the war why the Luftwaffe failed to prevent the serial invasion of Germany, Goering replied: "I most firmly believe that the reason was the success of the American Air Force in putting out a long-range escort airplane, which enabled the bombers to penetrate deep into the Reich territory and still have a constant and strong fighter cover. Without this escort, the air offensive would never have succeeded. Nobody thought such long-range fighter escort was possible." He had at first refused to believe, he said, that American fighters could fly escort even to Liege. It was still more incredible when they went as far as Hannover, but when they appeared over Berlin with the bombers he knew the results would be tragic.

Even if the GAF had been completely driven out of the sky there would have been yet another enemy for the bombers to battle. That was Nature, and she frequently played a deciding part in the success of a mission. Oftentimes weather determined the target to be attacked, routes to be followed, altitudes to be flown, and numerous other factors necessary in planning a raid. As a rule, weather in England and Western Europe seemed to conspire against the Allies. Throughout the year there was a procession of storms, fog, and cloud banks, and during the winter there was a severe storm on an average of once every three days in the region between London and Berlin. Even in the summer months cloud cover over Germany averaged 50 to 80 per cent. The AAF weather experts estimated early in the war that the maximum number of days per month that visual daylight bombing operations could be carried out would be 10, and the average that could be expected was six.

Nor was weather in the MTO any better. In the weeks following the Big Week in February the weather was so consistently bad that it was difficult to capitalize on the gains made in that week. It was not uncommon, therefore, in either theater for operational summaries to read: "Weather conditions over the continent were very poor and visual bombing of all primaries was impossible," "Solid cloud rising to as high as 24,000 feet prevented six combat wings from completing assembly," "Several attempts made to get through but overcast up to 25,000 feet forced all aircraft to return to base," or "All bomber operations cancelled due to weather at base and en route." Even in April, which was considered a good month, 65 per cent of the bombers in the Eighth which failed to make sortie or attack were prevented from doing so by weather. This was 16 per cent of the total number of bombers airborne that month.

Various techniques were developed and employed to circumvent the weather. One was improved weather forecasting. Regional weather offices were established to furnish the necessary data for the various operating units. In order to get as perfect forecasts as possible weather information was exchanged between theaters, between air forces in the same theater, and between the AAF and RAF. Some data also came from Russia and the Balkans. The available weather facts often had limited value, however, since they were gathered for the most part on the fringes of Axis Europe and accurate up-to-date meteorological information from enemy-held territory was lacking.

To remedy this defect weather reconnaissance was flown regularly by both air forces, P-38's usually being used for this purpose. In the spring of 1944 additional intelligence was acquired by the Eighth Air Force by briefing fighter pilots on combat missions to report weather conditions they encountered over enemy territory immediately upon return to their station. In this way bomber formations getting ready to take off had the benefit of the latest weather news. In May, this was improved upon by dispatching one Mosquito to each division area just prior to a heavy-bombardment mission. The commanding generals for the divisions were authorized to use these aircraft in any way they thought best to obtain up-to-the-minute weather data.

Techniques were also developed to allow missions to be carried out on days ordinarily considered nonoperational. There were various navigational and blind-bombing aids. While there were many of these, one of the most important was H2X. This equipment could be used for both navigational and bombing purposes. Its chief advantage over OBOE, GEE-H, and SHORAN was that it was not tied to any ground station, and therefore its range was limited only to the range of the aircraft carrying it. Actually H2X was a radar bomb sight which transmitted high-frequency electrical impulses downward through a revolving antenna. The objects on the earth reflected these impulses back to the plane where they were converted into light patterns.

H2X was first introduced in May 1943 and by the next month 12 hand-made sets had been installed in B-17's of the Eighth Air Force and were used as navigational aids. The first use of it for bombing was in the fall. In November, Brig. Gen. F. L. Anderson, Commanding General of the VIII Bomber Command reported that his bombers had been experimenting with it for bombing through overcast (BTO) of Wilhelmshaven, Bremen, and Ruhr targets. From this time on there was constant effort to improve on its use, train competent operators, and build up an adequate PFF in both theaters.

In general, the results obtained from H2X paid for the time, effort, and cost expended in developing it. A very large percentage of total sorties flown with such equipment was effective, and it also allowed the heavy bombers to operate on days when visual bombing was impossible. In January 1944, daylight missions were conducted on 11 days by the Eighth Air Force, and on seven of these and part of the eighth bombing was conducted by H2X methods. At least seven more full days were available for striking the enemy than there would have otherwise been. In February there were 18 daylight operations, and on seven days and part of three others the missions were BTO. The next month on 13 out of 23 days blind bombing missions occurred. In April there were 6 out of 21, and in May 10 out of 25.

One chief advantage which visual aiming had over H2X, however, was accuracy. Although there were constant efforts to improve the accuracy of blind bombing, visual bombing, if properly done, still remained the better method. There were, of course, instances when BTO missions were almost perfect and outdid those where the optical bomb sight was used exclusively. In March the Eighth flew a mission against the marshalling yards of Munich and the aircraft industry at Friedrichshafen; visual sighting was used at the former place and hits were scored on the post office, central revenue office, town hall, King Edward School, municipal hospital, a small factory, residential areas of the old town section, and royal palace and botanical gardens. At Friedrichshafen PFF aid was given at the target and results showed that the Dornier factory, railroad yards, a seaplane hangar and ramps, Lowenthal assembly plant, Manzell Do-217 seaplane base, Maybach Motorenbau factory, Zahnradfabrik plant, and some of the residential section all suffered bomb damage. In April an experiment was conducted in the Fifteenth Air Force to determine the practical value of H2X bombing. Bucharest was selected as the best site, and 14 groups were dispatched against it in daylight under good weather conditions. Six of the groups had their bomb sights disconnected, and all bombing was conducted by H2X methods with the operators sealed in without any outside vision. The other eight groups followed the conventional methods. A study of the strike photos showed that all bombs dropped by H2X fell within the city, their pattern was more compact, and the accuracy was better than for those bombs dropped by the eight groups using visual sighting.

These instances of accuracy, however, were rather the exception than the rule. H2X could rarely be depended upon for pin-point bombing of a particular factory or other single objective, but occasionally on the radar scope a large industrial plant would make a "blip" of its own which could be distinguished from the picture made by the whole city. A test conducted by the Eighth Air Force in May and June showed greater H2X accuracy against small coastal targets than against large cities. There were several reasons for this. First, although the H2X equipment did not show up the specific coastal target, it did show up the beaches sharply and clearly and these served as excellent check points. The edges of the cities, on the other hand, were fuzzy and indistinct and it was difficult to locate exact points in the city. Furthermore, crews over cities were not so concerned about dropping all bombs precisely on the aiming point, and this resulted in greater dispersion. A second reason was that bombing altitudes were lower for coastal targets, and accuracy varied inversely with the altitude. Thirdly, the size of the attacking force and bombing unit was always greater against cities, and the smaller the force and unit the greater he accuracy.

The question naturally arises as to what extent improved weather forecasting and blind bombing methods aided the prosecution of the CBO. It has already been shown that H2X increased the number of days on which the enemy could be profitably bombed. Better forecasting permitted improved advanced planning which enabled the Allies to step up the tempo and subject the enemy to an almost continuous pounding. He was not allowed to rest and gather strength with which to launch a counterblow.

Matters of defense and offense resolved themselves into a circle. Whenever the American air forces devised a new technique the Germans promptly set to work on an offsetting one, or when the enemy developed a new weapon the Allies instituted countermeasures. Each in turn spurred the other side to circumvent the new danger. The most effective defense the Germans had was their fighter force, and it was for this reason that the British and Americans finally turned their full attention to the job of destroying the Luftwaffe. It has already been pointed out that when long-range escort was limited, the USAAF had experimented with heavy-bomber formations designed to out down losses from fighters. The German employed every means he could devise to break or open up the formations so that he could attack the individual aircraft. Some of the methods used were serial – and ground-fired rockets, cable bombs, parachute bombs, and glide bombs. The firing of rockets from planes had been started in 1943. The technique was to stand out of range of the bombers' guns, 1200 to 600 yards away, and lob the missiles into the formation. Then when the formation was disrupted the fighters would close in and use their machine guns or 20-mm. cannon for the kill. Another method was to hide in the condensation trails left by the bombers and when within range of the formation let go the rockets before the tail gunners could see them distinctly. Although serial-fired rockets took their toil, the danger from them was never so great as from the 13-mm. or 20-mm, cannon of the fighters.

Ground-fired rockets were reported in use in the early spring of 1944. Each rocket upon exploding released five parachute incendiary bombs which burned for about a minute. B May the use of these was quite frequent but their accuracy or intensity was never great enough to be a serious threat to the safety of the American bombers. Cable bombs also were employed to some extent. Their use, however, was not new as they had been tried in World War I. The Germans revived the idea. In November and December 1943 American crewmen saw what they believed to be bombs towed by a cable, but it was not until January that there was complete confirmation. The difficulties of pulling the bomb through a formation, however, made this type of bombing ineffective.

The greatest danger to the American bombers came from the fighters. Prior to the lengthening of American fighter range, the German single-engine fighters were deployed along a thin line extending from Denmark to Bordeaux. This force could affect interception for a distance of from 175 miles to 200 miles inland from the coast, beyond the limits of the American escorts. When the range of the USAAF fighters was increased so that they could give long protection, the Germans were forced to redeploy their forces. They had to have depth as well as length, and in order to achieve this it was necessary to transfer fighters from the Russian and Italian fronts, where the pressure was less, to Western Europe where it was greatest. Twin-engine night fighters were also converted to day use, and it was from the twin-engines that most of the rockets were launched. As the Americans increased their range by use of auxiliary tanks, so did the Germans. New tactics were also evolved by the Germans. The bomber formations were attacked at the coast line and in the ensuing engagements the U. S. fighters were forced to use up their surplus gasoline and return to base, thus leaving the bombers with little or no escort. Then German fighters equipped with extra tanks could pursue the bombers unmolested. Until sufficient fighters were available for both escort and free lance fighting, the Americans ceased chasing the enemy and made his come to them if he wanted to fight. By spring sufficient fighters were available to allow some to go off seeking out the GAF and still leave sufficient force to protect the bombers. This force could affect interception for a distance of from 175 miles to 200 miles inland from the coast, beyond the limits for the American escorts. When the range of the USAAF fighters was increased so that they could give long protection, the Germans were forced to redeploy their forces. They had to have depth as well as length, and in order to achieve this it was necessary to transfer fighters from the Russian and Italian fronts, where the pressure was less, to Western Europe where it was greatest. Twin-engine night fighters were also converted to day use, and it was from the twin engines that most of the rockets were launched. As the Americans increased their range by use of auxiliary tanks, so did the Germans. New tactics were also evolved by the Germans. The bomber formations were attacked at the coast line and in the ensuing engagements the U.S. fighters were forced to use up their surplus gasoline and return to base, thus leaving the bombers little or no escort. Then German fighters equipped with extra tanks could pursue the bombers unmolested. Until sufficient fighters were available for both escort and free-lance fighting, the Americans ceased chasing the enemy and made him come to them if he wanted to fight. By spring sufficient fighters were available to allow some to go off seeking out the GAF and still leave sufficient force to protect the bombers.

As the GAF begin to feel the effects of the CBO it tried new tactics and tricks. Aircraft were sometimes painted to resemble P-51 or other American fighters. These would simulate escort tactics and then at opportune times attack the bombers. In general, however, the new tactics evolved from the need for caution and conservation. The enemy was unable to afford much wastage by the spring of 1944. Fighters hung around the edges of a formation waiting to pounce like wolves upon stragglers or cripples. Many times they showed great reluctance to engage in battle with the American escorts. When the weather was bad they often refused to come up through the overcast, depending upon ground defense to protect the target. At other times only one target would be strongly protected or en route only one combat wing would be aggressively attacked. Also the GAF by late spring ceased protecting certain areas and over these the dominance of the USAAF was practically uncontested. French targets were almost never defended by April, and attacks in Italy and Yugoslavia were virtually unopposed. Raids into Germany, Austria, and regions east of Yugoslavia, however, were vigorously opposed. When there was concentrated opposition it was usually agressive. German fighters were not cowardly at times were daring to the point of being foolhardy. Their reluctance to fight was born of the necessity for conserving air strength and not from fear.

The Germans were also led to develop new types of aircraft to counter the constant improvement of American planes. But this came too late to ward off the aerial invasion of Germany and save the Luftwaffe from destruction. As early as 1936 experiments on jet-propelled aircraft were begun by Heinkel, and in 1938-39 and jet-propelled aircraft program was initiated by the Air Ministry. The progress was slow, however, and it was not until 1944 when the shortage of high octane fuel became serious that production was stimulated. By this time, though, the shortage of trained pilots and the intensity of Allied bombardment along with the failure to iron out the mechanical troubles prevented jet-propelled aircraft from being a serious threat. The most successful of these planes was the ME-262, but its production was delayed by engine troubles and by Hitler's insistence that it be made into a fighter bomber, which kept it out of combat use for a number of months. The first models of this airplane had been accepted in March 1944 and by 8 May 1945 about 1400 had been received by the GAF. Only a few of them ever became operational, however, and their value was decreased by poorly trained pilots.

As the ability of the GAF to protect vital targets waned, more and more reliance was placed on ground defenses. Of these flak was the most efficient and was a constant threat to the Allied bombers throughout the war. After the fall of 1943, Hitler was convinced that the best defense against the increasing intensity of aerial attacks was not his fighter force but more and more flak, and by March 1944, because of the flak encounter, pilots no longer considered the hop to Calais a milk run. About 30% of the total

German output of guns in 1944 consisted of flak guns, and about 20 per cent of the ammunition of calibers from 7 cm upwards was AA shells. In the latter case the shortage of aluminum raised the question of whether this metal should be allocated to flak ammunition or to fighter aircraft. In the end a compromise was reached, but flak received preference. By D-day the flak personnel in Germany and occupied countries numbered one million with half of it in German proper. In spite of their imposing flak defense, Germany still did not have enough equipment to protect everything and many routes had to be left unguarded. Moreover, the strength and quality of AA units declined as the Allies advanced both on the ground and in the air. While bomber losses attributable to flak alone were usually not so great as those caused by enemy aircraft, the amount of damage inflicted was much more than that resulting from fighter attacks. For the first 10 months of 1944 about 25% of a bomber force could be expected to be hit by flak, but fortunately such damage was usually repairable in a short period of time. With better protection against flak the percent of damage and losses was cut considerably by the end of the war. From July 1943 to October 1944 in the Eighth Air Force, one bomber was lost for every 13 damaged, and by the end of the war the ratio stood one lost for every 22 damaged. The Germans also made use of considerable numbers of barrage balloons in conjunction with flak units. At the beginning of 1944 the heaviest concentrations were found around important industries, ports, and industrial cities. Synthetic oil and rubber plants were most heavily protected, with ports second, and then dams, bridges, and canals. By the end of April, however, a reversal of policy in their use was noted. The big barrages around places like Wilhelmshaven, Emden, Hamburg, and Bremen were materially reduced, and the barrages protecting the Ruhr cities of Homberg, Sterkrads, Essen, Gelsenkirchen, Huls, and Kamen were discontinued. The enemy also discontinued or reduced the size of the barrages at synthetic oil plants. The emphasis was now placed on protecting the road and railway bridges and lock gates of inland waterways in Germany; and in France, where several new barrages appeared, they were concentrated around power and transformer stations.

Another type of ground defense more or less successfully employed by the Germans was to obscure the bombardier's vision by a smoke screen. Smoke was commonly used to hide mouths of tunnels and other communication targets, such as marshaling yards, bridges, and junction points. It was also used to protect plants and cities, such as the Villar-Perosa ball-bearing factory at Turin, oil installations at Ploesti, or industrial centers like Frie-drichshafen. At first these smoke screens seriously affected bombing accu-racy, but in time it was possible to reduce their effectiveness by such methods as H2X and offset bombing.

Despite all German attempts to develop counter weapons and defense, the Allies were able to keep one or several jumps ahead. When the Germans began to use radar to warn them of the approach of American bombers or to determine the altitude and location of the formations for accurate sighting of the AA guns, the Allies jammed the enemy radar with WINDOW or CHAFF (strips of metal foil) or with CARPET or MANDREL (noise). Attacks were made on radar stations, and often fighters flew under the radar curtain to surprise and beat up an airfield prior to the arrival of the bomber formation. By this means the heavies were assured of negligible interference en route to their target. Larger and larger air armadas continued to fly against strategic targets and gradually the German ability to fight was ground down. When D-day arrived and the invasion of the Continent got underway, the Army Ground Forces found their task made easier by the success of the CBO.

10

ATTACK ON AIRFRAMES, AERO-ENGINES, AND AIRFIELDS

The success of the CBO was dependent upon the ability of the heavy bombers to penetrate the enemy defenses and destroy those industries whose existence was vitally necessary to the German war machine. The chief protector of these industries was the enemy's air force, and therefore the destruction of the GAF, in being and in production, became an intermediate primary objective of the CBO. The attack on the aircraft industry was divided into two main phases. The first was the high-priority campaign from the middle of 1943 to the late spring of 1944, and the second was a low-priority campaign from D-day to April 1945. The period of high priority was further divided into four phases: (1) April-October 1943, (2) November 1943-January 1944, (3) February 1944, and (4) March-May 1944. During the first two of these periods the bombing of aircraft targets was slight because of need for equipment and personnel, particularly fighters to give adequate escort protection. Nevertheless, 58 aircraft factories were hit with varying degrees of damage in 1943. By February 1944, both the Eighth and Fifteenth Air Forces were able to operate with great effectiveness against German strategic targets. The total weight of bombs

dropped on the aircraft industry in this third phase of the high-priority campaign totaled just a little less than that dropped on the industry to that date.
It was during this same period, too, that USSTAF met its most vigorous
opposition, but the blow delivered against the GAF was such that it was
never able to recover its strength. From March to May 1944, it was possible,
because of the waning GAF, to give the German aircraft industry its heaviest
bombing, and by late Aril attention began to turn from these factories to
other strategic targets such as oil and transportation.

The main attack was carried out against the single-engine fighter factories, chiefly those producing Me-109s and FW-190's. These attacks
included all phases of manufacture, but emphasized airframes and final
assembly. By the end of September 1944 all known single-engine airplane
plants had been attacked from one to seven times. In January 194 twin-
engine fighter factories were added to the list, and in the first nine months
of 1944, 16 of these had been bombed from one to five times each. Long-
range and dive bombers, transport, and jet-propelled aircraft factories were
also made primary targets during the early months of 1944, and by D-day
practically every type of German aircraft manufacture had felt the weight of
Allied bombs.

The Germans had early recognized the threat of strategic bombing and
had started to expand their production of combat planes. The program as
worked out by April 1943 provided for an increase of fighters to reach 2230
per month by December of that year. By July, production had reached
about 1740 planes monthly, of which 910 were single-engine. Even the
comparatively small-scale operations of USAAF, however, emphasized the
need of accelerating and expanding the output to offset the rapidly growing
Allied air forces. A stepped-up plan was initiated in August and further
revised in October when the goal was set at a minimum monthly production of 4150 single and twin-engine fighters a month by December 1944. In
December 1943, however, Hitler was tired of being kept on the defensive
and wanted to be able to retaliate by again bombing England. Accordingly,
he ordered a reduction in the schedule for single-engine fighters to 3000 a
month and an increase in production of the four-engine heavy bomber – the
He-177. The German expansion program, however, did not reckon on the
success of American precision bombing, and by March 1944 production fell

to a low of 1320 airplanes of all types. From this time on, however, production rose steadily to 1950 in September, of which 1400 were single-engine. Altogether the GAF in 1944 accepted 39,07 aircraft, about 26,000 being single-engine fighters, but the expansion program came too late to save German industry from aerial destruction. More and more the GAF was forced into a policy of conservation, and this gave greater freedom to the Allies to attack oil and other war industries. As the effects of the raids on oil began to be felt, the effectiveness of the Luftwaffe was further reduced because regardless of how many planes were produced they were useless if there was no fuel to fly them.

The rise in aircraft production after March 1944 was due in large part to the reorganization of the industry. This involved several factors, one of which was dispersal of component manufacturing to many small plants including unused textile factories. A study of dispersal problems had been made in 1942 and the Air Ministry recommended the principle, but little was done along these lines until the latter part of 1943. The government itself did not institute a compulsory program of dispersal until after the disastrous February assaults. Dispersal on a small scale had started, however, after the 1943 attacks on the Focke-Wulf and Heinkel plants at Bremen and Rostock. Although these raids resulted in little or no loss of production, the enemy was smart enough to read the signs, and he began to move the Focke-Wulf factory to East Prussia and Poland. These areas were chosen because it was believed they were beyond range of effective Allied bombing and because there were facilities and an adequate labor supply for converting existing plants to aircraft production. Another example of dispersion was the Messerschmitt complex at Regensburg/Profening which, after suffering heavy damage in 1943, was moved in part to Regensburg/Obertraubling, and its component plants to Kottern, Kempten, and Dingolfing. The Wiener Neustadt Me-109 complex was originally centered in Werke I and II at this Vienna suburb with components coming from Eischamend, Belgrade/Zemun, Klagenfurt, Neudorfl, and Obergrafendorf and with repair work carried on a Atzgersdorf. They heavy attacks on these laces in early 1944 led to partial dispersal of assembly from Wiener Neustadt to Bad Voslau, Zwolfaxing, and Markersdorf. Several textile factories at Ebreichsdorf, Pottendorf, and Neunkirchen were converted to manufacturing airframe components to take the place of bombed-out factories of the original complex, and the Enzesfeld light-metal plant was retooled for making wings.

Other forms of dispersal, such as converting GAF airfields into assembly points and moving factories to underground locations, were also resorted to. When the official order for dispersal was given in February 1944, a government agency was established to locate suitable underground sites and prepare them for industrial use. The first of the manufacturing processes to go underground was that of the V –weapons. Then jet aircraft, especially the Me-262 engine plants, were moved to caves, tunnels, and other similar shelters, and they were followed by the conventional fighter-engine factories. In the spring of 1944, Daimler-Benz transferred parts of its Genshagen plant to a gypsum mine at Neckarelz near Heidelberg. In Czechoslovakia, Skoda moved part of its engine production into a granite quarry at Kabana near Budapest, and in June 1944, the Bayerische Motoran Werks began its move to a railroad tunnel at Markirch near Strasbourg.

The effects of dispersal were both good and bad. The moving of factories to forest sites afforded good camouflage. The breakup of manufacturing processes into small plants easily protected by bunkers lessened bomb damage. Underground factories were, of course, out of sight and hard to hit. The multiplicity of plants made it difficult for Allied intelligence to seek them out and their very number made it almost impossible to reduce production capacity to any great extent. On the other hand, the policy had serious disadvantages for the enemy. Supervisory management was spread thin and there was a resulting loss in efficiency and quality. Hermann Goering pointed out after his capture that fittings from dispersed plants were not always accurate enough for proper assembly or that unmatching parts, such as two different landing wheels, would be received. Dr Karl Frydag, chief of the airframe industry, gave similar testimony. Dispersal also placed an additional burden on the transportation system in bringing parts together for assembly. When concentrated attacks began on transportation, final assembly plants often found themselves without the necessary subassemblies, and although transportation was never completely disrupted, the delay involved worked to the disadvantage of the Nazis. In the end there was a reversal of policy, and concentration of industry, particularly in underground locations, was once more undertaken.

Another phase of reorganization of the aircraft industry was the transfer of the duties of the Director of Aircraft Procurement to Albert Speer's Ministry for Armaments and Munitions. At the very time when aircraft manufacturing was being dispersed, direction of the industry was centralized. Field Marshal Milch had taken over the office of Director of Aircraft Procurement under the Air Ministry in 1941 after the suicide of General Udet. In February 1944, the functions of the director were transferred to the Jaegerstab which operated under the Speer Ministry, and Sauer superseded Milch as Speer's representative. In June the final dissolution of the office of Director of Aircraft Procurement took place. From this time forward the Speer Ministry had full responsibility for airplane procurement, and by clever utilization of capacity, use of specialist to supervise the complexes, exchange of workers and material, and concentration on a few fighter types, acceptance figures tripled within seven months. Speer, however, liked big figures as proof of his efficiency, and a goodly portion of the planes listed as new production were probably repaired or rebuilt aircraft.

The attacks against the aircraft industry in January 1944 were very light in comparison with those delivered in the succeeding months. The Eighth Air Force made five attacks on airframe factories. The first of these was an attacks on the FW-190 assembly and FW-200 repair plant at Bordeaux/Merignac on 5 January. The 112 B-17s making the attack were escorted by 76 P-47s as far as La Pallice, the extent of the fighter range. The bombers met with strong opposition, 50 to 75 M ene-109's and FW-190's, and 11 B-17's were lost. Claims against the enemy were 24 destroyed, 5 probably destroyed, and 6 damaged. Despite almost 10 per cent loss of the attacking force, the GAF installations suffered extensive damage. The second was a triple attack on 11 January against the FW-190 assembly and components factory at Oschersleben, the Me-110 assembly at Brunswick/Waggum, and the Ju-88 wing plant at Halberstadt. Weather was bad en route, but over the targets it was clear and severe damage was inflicted on the factories in spite of strong enemy fighter opposition. On 30 January, 778 bombers were dispatched against the Me-f110 components factory at Brunswick/Wilhelmitor. Again the weather was bad and with a 10/10 cloud over the entire Continent it was necessary to use PFF equipment. One combat wing lost contact with the other formations and bombed Hannover instead. Opposition was heavy and the enemy employed rockets fired from both single- and twin-engine planes. Cable, parachute, and serial bombs were also used.

The Fifteenth made two major attacks against airframe factories in January. The first was on 8 January when 109 B-17's dropped 324 tons of bombs on the Reggiane fighter (Re-2005) and SM-79 assembly plant at Reggio Emilia. It was estimated that the damage inflicted would substantially reduce production for the next six to eight months. The second attack was against the Me-109 components factory at Klagenfurt – part of the Wiener Neustadt complex – on 16 January. Sixty-one B-17's dropped 201 tons of bombs inflicting moderate to severe damage on the factory, warehouses and railroad tracks. These attacks of the Fifteenth appeared puny in comparison with those of the Eighth, but the former Air Force was still in process of being built up and its strategic efforts were dissipated to some extent by the exigencies of the Italian campaign.

The RAF was also busy supplementing the destruction brought about by USSTAF. Most RAF attacks were area ones, but the target list complemented that of USSTAF. For example, the RAF Bomber Command followed up the Eighth Air Force attack of 11 January on Brunswick with a fire and high-explosive raid of its own on 14/15 January. On 2/3 January, the RAF attacked Berlin in an area raid seriously damaging the Henschel Hs-126 assembly plant at Johannisthal. Other January attacks hit the FW-200 components factory, the Flettner plant engaged in assembly and repair of trainers and gliders, and the aircraft research establishment of the Deutsche Versuchen Anstalt, all at Berlin/Treptow. In the Mediterranean the 205 Group, RAF preceded the American attack on the Reggiane factory on 8 January with a raid on Reggio Emilia on 7/8 January.

February started out inconspicuously enough, but hopes were high. Maj. Gen. F.L. Anderson wrote t. Gen. Ira C. Eaker that the future looked bright in the Eighth Air Force if the weather would just clear up. The results of combat crew training given in November and December had begun to show, and the advent of the P-51 had extended the bomber capabilities tremendously. Before the end of the month it was contemplated the Eighth could put 1000 bombers in the air for a single operation and most missions would average about 900 bombers. A few clear days, plus good bombing and a willingness to take some extra losses, would enable the Air Forces to finish off the German fighter factories.

The bad weather of January carried over into February, and for nearly three-quarters of the month operations against the aircraft industry were at a minimum. On 5 February, 113 B-17's escorted by P-47's made a successful attack on the Ju-52 assembly and FW-190 repair base using visual methods and 380 tons of general purpose (GP) and incendiary bombs (IB) were dropped with excellent results. On 14 February, the Fifteenth Air Force made a small attack with five B-17's against the Piaggio Pi-108 and G-55 assembly factory at Pontedera, and in spite of the small size of the force serious damage was inflicted.

These attacks by the USSTAF were secondary in nature, however, and the factories bombed were of minor importance. The RAF Bomber Command in its night area raids was able to damage more important aircraft industries during this period of inclement weather. On 15/16 February it attacked Berlin, damaging the FW-200 components plant and the Flettner factory at Berlin/Treptow, and the Hs-12 assembly plant at Berlin/Johannisthal. In the 19/20 February attack on Leipzig the Erla Me-109 components factories were heavily hit.

Toward the end of the month weather forecasts indicated a few days of good weather, and Spaatz set about to cram as much bombing as possible into these few days. Several coordinated attacks by the Eighth and Fifteenth Air Forces were planned, but only three were carried out (see Table 7, page 62). Despite this, for six days, 20 to 25 February (the Big Week), the enemy aircraft industry received the worst pounding of its life, one from which it never fully recovered. The success of the Big Week assured Allied air superiority for the rest of the war. A coordinated attack had been planned to take place on the next day of good weather in the ETO, but on that day, 20 February, the bombers from the Fifteenth Air Force failed to reach their target of Regensburg because of icing conditions over the Alps. The Eighth Air Force, however hit the plants making the Me-109 assembly and fuselage and the Ju-88 and Ju-52 assembly factories at Leipzig/Fockau and Leipzig/Weiterblick; the IAG Me-110 components and tank plants at Brunswick/Neuperiter and Brunswick/Wilhelmitor; the FW-190 assembly and components at Oschersleben; the Junkers Ju-83, Ju-188, Ju52 assembly plants, the

Gotha Me-110 and Go-343 assembly at Gotha; the Heinkel assembly and components at Rostock, Rostock/Warnsdorf; and the Arado FW-190 assembly at Tutow.

The attacks continued on the next day with the Eighth striking the Me-110 factories at Brunswick once more. On 22 February it was out again in force against the Junkers assembly components plants. This day was also the first successful coordinated attack of USSTAF. While the Eighth was hitting the above-mentioned places the Fifteenth struck the Me-109 components factories. With simultaneous attacks from the west and the south the GAF was hard put to protect all the targets. Enemy aircraft were encountered by the Eighth and the Fifteenth. The Eighth Air Force lost 38 out of 289 bombers and eleven of its fighters, but it claimed 91-25-43 enemy planes. The Fifteenth lost 19 out of an attacking force of 233 bombers and fighters and made claims of 30-18-5 against the enemy.

The following day weather forced the Eighth Air Force to cancel its part of a coordinated attack, but the Fifteenth was to dispatch 108 B-24's against the Me-109 components factory of Daimler-Puch at Steyr. The bombers met with intense flak over the target but dropped 214 tons of bombs with good results. About 120 enemy fighters plagued the formation until the P-38 escort met it at the Alps on withdrawal. Sixteen bombers were lost, but bombers and escort claimed a total of 3-10-13 of the enemy.

On 24 February USSTAF staged another successful coordinated attack. The Eighth returned to Gotha to finish the job begun on 20 February. The Fifteenth Air Force struck the Daimler-Puch factory at Steyr again. That night, 24/25 February, the 205 Group, RAF, hit the same plant. The next day brought the Bi Week to a close, and it also marked the last of USSTAF's successfully completed coordinated attacks until July. That day also was notable because it marked the first time when both Air Forces were over the same target on the same day. The Fifteenth dispatched a force of 149 heavy bombers (111 succeeded in reaching the target) to bomb the Regensburg factories at Pruffening and Obertraubling. Several hours later, 268 heavies of the Eighth arrived over the same targets and proceeded to complete the destruction. The total tonnage delivered on these places that day was 948 tons of GP, IB, and fragmentation bombs. The Fifteenth met with heavy and aggressive opposition, encountering about 200 enemy fighters, and lost

39 bombers and 4 fighters against claims of 93-17-15. The Eighth Air Force found the stinger pulled when it arrived, since it encountered only 35 to 50 enemy aircraft. It lost only two B-17's and made claims of only 13-1-7. While part of the Eighth was attacking Regensburg, other formations attacked the Bachmann Me-110 components factory at Furth and the Messerschmitt Me-410 assembly at Augsburg. The RAF Bomber Command followed up with a raid on the latter place that night, 2/26 February.

The Big Week was now concluded. Weather closed in and operations against the aircraft industry were curtailed. It was not until the last day of the month that it was again possible to attack the airframe industry. On 29 February, 226 B-17's were dispatched to attack the Me-110 components factories at Brunswick. A 10/10 cloud made it necessary to se PFF techniques and results were unobserved. A significant feature of this raid, however, was that no enemy fighters attacked the bomber formations, and in fact escort pilots reported seeing only 18 German planes, which would not do battle. One bomber was lost to flak, and four fighter pilots were lost to causes other than enemy action.

The attacks during the Big Week were not confined solely to airframes. Aero-engines, ball bearings, airdromes, transportation, and other industries were also hit. RAF bombing was area in nature and its effects extended to residential as well as industrial sections of a city. But all in all airframe assembly and components factories were given the heaviest dosages of bombs. In the 10 days from 15/16 February to 25/26 February, 41 attacks were made on the aircraft industry, 26 of which were by the Eighth, 6 by the Fifteenth, and 9 by the RAF. The total number of tons dropped in these 41 attacks amounted to nearly 16,000. The Eighth Air Force delivered almost 5240 tons, the Fifteenth about 1168 tons, and the RAF in its area attacks approximately 9500 tons. The total tonnage for the whole month of February delivered against all targets by the entire Eighth Air Force was 18,436 tons; for the Fifteenth it was 5901 tons; and for the RAF (both the Bomber Command and the 205 Group) it was 15,319 tons.

The success of the Big Week was not obtained, however, without cost. Out of 8572 bomber sorties in February by the Eighth, 299 bombers were lost. Of these, 156 were lost during the six days of 20/25 February. In the Fifteenth Air Force there were 3981 bomber sorties and 115 bombers were lost, 95 of these during the period of the Big Week. These losses were not uncompensated, however, for in addition to the destruction of aircraft production the FGAF suffered crippling losses in its operating strength. The combined bomber and fighter claims of the Eighth and Fifteenth Air Forces for February were 992 enemy aircraft destroyed, 224 probably destroyed, and 468 damaged, and of these 641-177-264 were claimed for 20/25 February.

The February attacks, despite heavy Allied bomber losses, paid high dividends in the long run. Production was slowed down at the moment. It was estimated that effective production at Bernburg was lost for 10 weeks, at Oschersleben for six weeks, at Regensburg/Obertraubling for months, at Furth for two months, and at Augsburg for three weeks. It was also estimated that over-all productive capacity was out from 900 airplanes per month on 1 February to 450 per month after the Big Week. In spite of future increases in production and acceptances, the first line of operational strength was never able t grow at a rate sufficient to offset the growing intensity of Allied bombing. Operational strength of the GAF on all fronts was cut from 2638 planes on 28 January to 207 on 25 February. By the end of March this had risen to 2613 in April to 2646, and by 1 June to 2721. In order to combat the threat to her war industries from USSTAF and the RAF it was necessary for Germany to keep from 60 to 70 per cent of her fighters on the western and south German fronts, thus leaving her armies in Italy and those facing the Russians with only token air support.

Although the reduction in production capacity had a hindering effect on the GAF, it was not so serious in the long run as the corresponding loss of trained pilots. Planes could be produced faster than competent flyers. In order to meet the ever-increasing shortage of fighter pilots, training time in 1944 was cut to almost half of what it had been in 1942 and to about 25 hours less than in 1943. Bomber and staff pilots and instructors were also converted into fighter pilots in a space of 30 days. These efforts succeeded in maintaining a balance between the number of aircraft and pilots, but the quality of the pilots, like that of the airplanes, grew progressively worse. The peak of the GAF strength and efficiency had passed.

The heavy February attacks and succeeding bad weather left slim pickings in airframe production for both the Eighth and Fifteenth Air Forces in

March. There was little reason to repeat the bombing of most factories until sufficient recovery had taken place to warrant a return engagement. The Eighth, nevertheless, attacked airframes on six days. The first of these was on 15 March when 344 heavies were dispatched against aircraft factories at Brunswick-328 actually making the attack. A 9/10 to 10/10 cloud cover obscured the targets, however, and the bombers bombed the city instead, dropping approximately 40 tons of mixed bombs by aid of PFF equipment. Some damage was inflicted on the MIAG Me-110 components factory at Wilhelmitor. The city was revisited on 23 and 29 March with dense clouds again hiding the targets, but later reconnaissance showed that the Me-110 factories at both Wilhelmitor and Neuperiter suffered additional damage. On 16 March, 195 B-24's dropped nearly 500 tons of GP and IB bombs on Friedrichshafen by PFF means though 4/10 to 10/10 cloud and heavy smoke screen. The Dornier FW-190 components factory and the Zahnrad-fabrik at Manzell received some damage. Two days later 189 B-24's returned to drop another 48 tons of bombs on the city, hitting again the same installations at Manzell and slightly damaging the Do-217 assembly and FW-190 tool factory at Lowenthal. On this same day, 18 March, 136 B-17's dropped slightly more than 300 tons of bombs on the Dornier Me-410 and Do-217 assembly plant at Oberpfaffenhofen. 27 March the Eighth dispatched 707 heavy bombers to attack a number of German and French targets. Included in the list were the SNCA FW-189 assembly and FW-200 repair base at Bordeaux/Merignac and the Liotard FW repair plant at Tours/Usine. At the former place, 124 bombers dropped almost 210 tons of GP bombs and 84 tons of fragmentation clusters. Although the assembly plant was hit, the hangars, barracks, airfield, and parked airplanes received the brunt of the attack. Thirty-five B-17's attacked the Liard installation at Tours with 107 tons of GP bombs, inflicting moderate damage.

In March the main emphasis of the Fifteenth was placed on airdromes and marshaling yards, although several successful attempts were directed against aircraft factories. On 1 March, a large force of B-17's and B-24's was dispatched to the Wiener Neustadt Me-109 complex plants at Fischamend and Schwechat. None of the 125 B-17's were able to reach their targets because of weather. A force of 192 B-24's reached the vicinity only to find everything hidden by dense clouds, so they dropped 379 tons of mixed bombs on the city of Vienna by estimated-time-of-arrival technique. Twenty-six other B-24's dropped 64 tons of bombs on scattered targets of opportunity with unobserved results. Two days later weather prevented an attack of the Daimler-Puch factory at Steyr, and a second mission on 23 March was recalled for the same reason. A third operation against Steyr on 26 March was turned back over Yugoslavia because of deteriorating weather, and the bombers attacked instead the port of Fime, Rimini marshaling yards, and Udine airdrome, all with poor results. The 205 Group, RAF was able to inflict some damage on the Cant aircraft factory, however, in connection with its raid on the submarine base at Monfalcone on the night of 19/20 March.

In April improved weather conditions and partial recuperation of the German aircraft industry through reorganization and dispersal allowed USSTAF to intensify again its attacks against airframe production. Single-engine fighter factories were still the main focal point of attack, with the Eighth emphasizing destruction of FW-190 factories and the Fifteenth trying to clean up the remaining Me-109 plants in south Germany and the Balkans. Attacks against twin-engine fighters were continued and long-range heavy bombers were added to the list. Both Air Forces were able to operate on nine days against airframe factories. T Eighth made 29 attacks against 27 targets, and the Fifteenth launched 21 attacks against 14 targets.

On 8 April the Eighth dispatched over 600 bombers to attack GAF installations and factories in the Brunswick and Oldenburg areas. At the former place 192 B-24's dropped 476 tons of bombs on the Me-110 components factories in Wilhelmitor and Waggum with excellent results. The next day 542 planes flew against the FW-190 components plants at Tutow, Marienburg, Posen, Warnemunde, and the FW-190 assembly and repair factory at Gdynia/Rahmel. A total of 958 tons of bombs was dropped on these places with generally good results. The bombers were attached, however, by 225 to 300 enemy fighters which in many instances were vicious and persistent and a total of 31 bombers was lost. On the other hand, the fighter escort found the enemy unwilling to engage in combat with it, and so after completing their escort duties the pilots attacked various ground targets From these operations they claimed 8-0-4 locomotives, one freight train, 11 factories, several antiaircraft installations, and 15-0-5 aircraft on the ground, against a loss of 10 fighters. The combined bomber and fighter claims of German airplanes destroyed in the air was 65-9-20. On 10 April the Eighth paid some attention to minor factories in France and Belgium. On that day 158 planes dropped 466 tons of mixed bombs on the SNCA Se-204 assembly and repair plant at Bourges, France, and 122 bombers left 296 tons of bombs on the Every He-111 repair factory at Brussels. No aircraft were lost and severe damage resulted at both places.

Another big day for the Eighth was 11 April when 917 four-engine bombers out of an available force of 1077 were dispatched against six assembly and components factories in eastern and central Germany The airframe targets hit were the FW-190 assembly plants at Sorau, Cottbus, Oschersleben, the Ju-88, Ju-13, and Ju-32 assembly at Bernburg, the Ju-88 components at Belberstadt, and the He-111 components plant at Rostock. Adverse weather, however, necessitated some PFF bombing, and some of the results were not so good, especially at Gorau and Bernburg. In general, results were fair to good. On this mission the bombers met with severe and well-coordinated attacks by the GAF, although fighter escort reported that the enemy avoided combat with it when possible. Antiaircraft fire over the target areas was also intense and accrete. Once again when their escort duties were finished the fighters descended to attack ground targets and claimed 64-7-63 planes on the ground, 18 locomotives and 8 trains, 2 hangars, 2 factories, flak towers, a radar station, barracks, and gun emplacements damaged.

On 13 April the Me -410 assembly plant at Augsburg was attacked by 230 heavies which dropped 32 tons of bombs with good results although 18 bombers were lost. A part of the forces also inflicted severe damage on the Lechfeld airdrome, a Messerschmitt training and jet experiment field just south of Augsburg. A small force of 60 aircraft dropped 149 tons of mixed bombs on the Dornier Me410 and Do-217 assembly plant at Oberpfaffen-hofen with but fair results and the loss of six of the bombers.

On 18 April a force of 768 bombers flew against numerous targets in the Berlin area. The airframe objectives were the He-111 and He-177 assembly plant at Oranienburg/Annahof, the Me-177 assembly at Granienourg/Ger-mandorf, the Arado He-177 assembly at Brandenburg, and the Arado FW-190 components factory. A total of 1091 tons of bombs was dropped on these places. The next day 209 aircraft dropped 41 tons of high explosive and incendiary bombs on the Fieseler FW190 components plant at Kassel/Bettenhausen and FW-190 assembly at Kassel/Maldau, resulting in an estimated loss of three months' production. The Do-217 assembly and FW-190 components factory at Friedrichshafen/Manzell and the Do-217 assembly and MW-190 tool plant at Friedrichshafen/Lowenthal were bombed by 211 planes on 24 April. A total of 494 tons of bombs was dropped, but results were disappointing. The Manzell targets were not hit, although extensive damage was inflicted on the Ashnredfabrik gear factory. At Lowenthal results were only fair. On this same day, 34 bombers paid a return visit to Oberpfaffenhofen, dropping 192 tons of bombs with accuracy. Also, 95 aircraft dropped 248 tons of bombs on the Leipheim airfield where Messerschmitt had a jet-aircraft assembly plant. The last attack against airframes by the Eighth in April was on the 29th when 10 B-17's out of a much larger force headed for Berlin returned to Brandenburg to lay 12 tons of bombs on the Arado He-17 assembly plant.

The RAF Bomber Command also aided in the destruction with its night raids. On 5/6 April, 141 British bombers attacked Toulouse with 673 tons of bombs and heavily damaged the Ateliers de L'Air Industriel (AIA) Heinkel repair plant the Dewoitine trainer factory of SWCA, and the S.A. Ateliers D'Aviation Louis Areguet, which manufactured the Latecoere-298 and experimented with jet aircraft. On 22/23 April, 237 aircraft bombed the city of Brunswick with 729 tons of bombs, adding fresh damage to the aircraft factories there. The Bomber Command also hit the Ejeller Messerschmitt airframe and Daimler-Bens engine repair factory at Oslo with 50 airplanes and 210 tons of bombs on 28/29 April. The next night 53 bombers put 217 tons of bombs on the Alnet factory airfield at Clermont-Farrand which was engaged in repair work.

The April campaign against airframes in the Mediterranean began on the night of 1/2April when 55 bombers of the 205 Group, RAF attacked the: assembly plant at Verose, Italy with 92 tons of bombs. As a part of a widespread attack on Budapest by the Fifteenth Air Force on 3 April, 111 B-17'sdropped 362 tons of bombs on the Duna aircraft factory located on Isepol Island near the town of Szigetszentmiklos and on the cage of the Tokel airfield. Enemy opposition was weak, and although there was intensely heavy flak over Budapest only three B-17's were lost against total bomber and fighter claims of 24-4-10. Ten days later the factory was again bombed, with 93 B024's dropping 213 tons on the components plants scattered in the woods and 125 bombing the assembly plant on the edge of the Tokel airdrome with 200 tons. Another125 B-24's also attacked the Budapest/Veeses airdrome with 186 tons of fragmentation bombs. This installation was used as a storage field and repair base. It was also capable of performing final assembly, and it was supposed to partially engaged in Ju-52 assembly. While these installations were being attacked, 163 B-17's raided the Hungarian Wagon works at Gyor where e-109 components were made. Severe damage was inflicted by 31 tons of bombs which were dropped on the factory and adjacent airfields.

Two nights before, on 11/12 April, the 205 Group, RAF hit the Macchi factory at Varese again. It was a very light attack, only three tons being dropped through a 10/10 cloud cover which forced most of the aircraft to seek targets of opportunity. The following day the Fifteenth turned its attention to the great Wiener Neustadt Me-109 complex at Wiener Neustadt, Werke I was so extensive that it was unnecessary to return to it before 10 May. The assembly plant, however, was not so heavily hit. A formation of 172 B-17's dropped 465 tons of bombs on the Fischamend components factory, covering the target so well that it was unnecessary to bomb it again. At Voslau 140 B-24's put 259 tons on the assembly plant, severely damaging the important installations chosen for attack.

In the middle of the month the Fifteenth extended its operation against aircraft production in the Balkans. On 16 April, the Rogozarski Me-109 assembly plant at Belgrade was attacked by 116 B-17's and 2 B-24's which dropped 397 tons of bombs on it. The same day the IAR Me-109 assembly and aero-engine factory at Brasov was severely damaged in an attack on that city's marshaling yards. On 17 April, the Fifteenth returned to Belgrade and dropped another 81 tons on the Rogozarski factory and 74 tons on the Ikarus Me109 assembly plant. The later was paid a return visit on 24 April, when 19 B-17's laid on it another 56 tons of 500-pounders.

Another strike against Werke I at Wiener Neustadt and the Bad Voslau factory was made on 23 April. Werke I had escaped for all practical purposes in the bombing of 12 April, and although Bad Voslau suffered heavy damage

on this same attack , portions still remained which needed further working
over. These plants were the two most important airframe production centers left within the range of the Mediterranean forces. A total of 171 airplanes of the Fifteenth Air Force attacked Were I with 513 tons of well-
aimed bombs. Only 30 to 45 energy fighters were encountered and only 2
B-17's were lost. . At Bed Voslau 170 B-24's dropped 125 tons of "frags" and
22 tons of 500 pond FP bombs with excellent results. Five of the attacking
Liberators were lost, but the GAF suffered losses of 165-8. Thirty-three
B-24's also bombed the Wiener Neustadt north airdrome with 36 tons of
frags, but o fresh damage was inflicted on the installations there. Another
force of 143 B-24's attacked the Heinkel factory at Schwechat, and 646 tons
of 500-pounders were dropped with good concentration on the target. This
plant was of importance because it was the only it was the only one producing the Me-210, and it was also engaged in work on jet-propelled aircraft. Enemy opposition was very light; only three fighters were encountered, but four B-24's were lost, one of them crash-landing at the base.

On 25 April the Fifteenth again turned its attention to the Italian factories, and 188 B-24's attacked the Fiat assembly plant at Turin with 291 tons
of bombs. Numerous workshops and hangars were hit and a number of
planes were destroyed on the ground. The Fiat factory was a Fiat subsidiary
and was one of the most important aircraft production centers in Italy in
which the Germans were interested. Enemy opposition was not very strong,
however, only 41 fighters, 16 of which were over the target, being encountered; but flak at the factory was moderate, accurate, and heavy. The claims
against the enemy were -2-2, but American losses were seven bombers and
one)-47. The last attack against airframes in April was on the 30th and again
it was directed against Italian factories. Fifty-three B-17's dropped 153 tons
on the Breda factory at Milan/Bresso, and 67 Fortresses delivered 201 tons
to the Macchi factory at Varese. In these two operations four bombers were
missing, but claims against the enemy of 18-11 were made. The April
attacks by both the Fifteenth and 205 Group, RAF "wrote off" practically all
Italian aircraft production and left very little destruction to be accomplished
in the following months.

May was the windup month before OVERLORD. The Eighth Air Force
was preeminently occupied with this operation, and the Fifteenth, in addi-

tion to its strategic bombing operations, had additional assignments in the campaign to take Rome. Yet, in order to cinch the gain in air superiority, attacks against aircraft production continued. Some factories had recovered, in part at least, from previous bombings, and these played host again to returning bombers. New sites to which production had been dispersed were discovered and added to the target lists. By D-day, 6 June, every known major components and assembly plant had been hit and in most cases severely damaged during the first half of 1944.

The majority of the attacks against airframes in May came in the last half of the month. Each Air Force made three attacks prior to 15 May. On 6 Ma, the Fifteenth dispatched 161 B-17's against the IAR Me-109 components factory at Brasov, Romania. Of that number, 154 bombers succeeded in reaching the target and dropping 369 tons of bombs in a well-concentrated pattern on the objectives. In the Eighth Air Force raid on Berlin on 8 May, 10 B01's dropped 25 tons of 500-pound GP bombs on the Arado Me-177 assembly plant at Brandenburg as a target of opportunity. Two days later Wiener Neustadt was again the target for the Fifteenth Air Force. A force of 174 B-17's and 126 B-24's dropped 95 tons of bombs on Werke I and Werke II, with more damage resulting to the latter than to Werke I. Another 102 Liberators hit Wiener Neustadt north airdrome with 212 tons of frags with fair results. Altogether about 150 German fighters were encountered over the target areas and flak was intense and heavy. Twenty-eight of the bombers and three of the escort fighters were lost, and claims against the enemy were 50-22-23. On 12 May, 58 B-17's from the Eighth put 142 tons on the FW-190 factory at Evickeu, damaging all buildings except one. The same day, the Fifteenth flew against the Fiat airframe factory. On 13 May, 225 heavies from the Eighth, using PFF equipment, struck at the Tutow factory airfield with 559 tons of high explosive and incendiary bombs, further damaging the already partially destroyed FW-190 assembly plant.

No further raids against airframe production were made by either Air Force until the 19th. On that day 272 planes of the Eighth attacked the Me-110 components factory at Brunswick/Wilhelmitor. A total of nearly 803 tons of mixed bombs were dropped, adding fresh damage to this already well-bombed plant. The following day, 73 bombers struck the Ju-52 assembly and FW-190 repair base in the Paris suburb of Villacoublay with

103 tons of bombs. This installation had not been attacked since 8 February and much new damage resulted. On 23 May, the Eighth again bombed the Se-204 assembly and components plant at Bourges with 84 planes and 250 tons of bombs.

The next day the Fifteenth attacked the Ammo-Lutner-Seck Me-109 components factory at Atzpersderf, a suburb of Vienna, with 123 B-17's. Poor weather, however, made it necessary to drop the 384 tons of bombs by PFF methods, and results were underserved. In the 25 May raid by 61 B-24's on the Harbor, on which 140 tons were dropped, an assembly plant that was severely damaged.

The Eighth resumed its attacks against airframes on 25 May when 15 bombers paid a return visit to the G. Brasser plant at Wiekeu and 48 attacked the Ju-52 and Ju-58 assembly factory at Bessau. The former place, a target for a main attack on the oil installations at Ruhland, and Zeitz, received 26 tons of bombs. Dassau, which had a primary target on the same mission, was hit with 102 tons.

The month ended in a blaze of glory, when in two days, 29th and 30th, a total of 2025 bombers from both Air Forces dropped 4000 tons of bombs on 18 airframe targets. This tonnage represented 70 per cent of that dropped on this type of objective during the last half of May, and 6 per cent of the total tonnage dropped on all targets in the whole month by the Eighth and Fifteenth Air Forces. In these May attacks, particularly, those of the 29th and 30th, the German aircraft industry received a very serious set-back. The emphasis put on the destruction of components factories assured a much slower recuperation than in the past, when final assembly plants had been the priority targets. Improvisation which would allow work to con-tinue in the latter was much more simple than it was in the parts factories.

During the first part of June the major portion of the Eighth's efforts was devoted to the support of landing operations and ground activity in Nor-mandy. Its strategic work was confined chiefly to sitting airfields to prevent the GAF from interfering with the invasion, and between 1 June and D-day eight of these, chiefly in the Paris area, were attacked. One airframe factory was struck, however, during this period. On 4 June, 23 bombers revisited the SYCA Se-204 plant at Bourges with 28 tons of fragmentation clusters. Some new damage resulted. The Fifteenth Air Force was chiefly engaged in hitting important railroad junctions and bridges in support of the Italian campaign and the Russian advance in the Balkans. Its first attack on aircraft production after 30 May was on 9 June when 30 bombers struck the Dornier factory at Munich/Neuaubing with 57 tons of bombs. By D-Day, however, German aircraft production had been reduced to such a low level that the task of the Air Forces became one of policing to see that this level was maintained and primary attention was turned to other target systems.

As a corollary to airframes, aero-engines were seriously attacked in 1944. They became priority targets early in the year and by the end of September, 21 of the 22 major factories producing Bayerische Motoran Werks, and Daimler-Benz engines had been damaged. The end result was to limit both replacements and installations in new aircraft. At the beginning of 1944, the GAF had a surplus of 10,000 engines and an increasing monthly production which reached a peak of 6000 in April. This provided for a balance between production and requirements until May, when requirements began to exceed production. In October production had been reduced to 2700 a month and the surplus had fallen to less than 1000. There was some recovery from this time on, due in part to removal of factories to disperse and underground sites, until about 4200 engines a month were being produced by the end of the year. While this helped, it was not enough to meet the requirements.

The concentrated attack on aero-engines did not take place until the latter half of 1944. From January through May there was a total of 48 strikes, 16 by the Eighth Air Force, 5 by the Fifteenth, and 21 by the RAF. Many of the factories bombed in this period received their damage from area rather than precision raids. This was particularly true in the case of the RAF missions. The Eighth was also able to hit some engine plants by bombing, although the particular factory involved was not pin-pointed. The damage inflicted on the Fischer A. G. Jumo carburetor plant at Frankfurt was an example of this. In some instances an engine factory, such as the BMW plant at Eisenach which was raided by the Eighth on 24 February, was attacked as a part of a raid on an airframe establishment – in this case the Me110 assembly at Gotha. The Fifteenth's attack on the Daimler-Benz (DL) engine components at Steyr was in connection with the raids on the ball-bearing industry.

Not all precision attacks were successful. On 21 February the Neider-sachsische Rotoren Werke at Brunswick/Querm was the target, but the bombs fell wide of the mark and practically no damage resulted to the primary objective. Although only 36 per cent of the total tonnage of 5534 tons dropped by the Eighth specifically on aero-engines was dropped prior to June 1944 (937 tons from April to December 1943, and 1028 tons from January to May 1914), these attacks hastened the dispersal of the factories with the resulting loss of quality and quantity and added to the problems of the already harassed GAF.

Allied with the campaign against aircraft production was the destruction of the enemy's airfields. Not only were these installations fighter bases from which the GAF could dispatch planes to intercept the bomber formations but they also served numerous other purposes. The Zemun airdrome at Belgrade, for example, was an important stop-over point for German transports flying supplies to the Russian front from northern Italy, Yugoslavia, and Greece. Some fields, such as those at Avieno, Villaorba, and Piacenza served as ferry bases for aircraft flying from the production lines to the Italian battle areas.

Other airfields were used as repair bases, and practically every final assembly plant had an adjacent airfield for testing and storage. For example, an airdrome not only was a long-range bomber base but would also be equipped with extensive repair and conversion facilities. The airfield adjoining the Messerschmitt components plant was not only a point in the first line of defense of southern Germany, but also a storage depot and repair base. As the destruction of Luftwaffe production increased in intensity the airdromes having repair facilities increased in importance. It became necessary to recondition and return to service many airplanes which normally would have remained grounded. An example of this was the Wollersdorf airfield at Wiener Neustadt. This installation had always been the chief GAF air stores park in Southeastern Europe for supplying Italy and the Balkans, but after the severe damage inflicted on Werke I and Werke II Messerschmitt factories at Wiener Neustadt, its importance as a repair base grew rapidly.

Attacks on many airfields were tactical in nature rather than strategic. The Eighth Air Force sorties against man of the French, Belgian, and Dutch installations, such as Chateaudun, Caen/Carpiquet, Romilly, and Biarritz in France, Catend, Brussels/Le Culot, and Brussels/Le Culet, and Brussels/ Melsbrock in Belgium, and Gilze-Rijin and Lindhoven in Holland, were designed not only to render them unserviceable as bases from which to fly against the heavy bombers but also to prevent their use for repelling the cross-Channel invasion when it got under way. In the Mediterranean where a land battle was already in progress, the Italian and southern French air- fields had a particular tactical significance. Gradually the German fighter operational fields were pushed farther and farther back from the front lines as both the Fifteenth and Twelfth Air Forces poured tons of bombs on the fields. By the middle of February, the GAF could use the bases in the Rome area, such as Viterbe, Terquinia, and Orvieto, only as advanced landing grounds. The airfields in southern France, such as Montpellier/Frejorgues, Istres Le Tute, and Salon de Trovenee, served as long-range bomber bases from which the GAF operated against Mediterranean shipping and the Anzio beachhead, and it was necessary for the Fifteenth to neutralize them not only to protect shipping and Anzio but also to assure the success of ANVIL.

Not only were the airfields attacked by the four-engine bombers of USSTAF, but as the strength of the Luftwaffe waned and the number of American fighters increased, the fighter escort, freed from close watch over the formations, often descended to shoot up fields either as primaries or as targets or opportunity. By the end of April, it was common procedure for fighters to strafe any fields they could find when relieved of escort duties. The effectiveness of these bomber and fighter strikes is attested to by the great number of fugitive sorties flown by the Germans on the approach of Allied formations. The attacks, in addition to destroying and damaging air- craft on the ground, facilities, and supplies, also furnished the GAF with a varied assortment of transportation, repair, and morale headaches. Prob- lems of personnel evacuation, conscription and transportation of sufficient labor for repair work, and maintenance of discipline caused trouble long after the bombs had fallen. After the 5 February attack on the Chateauroux/ Martineri airfield by the Eighth, the Germans requisitioned several hundred workers from the usual sources to assist with the repairs. Unable to get more than a fraction of the number needed, however, the Germans drafted laborers from factories in the vicinity. The difficulties were not lightened by the fact that a week after the attack 40 to 50 unexploded bombs were still on the airfield. Altogether in the first nine months of 1944, assaults on airfields accounted for 76,700 tons of Allied bombs, with USSTAF and the RAF making 531 attacks on 257 targets – 135 in France and the Low Countries, 75 in Germany and Austria, and 47 in Italy and the Balkans.

The Luftwaffe did not take these attacks lying down, but as its strength declined it had to develop techniques for conserving its operational aircraft. As early as January the Germans resorted to a new dispersal policy on airfields in occupied countries, placing dispersal areas as far as a mile and a half from the main field. This made it more difficult to destroy or damage planes on the ground and divided the Allies' efforts. Another trick was to plot the approaching fighters and order all aircraft on the field to go up and hover over near-by woods where their color blended with that of the forest. Often the American fighters would not see these camouflaged planes in the air and would pass them by, and seeing no aircraft on the ground would do little or no strafing. If one of those hiding formations was spotted, however, the Americans descended on them like wolves on a herd of sheep.

The USAAF also developed tactics of its own to secure the most efficient results from attacks on enemy airfields. In order to prevent the GAF from rising against bombers on their way to a targets, a number of fighters would precede the bomber formation by about 15 minutes. They would fly low enough to come under the enemy's radar curtain, and arrive at the field undetected in time to catch the German fighters getting ready to take off to intercept the heavies still miles away. Another tactic developed was for the escort to slide to one side of the bombers when the latter prepared to drop their bombs on an airfield. Then as soon as the bombs had exploded and before the flak guns could be fully manned, the fighters would sweep in and shoot up the rest of the field. By this technique it was possible to stay over the field for about five to 10 minutes before it was necessary to pull out.

The results of the attacks on aircraft production are confusing and paradoxical. In spite of this damage inflicted (146 assembly, component, repair, and aero-engine plants were damaged in the first nine months of 1944) production rose sharply after March, and during the whole ear 39,807 aircraft of all types, of which 25,860 were single-engine fighters, were accepted by the GAF. It must be remembered, however, that an increased production had been planned and provided for in 1943, and only a guess can be made as to how much greater the output would have been if the Allies had not given the aircraft industry the high priority it held. Reichsmarshal Goering explained that increased total numbers meant little unless the types were also considered. The change from bomber to fighter planes alone allowed for greater numbers. Four fighters, he said, could be built out of what it took to construct one Be-177. Goering also stated that after the Ministry took over procurement more raw material was available, and this coupled with large-scale dispersal naturally permitted increased production. The effects of bombing were, as Goering said, partially offset by dispersal and conceal-ment of factories in underground sites.

After eliminating other factors which contributed to reducing produc-tion, responsible German officers agreed to the effectiveness of the Allied bombing policy in general. Field Marshall Milch claimed the attacks had a noticeably crippling effect as early as July 1943. An operations officer in Italy estimated that 18 per cent of the aircraft industry failed. "We were con-fronted," he said "with insurmountable difficulties – moving the industry underground, using every available workshop, no matter how small, every garage to produce parts. Replacement of workers moving and housing workers, difficulties with our foreign laborers, the transportation difficulties and securing the alloys and other materials which go into an aircraft were but a few of our Gargantuan tasks. In this respect your strategic bombing program was of course successful, you forced us to the limits of our endur-ance, ability and energies, and had it not been that we were fighting a des-perate, fanatically defensive war, our aircraft industry could never have over-come your bombings." Another staff officer admitted that the industry was badly damaged and that it was a tremendous task to assemble the arts from widely dispersed locations where they were being made, but said he, "somehow we managed."

A very important effect of the war against the aircraft industry was to deny organizations enough new planes to keep them up to the authorized operational strength. The Jagdgeschwader 7 (fighter wing) which was to be re-equipped with the famous je-propelled Me-262 was forced to twiddle its thumbs because of a lack of planes. Deliveries were delayed for a long time because and important tool supply, necessary in construction, had been destroyed in the Regensburg raids. Since the Jagdgeschwader had already relinquished its old planes to other units, the training and transition to the Me-262 was considerably slowed down, and many pilots and ground crews were forced into idleness. Some conventional groups, in addition to lacking new planes, also suffered from a shortage of replacement parts, such as propellers.

The Germans themselves should be given some credit for their reduced production. Hitler, stubbornly refusing to recognize that the GAF was no longer an offensive but a defensive organization, insisted that the Me-262 be converted to a fighter-bomber, and on his personal orders production on this plane was held up at a time when the Germans needed every fighter they could get. He likewise relinquished its old planes to other units, the training and transition to the Me-202 was considerably slowed down, and many pilots and ground crews were forced into idleness. He likewise ordered a cut in the fighter production program in order to make materials available for an increased four-engine bomber program. There was also friction within the German organization and too much competition in matters of materials, tools, and manpower. Apparently there was no effective priority system. From this it would appear that priority positions depended upon the personal whims and influence of governmental officials instead of on objective ratings.

The Americans themselves were guilty of mistakes which lessened the effectiveness of the bombing of the aircraft industry. One was in the choice of bombs used. The attacks on airframe factories often resulted in more structural damage to buildings than destruction of essential machinery. Certain precautions taken by the Germans, such as leaving windows open during a raid to reduce the force of the blast and removing undamaged or slightly damaged machinery immediately to a rapidly improvised workshop such as a hangar, allowed production to go on. It had been supposed that aircraft factories were not particularly vulnerable to fire, but postwar surveys show that a high value target was machine tools. The chief objection to the 500-pound bomb was that they were too light to wreck important structures completely. They dug craters in the floor but did little damage to the machinery. Technicians agreed that maximum damage was created when the

bomb explodes just beneath the roof, but proper fuses for this type of detonation were not available even in limited quantities until the last half of
1944. The emphasis placed on final assembly at first was designed to prevent finished aircraft from reaching the front lines, but the recuperative
capacity and ease of repair or improvisation kept this from happening and
there had to be many return attacks. Goering generally agreed that earlier
attacks on aero-engines and components would have affected final assembly
more disastrously than the destruction of final assembly facilities themselves.

The attacks on airfields were generally effective, but in the opinion of
Goering they were not a major factor in the destruction of the Luftwaffe.
Runways were, of course damaged, but these could be more or less easily
put into operation again. This the Germans called "the race between the
shovel and the bomb." A large number of grounded planes at these places
were destroyed also, and although the bombing of these airfields might not
have been a major factor in Germany's defeat, it certainly was a contributing
one.

Regardless of the faults inherent in the bombardment policy of the
German aircraft industry, it did accomplish in the end certain important
results. First, it forced the Luftwaffe to change from an offensive to a defensive organization, and the Luftwaffe was not adequately prepared for an
effective quick readjustment. It also necessitated the reshifting of forces so
that the heaviest disposition was in western Europe and Germany, thus
leaving the ground forces in Italy and on the Russian front with diminished
air protection. A captured officer explained: "Why don't we see any of our
planes? Because we don't have any! If you're in Russia you're told that the
Air Force is in Italy; if you're in Italy, then you are told it is in the West and
if you're in the West, then you're told that it is in Russia. I saw something of
the situation. At Bologna there were exactly 16 planes! It made my hair
stand on end!"

Another important effect was to eliminate serious air opposition to
OVERLORD. The extent to which the GAF was knocked out is illustrated
by the lament of General Jurck, commander of the fighter defenses in the
French invasion area. His statement was corroborated by Goering, that on
D-Day he had only 160 aircraft, 80 of which were operational, to oppose the

invasion. During the first five days of June 1944, 3300 bomber crews and 2312 fighter pilots of the Eighth Air Force reported that scarcely an enemy plane was seen. The total GAF reaction to nearly 6000 sorties was an attack by 10 Me-109's on their straggling B-24's on 4 June but even these fled from the P-51 escort.

A third result of the air attack on GAF production was to force the Germans into a weakening policy of plane conservation and to make more vulnerable other portions of the enemy's air industry. This lack of air opposition in turn considerably reduced the costs during the latter months of the strategic bombing and allowed an economical destruction of oil, transportation, and other vital targets.

11

ATTACK ON THE BALL
BEARING INDUSTRY

Allied with the bombing of aircraft factories were the attacks on the anti-friction-bearing industry. In these days of mechanized warfare and high-speed moving machine parts the ball and other types of bearings play an important role. Thus it was hoped that the destruction of the sources of supply for the ball bearings would affect the production not only of airplanes but also of motor vehicles, tanks, machinery, and other war equipment. The RAF had opened the campaign on 14 April 1943. The Eighth Air Force inaugurated its daylight offensive against ball bearings when it attacked the Schweinfurt plants on 17 August of that year. Its next attack was a month later, 15 September. On 14 October Schweinfurt was again raided by the Eighth and before the end of the year the bearing factories at Turin and Villar-Perosa were attacked by the Fifteenth.

By the middle of January 1944 it was estimated that ball-bearing production in Germany had been cut somewhat over 20 per cent, and General Arnold was anxious that the complete destruction be accomplished as soon as possible. He estimated that the effects would be seriously felt within a month after production ceased. Schweinfurt still remained the chief producer even after the two heavy bombings in 1943, and in the ensuing months it received the most attention. The three plants (Kugelfischer, VKF, and Fichtel and Sachs) located there still produced a little over 38 per cent of the bearings. Outside of Germany, the biggest manufacturer was the Steyrwaffen Walzlagerwerke, a Daimler-Puch factory, which had produced nearly 10 per cent of the pre-attack supply. With the elimination of other sources of supply this was stepped up to about 14 per cent by the end of the first quarter of 1944.

The Fifteenth Air Force began the 1944 campaign against the bearing industry with an attack by 53 B-17's on the RIV factory at Villar-Perosa on 3 January. A total of 171 tons of bombs cascaded down on this plant which had supplied 1.4 per cent of Germany's normal supply. Between 20 and 26 February, seven large-scale attacks were launched, three by the Eighth Air Force, one by the Fifteenth, and three by the Bomber Command.

In April, only two ball-bearing centers were attacked in three raids. The first of these was on 2 April by the Fifteenth against Steyr, and on 15 April the Eighth Air Force returned to Schweinfurt and dropped about 345 tons of mixed bombs. With these attacks, there came a lull in the campaign against ball bearings. In May, there was only one attack on the industry.

The Allied campaign against the antifriction-bearing industry continued almost to the end of the war. No attacks were made in June, but eight were launched in July. Then there was another letup until October and the last attack came on 23 February 1945 when 12 B-17's dropped about 36 tons on Schweinfurt in an area raid. During the main period of the attack, 17 August 1943 – 30 September 1944, USSGAF mad 26 attacks on 14 factories producing about 84 percent of the Axis supply of bearings. The bombs dropped on these plants represented 1.2 per cent of the total effort of the U.S. Strategic Air Forces in these 11 months. In the first half of the period, August 1943 – February 1944, it was estimated that those attacks, along with the loss of imports, caused a 20 per cent reduction in the German pre-raid supply. In the next seven months the reduction amounted to 30 per cent.

In spite of the high hopes entertained in the beginning that disastrous effects would be achieved by the attacks on ball bearings, the results were not as fruitful as desired. Experience showed that it was very difficult to put factories out of operation. Even the destruction of a vital process could not stop production, since the organization of the plants into departments doing one complete phase of manufacture allowed continuation of work in other departments when one was bombed out. This, along with the failure to destroy or disable machinery and the inability to harm raw materials or finished and semi-finished stocks, permitted a certain supply to keep flowing to users. The greatest damage was to buildings. Almost half of the pre-raid floor space was destroyed and another half was heartily damaged. Even in April 1944, when supply fell to 47 per cent of pre-attack levels, 50 per cent of the requirements were met. The average supply for the first six months of 1944 was 58 per cent of pre-attack days, and this was sufficient for 75 per cent of the needs.

German leaders themselves did not believe that the Allied campaign against ball bearings was too effective. Goering claimed that dispersal, underground factories, and use of substitutes made it possible to keep a pipe line open to the users and bridge the gaps in production. Speer's testimony corroborated that of Goering and Gilch. Gilch stated that the bombing forced the Germans into a policy of dispersal which caused at least a temporary shrinking in production. .

Despite the fact that the campaign against ball bearings did not bring the full amount of desired results, the theory behind the decision to strike at this industry was sound. It was in part unforeseen developments, such as Swedish supply of bearings, lack of intelligence on the full condition of the industry, and some tactical errors on our part which prevented the end results from being completely successful. Albert Speer testified that the effect on armaments production would have been disastrous and the entire armaments industry would have been brought to a complete standstill if: (1) all ball-bearing plants had been attacked simultaneously; (2) repeat attacks had been staged at short intervals, about every 14 days, until production stopped; and (3) each attempt at reconstruction had been attacked every two weeks for six months.

Whether Speer's advice could have been followed is a question for tacticians. It was an accepted fact among Allied airmen that repeat bombings at regular intervals were usually necessary to knock out a large target completely, but incidents of weather, shortage of equipment, availability of personnel, incorrect interpretation of previous damage, and other human failings often interposed to alter a line of action. It is easier to see mistakes after they are committed.

12

TRANSPORTATION

Next to aircraft production transportation held highest priority, and when the success of the counter-air -bombing in the spring of 1944, transportation rose to first place. The reason for placing it at the head of the list of target systems at this time was to give as much direct support as possible to the forthcoming invasion of the Continent. The campaign against the transportation systems, however, can be placed into three distinct areas of operation: (1) the Italian peninsula; (2) western Europe; and (3) southeastern Europe and the Balkans. In each of these there was a specific purpose to be accomplished, and for this reason the attack on transportation lacked the singleness of purpose which characterized the fight to gain air superiority. Furthermore, transportation included more than railroads, although these were the targets most frequently attacked. The other transportation features also bombed were harbors bridges, viaducts, and canals, while rivers and coastal areas where radar installations were the this target system and were the responsibility solely of the strategic air forces. The tactical air forces, such as the Ninth had their share of marshaling yards, bridges, tunnels, and viaducts which were located within their range, and in the Mediterranean theater the Coastal Command was engaged in striking at shipping both in harbors and at sea.

Unlike other target systems, transportation is one where it is difficult to draw a clear line of distinction between strategic and tactical attacks. This was particularly true of the Fifteenth Air Force, which during the period covered by this study was actively engaged in supporting the land battle raging in the Italian peninsula and the advance of the Russian armies in Southeastern Europe. The same was true of the Eighth Air Force after the invasion of Normandy. Generally speaking, however, strategic attacks were those designed to strike at facilities well behind the enemy's forward lines and were not intended to isolate specific units engaged in battle, and they might have an adverse effect on industry as well as a long-range tactical benefit.

In the Italian theater the line of demarcation between strategic and tactical operations was roughly that of Rimini-Pisa. The Fifteenth Air Force, as discussed in Chapter IV, was often called upon, however, to fly missions south of this line. The general plan for the strategic disruption of rail communications in Italy by MASAF at the beginning of 1944 was two-fold: (1) to strike at the northern marshaling yards, and (2) to interdict lines in the La Spezia-Rimini area. With the marshaling yards knocked out the movement of goods and personnel into and out of Italy, would be eliminated or at least greatly hindered, and the cutting of the lines from the marshaling yards to the forces in central Italy would prevent the enemy's troops in battle areas from receiving equipment and reinforcements already gathered at distribution points.

In the interdiction program six specific areas were chosen for attack. One was the Genoa-La Spezia railroad, particularly the Recco viaduct which was the longest of four such structures on this line. The task of knocking this out was given primarily to the Coastal Command and the Navy, although the strategic forces also worked on it. In the Rimini-Ancona sector the work of destroying the bridges at Fano and Falconara and the Cesano River bridge was assigned to the fighters and fighter-bombers. The other four areas, Parma-Aulla, Bologna-Pistoia, Bologna-Prato, and Faenza-Borgo San Lorenzo, were assigned to MASAF. On each of these lines there were important bridges, viaducts, and transformer stations, and it was hoped that successful attacks on these targets would create a serious bottleneck. All of them were in difficult terrain and far away from railway repair centers. Furthermore their distance from combat zones would not make transshipment by motor transport feasible. Goods would then tend to pile up at marshaling yards and thus create a still larger traffic jam and offer spectacular targets.

During the month of January the total tonnage of bombs dropped on railroads and marshaling yards by MASAF was 4325. Most of the transportation targets hit were within a radius of 200-300 miles of Foggia, with the marshaling yards in the Florence area, such as Prato, Certaldo, Poggibonsi, Pontassieve, and Pistoia, receiving the heaviest blows. Although the line for separating the activities of the strategic and tactical Air Forces was roughly Pisa-Rimini, MASAF struck a number of railroad targets and marshaling yards, such as Arezzo, Siena, Orvieto, Perugia, Tesi, Terni, and Porto Civitanova, which were considerably south of this border. Above the line the important marshaling yards hit were Isa, Ferrara, Pontedera, Verona, Bologna, Turin, and Rimini. Several of the targets were attacked more than once, and not all were primary targets but were raided as secondary or targets of opportunity when weather conditions obscured the primaries.

In February, the bulk of the bombing effort against rail transportation was expended in approximately the same area as in January – between Ancona-Civitavecchia and Pisa-Ferrara. Tonnage was reduced, however, to less than half (2087 tons – 1994 tons by the Fifteenth and 93 tons by the 205 Group, RAF) of the January total, but it represented 30 per cent of all of ASAF's bombing. A good many of the raids could be called tactical since they had as their primary purpose the giving of direct aid to the ground forces. For example, on 16 February the Fifteenth dropped approximately 358 tons of 500-pound GP on the rail lines, bridges, and marshaling yards of Prao, Pontassieve, Certaldo, Poggibonsi, Rieti, Siena, and Cecina, and on 20 February it let loose 182 tons on the road and rail communications in the Santé Marie/Tagliaozzo area. In the first half of the month, however, MASAF did bomb a number of the more important yards and rail communications in the north, such as Padua, Verona, Ferrara, Mantua, Vicenza, and Modena. These were key points in routing traffic into Italy and southward to the battle zone.

The Fifteenth also struck several railroad targets outside of Italy, but these were in conjunction with attacks on other objectives. On 4 February, as a part of the Toulon Harbor raid, 87 tons of bombs were aimed at the

Antheor viaduct, just east of the harbor, but with no success. On 22 February, 42 tons of bombs were dropped by 21 B-17's on the Etershausen marshaling yards, which were a secondary target on the Regensburg/ Prufen-Regensburg, 16 B-24's hit the yards at Zell-am-See, 100 miles northwest of Klagenfurt, as a target of opportunity. The same day, another 16 B-24's dropped 37 tons on the Fiume marshaling yards and docks as a secondary target.

About the middle of the month it was definitely stated, however, that the second priority for MASAF (counter-air program of POINTBLANK being first) would be the disruption of Italian rail communications, including repair shops and other services as well as marshaling yards, at the following points, listed in order of priority: Padua, Verona, Bolzano, Turin, Genoa, and Milan. When visibility did not permit attacks on these places, alternate targets would be: Treviso, Mestre, Vicenz, and Alessandria. If weather was such that none of the 10 targets could be attacked, other communication centers north of the Pisa-Florence-Rimini line would have priority in accordance with the size of their marshaling yards and repair facilities.

This new directive meant that generally speaking the Fifteenth Air Force and the 205 Group, RAF henceforth would devote their main attention in matters of rail transportation to integrated systems rather than to individual engineering structures involved in interdiction and that the attacks would be less immediately associated with the front lines. Although the plans for March were to concentrate on the northern yards as supplementary to the attacks of the Twelfth Air Force closer to the battle areas, MASAF continued occasionally to bomb single targets, such as bridges or marshaling yards in the area south of Pisa-Rimini. For example, on the night of 2/3 March Wellingtons of the 205 Group, RAF struck at the Orbetello marshaling yards and railroad targets in the vicinity of Montalto di Castro. The Fifteenth sent a number of its heavies on 3 March against the Rome/Littoria and Rome/Tiburtina marshaling yards with fair results. Later in the month, on 28 March, the Fifteenth bombed the bridges at Fano and Cessno. The major transportation attacks of MASAF were directed, however, against such places as Padua, Genoa, Verona, Bologna, Rimini, Milan/ Lambrate, Turin, and Bolzano. The biggest day for the Fifteenth Air Force was on 28 March, when 1061 tons of bombs were dropped on communication targets in Italy. This was the first "1000 ton day" for this organization. Altogether the Mediterranean strategic Air Forces dropped nearly 6000 tons of bombs on railroads and marshaling yards (4939 tons by the Fifteenth and 1000 tons by the 205 Group, RAF) in March. This was 55 per cent of all MASAF tonnage that month.

In April, MASAF's total tonnage delivered against all targets almost doubled (from 10,767 tons in March to 21348 tons in April), but the amount dropped on rail transportation targets was down to 46 per cent. These 9882 tons, however, represented more than half of the total tonnage (17,062 tons) dropped by all components of MAAF on railroads and marshaling yards. The bombing pattern was pretty much the same as it had been in March, with the northern transportation centers receiving the most attention. The 20 Group, RAF hit such railroad centers as Micenza, Genoa, La Spezia, Alessandria, and Piacenza. The Fifteenth Air Force bombed, mostly with good results, the marshaling yards at Treviso and Mestre in the Venice area, Ferrara, Bologna, Parma, Milan, Alessnadria, Vicenza, Padua, and Trieste/Opicina. Some of these targets were struck several times, demolishing repairs as soon as they were made and thus allowing only a small amount of traffic to trickle southward to the Florence area. Below Florence the tactical Air Forces had to bomb individual engineering structures and targets south of Pisa-Rimini. These were for the most part, however, either secondary targets or targets of opportunity. For example, on 20 April, some of the forces from the Fifteenth, finding their primary targets cloud-obscured, dropped their bombs on Ancona and Fano marshaling yards as secondaries, and hit the railroad bridge over the Tagliamento River at Casarsa as a target of opportunity.

During April the Fifteenth introduced a new type of bomb to the European theater. This was the Azon which consisted of a special radio tail attachment for 1000-pound bombs and a radio transmitter in the airplane, by means of which the bombardier could control the azimuth movement of the bomb. As early as February, Headquarters, AAF had decided to use at least 100 of these bombs against special targets in the ETO, and plans were made to ship necessary equipment and personnel to the Eighth Air Force by 1 March, Experiments at Eglin Field had led the planners to believe, however,, that this weapon was not a suitable one against the selected objectives on the French invasion coast. Since they were controllable only in azimuth, they could be used more efficiently against long targets, such as bridges, docks, and marshaling yards, where range was not particularly important. For this reason it was recommended that the project be transferred to the Fifteenth Air Force, which was doing considerable bombing of transportation targets. The recommendation was accepted, and a six-plane, 200-bomb, Azon project was scheduled to leave the United States for the MTO by 15 March.

The first shipment did not leave until early April, but by 19 April everything was in readiness in the theater to start operations at an early date. The first mission took place on the 24th when five Azon-equipped B-17's attacked the Ancona-Rimini railroad with eight tons of bombs. The bombers met with no opposition, there were no losses, and the results were considered good since hits were scored on the tracks and on the approaches to a bridge. The next mission was on 29 April. Again five B-17's participated, dropping 12.5 tons of 1000-pound RDX Azon bombs on the same railroad. There was a direct hit on the bridge at Senigallis, a cut in the line, and numerous near misses. The average deflection error was estimated to be 150 feet and for range about 500 feet and it was hoped that further experiment would decrease the number of misses.

On 13 May, four B-17's, Azon-equipped, participated as leaders in an attack on the Avisio viaduct (a few miles north of Trento on the Brenner Pass rail line) by the 301st Group of the Fifteenth Air Force. Out of the 2 Azon bombs released, four were direct hits. The rest of the group, using normal methods, released their loads of 1000-pound GP simultaneously with the Azons. Photo interpretation showed a 0-foot gap in the viaduct, which would effectively block traffic through the vital Brenner Pass. At the same time that Avisio was being bombed other planes were attacking the Bolzano marshaling yards, thus causing more interruption on this link between Germany and Italy.

It was not until the last of May that the Eighth Air Force was equipped with Azon bombs, although it had requested them in early April. The Eighth felt that these bombs could be successfully used against the increasing number of CROSSBOW, communication, and tactical targets it would be called upon to destroy prior to and after D-day. Headquarters, AAF replied that the current procurement contract called for only 10,000 Azons and a decision to manufacture more would depend upon the success obtained by the Fifteenth. Nevertheless, the Eighth was advised to observe the operations in the MTO practical date. On 8 May, Spaatz requested 10 B-24's equipped for Azon bombing, and two days later he was notified that this number was being diverted from the China-Burma-India theater to the ETO. Upon arrival these were assigned to the 96th Combat Wing of the 2d Bombardment Division. The first mission in which they were used was on 31 May when 14 out of 2 Azon bombs were released against French bridges with fair to good results. Five of the bombs were jettisoned over the English Channel and six were returned to base. Three days prior to this, uncontrolled glide bombs were used in a raid on Cologne, but the unsuccessful results led to a recommendation that no more of these bombs be ordered for the Eighth Air Force.

In May, which saw the beginning of the concentrated drive on Rome (DIADEM) and the final preparations for a cross-Channel invasion of France (OVERLORD, the operations of MASAF against rail transportation were divided largely between Italian and French communication centers. It was on 12 May, too, that the Fifteenth Air Force celebrated its first "1000 sortie day" and dropped the record tonnage of the year to date. On that day, 1143 sorties were flown in cooperation with the round forces in Italy, and 1912 tons of bombs were rained down on a combination of railroad yards, airfields, and other military targets. Although the percentage of bombs dropped by MASAF on railroad installations in May was less than half of the total for all targets (45.8 per cent), the total number of tons (13,910) was greater than at any previous time and no other target system received nearly so much. Of the total, the Fifteenth dropped 1,257 tons and the 205 Group, RAF dropped 653 tons. In addition to the railroads, MASAF also attacked other transportation facilities, putting 3726 tons on harbors and docks and 872 tons on highways.

The 205 Group, RAF started the May campaign off on ½ May with an attack on the Alessandria marshaling yards and the Genoa docks and rail yards. This was followed on 2 May by Fifteenth Air Force raids against Castelmaggiore, Parma, Ancona, and La Spezia marshaling yards and the Orbetello and Faenza railroad bridges. Generally, the important transportation

targets were north of Pisa-Rimini, although some south of this line were singled out for attack in direct cooperation with the ground armies. The Flor-
ence-Rome routes were attacked at Arezzo, Orvieto, and Fornovo di Taro.
On the east coastline from Rimini southward strikes were made at Ancona,
Fano, Porto Civitanova, Porto San Giorgio, San Benedetto, Giulianova,
Teramo, Tortoreto, Montesilvano, and Roseto. Southeast of Rome, the railroad and highway junction at Valmontons was bombed.

In the north there was a systematic hitting of key junction points and
then a blocking of the lines between these places. On the through rail line
between Piacenza and Rimini, these two cities and the chief junctions with
the Brenner Pass and east-west railroads such as Parma, Modena, and
Bologna were attacked to check traffic entering this region for transshipment southward. Then between these places, marshaling yards and other
railroad installations at Cesena, Fidenza, San Rufillo, Faenza, Imola, and
Forli were bombed. On the west coast, the Recco viaduct was attacked
again as well as both Genoa and La Spezia. These attacks effectively slowed
rail movements of supplies and reinforcements to the battle areas at a critical time.

In order to prevent east-west traffic from leaving or entering Italy, Alessandria, Milan/Lambrate, and Vercelli in the northwest, and Casarsa, Lati-
sana, Padua, Vicenza, Treviso, Mestre, Ferrara, and Mantus in the northeast were attacked. The eastern points, such as Padua and Vicenza, not only
connected with the Balkans but also with the Brenner Pass, and such places
as Ferrara and Mantua fed northern traffic to the Piacenza-Rimini line. The
third transportation system attacked was the Brenner Pass railroads, which
were the most direct avenues to Germany. The rail installations to receive
the chief weight of Allied bombs were those at Bolzano, Borgo, Bronzolo,
Colle Iscara, Trento, and the Avisio viaduct.

In the latter part of May a system of priorities within each of four groups
of localities was established for railroads in southern France. These were,
according to priority: (1) Chambery, Grenoble, and Amberieux; (2)
Toulon/Carnoles and then Nice; (3) Lyon/Mocha, Lyon/Venissieux,
Lyon/Vaise, St. Etienne, and Badam/Givors; (4) Avignon, Marseilles/St.
Charles, Marseilles/La Blaneharde, and Nimes. In addition certain bridges
on the routes to Italy were to be attacked in conjunction with raids on the

above-named places. These bridges were near St. Pierre Albigny over the Isere River on the Modane rote or, as an alternate, the Meana viaduct on the Italian side of the same line. On the coastal line the Var River bridge just west of Nice or the bridges at Ventimiglia and Taggia were ready for reattack.

The campaign against French railroads began on 25 May when 575 aircraft of the Fifteenth were dispatched against the marshaling yards at Amberieux, Toulon/Carnoules, Lyon/Venissieux, and Givors to interdict traffic to southern French ports and to Italy over the Mt. Cenis line. A total of 858.75 tons of bombs were dropped with Lon/Venissieux receiving 367.5 tons, Toulon/Carnoules 265.25 tons, Givors (just south of Lyon) 128 tons, and Amberieux (northeast of Lyon) 98 tons. The next day the Fifteenth was out again in force and put 248 tons on the Lyon/Vaise marshaling yards, 247 tons on Lyon/Mouche, 180 tons on Chambery, 158.75 tons on Grenoble, 439.5 tons on St. Etienne, 242.75 tons on Nice/St. Roch, and 94.5 tons on the Var River bridge. On 27 May four more marshaling yards were attacked. Avignon received the largest tonnage (274 tons), then Nimes (234.75 tons), Marseilles/St. Charles (165.5 tons), and Marseilles/ La Blanchard (119.75 tons). In these three days the Fifteenth hit 14 of the most important marshaling yards in southern France with a total of 3198.75 tons of bombs, seriously crippling transportation in that area while still maintaining pressure on the Italian rail communication system.

For the first three days of June no attacks were made by MASAF on Italian or French railroads. Then on 4 June, the day Rome fall, the Fifteenth made a series of attacks against the lines leading from France to Italy. The Var River bridge was raided with 79 tons of bombs. The Antheor viaduct received 84 tons which did practically no damage. On the Modane route to Turin, the Oreille railroad bridge on the French side was bombed with 80 tons of GP, and on the Italian side the Gad railroad bridge was struck with 16 tons. The Recco viaduct was bombed with 117 tons of general purpose bombs as a part of the mission against Genoa. The marshaling yards attacked were Turin (262.75 tons), Genoa (1712.5 tons), Savona (69.35 tons), and Novi Ligure (6.5 tons).

The following day the Fifteenth turned its attention again to the Piacenza-Rimini railroad system. A series of bridges on lines south to La

Spezia, Florence, and other points were attacked with a total of 471.5 tons of bombs, with results varying from poor at Pioppi to excellent at Vado. These bridges were at Fornovo di Taro (100 tons), Pioppi (8.5 tons), Vado (59 tons), Marradi (114 tons), and Rimini (120 tons). The marshaling yards which were attacked on 5 June were: Ferrara with 131.8 tons, Ferli with 64 tons, Faenza with 74 tons, Castelmaggiore with 188.25 tons, and Bologna with 169.5 tons.

In the European theater there was no land battle actually in progress as there was in Italy, and therefore USSTAF attacks were not very heavy during the first quarter of 1944. After the Eighth Air Force came under SHAEF in April the weight of the attacks increased, but generally speaking, the bombing of French and German rail communications by the strategic Air Forces was subordinate to other target systems in POINTBLANK,. The responsibility for transportation was largely that of the tactical Air Forces and the RAF until just before and after D-day, when a systematic attempt was made to interdict all traffic to the front lines.

Prior to April most of the damage inflicted by the Eighth Air Force on rail transportation resulted from PFF bombing of industrial centers, from attacks on secondary targets and targets of opportunity, or from bomb falls incidental to attacks on aircraft factories and other industrial objectives. Examples of the first type are the PFF bombing of Munster on 4 January, of Frankfurt on 2 March, and of Berlin on 6 March. In all these cases the rail lines suffered varying degrees of damage. In several instances rail transportation was attacked as a target of opportunity. On 1 January, 70 tons of bombs were dropped on the rail and engineering components center of Bielefeld, 26 miles southwest of Osnabruck, as a target of opportunity (T/C). The same day the rail and armament center of Meppen, north of Lingen on the Dortmund-Ems Canal, was hit with 154 tons as another T/O. The Poix viaduct on the Amiens-Rouen line was another such target on 14 January and received 27 tons. Other targets of opportunity during the first three months of 1944 in which either rail lines, marshaling yards, or repair facilities were damaged were: Helmstedt, 20 February; Lingen, 21 February; Hamm, 23 March; and Osnabruck, 23 March. Of these places, Hamm was by far the most important. It was the largest yard in Germany, dealing in general traffic and handling most of the business between the Ruhr and north and central Germany. It had a capacity for 10,000 freight cars a day. Sixty-nine tons of incendiaries and 143 tons of GP were dropped on the marshaling yards, causing fairly severe damage.

Often in the Eighth Air Force's attacks on aircraft or ball-bearing factories rail transportation or repair facilities suffered some damage. On 24 February the locomotive factory at Gotha was hit in the attack on the aircraft factories in that city. The same day the marshaling yards at Schweinfurt were the recipients of some bombs in the raid against the VKF and Kugelfischer ball-bearing works. At Furth on 25 February about 28 miles of track were either destroyed or displaced in the attack against the Messerschmitt plant. In the attack against the VKF installation at Berlin/Erkner on 8 March, the Schwarzkopf locomotive works and railroad station at Berlin/Waldau and the Grunewald yards were heavily hit.

The Eighth did have one marshaling yard as a primary target in March. This was at Munster, a strategic railroad junction of east-west lines. The first attack was on 11 March. The target was completely overcast, however, and it was necessary to use PFF equipment to drop the 78 tons of GP and 157.5 tons of IB bombs. Munster was attacked again on 23 March as a secondary target on the Brunswick mission of that day. Only a fair amount of harm was done by the 132 tons of mixed bombs.

More damage was inflicted by the RAF Bomber Command than by the Eighth, during the first three months of 1944. The area attacks of the British naturally damaged some railroad installations and during March itself the RAF attacked seven marshaling yards as primary targets. The first of these was on 6/7 March when 263 planes dropped 1407 tons of bombs with excellent results on the Trappes marshaling yards southwest of Paris. The next night the yards at Le Mans, between Paris and Nantes, were bombed, and were rebombed on 13/14 March with heavy damage resulting from both raids. The Amiens/Longeau marshaling yards were extensively wrecked on 15/16 and 16/17 March, and then followed attacks on the railroad yards at Laon (23/24 March), Alnoys (25/26 March), Courtrai (2/27 March), and Vaires (29/30 March). In these nine raids 1314 RAF planes participated and 6873 tons of bombs were dropped. This was 26.4 per cent of the total RAF Bomber Command tonnage for March.

Although it was obviously impossible to knock out completely the whole Nazi rail transportation system, the British Ministry of Economic Warfare (MEW) reported that the series of attacks on the French railways had considerably limited traffic and created a heavy demand for switches, crossings, rails, ties, wire, cable, and other equipment – all of which were difficult to procure. Coal distribution had also been seriously affected, and at one time the coal stocks of the Paris gas works were down to a few hours' supply. One of the largest running sheds in the Region Est had a half day's supply. MEW also stated that there was a great increase in the number of trains held up in the yards and sidings because of the inability of other yards and stations to handle them. In the middle of February it was estimated that this number was about 20, and by the end of March it had risen to between 500 and 550.

During the first half of April, the attention of the Eighth was still focused on aircraft factories, airdromes, and supporting installations and no transportation was attacked as a primary target. Some damage was done to a rail line in Strasbourg when that city was attacked as a TO on 1 April. In the attack on Posen on 9 April some IB were seen to fall on a locomotive works and in the marshaling yards which handled freight going to the Russian front. The chief damage, however,, was to buildings. On this same day, one B-24 also bombed the Tullic marshaling yards as a target of opportunity on the Marienburg mission.

In the last half of the month, however, the Eighth reinforced the RAF attacks with four raids on marshaling yards as primary targets. The first of these was against Hamm on 22 April, when 638 aircraft loosed 1551 tons of mixed bombs on the marshaling yards, creating huge fires among rolling stock and buildings, and wrecking the tracks in sidings, through lines, sorting yards, and hump and choke points. Three days later, nearly 600 bombers were dispatched against GAF installations in France and Germany and against the Mannheim marshaling yards. Because of bad weather only seven planes were able to find and bomb the latter place, and only 12. Tons of GP and four tons of IB were dropped. The resulting damage was very slight, since most of the bombs dropped outside the target area. On 27 April, 118 aircraft heavily damaged the sidings and locomotive sheds and repair shops with 341.75 tons of bombs at the Blainville-sur-l'Eau marshaling yards on the main route from Germany to Paris. The same·day, 72 bombers hit the yards at Chalons-sur-Marne, on the Paris-Stuttgart line, with 215 tons of general-purpose bombs leaving severe damage in their wake.

Some further damage was inflicted on transportation in attacks on targets of opportunity and secondary targets. On 18 April four bombers put nearly 10 tons on the Limburg marshaling yards, and other planes temporarily disrupted traffic at Velsen, Salzwedel, Bad Wilsnack, and Buchalz. The next day five aircraft attacked the yards at Soest, but the 10 tons dropped missed the target. Also on 19 Aril, eight planes hit the Coblenz railroad yards, a secondary target, with 16 tons of GP bombs, with the engine sheds being hardest hit. This same target was struck as a T/O three days later when 50 aircraft dropped 58.6 tons of bombs, but very little additional damage occurred. Installations at Landau marshaling yards, on the Karlaruhe-Zweibrucken route, were damaged by 16 bombers dropping 40 tons of GP, but the through lines were not cut. The fighters also contributed to the general attack by strafing yards, locomotives, trains, and other transportation facilities. For example, on 8 April, 68 fighters shot up 15 locomotives, marshaling yards, and factories in the Mannheim and Coblenz areas, and from 18 to 29 April they accounted for 35 locomotives. Again it was the RAF Bomber Command which contributed the most toward the destruction of rail communications. During the first two weeks of April seven of the eight major RAF attacks were against the marshaling yards on the France-Germany routes, and in the last half of the month 11 yards were struck. Altogether 3236 planes took part in these raids and 16407 tons of bombs were dropped. This was 53.4 per cent of the RAF's total tonnage for April.

In the middle of April, 25 French and Belgian marshaling yards were put in third priority for the Eighth Air Force – GAF and CROSSBOW targets preceding them. The destruction of these yards was a part of a joint effort b the Eighth, RAF Bomber Command, and the Ninth Air Force to disrupt transportation to such an extent that the Germans could not readily move reinforcements and supplies to the battle areas when the Normandy invasion began. The Eighth Air Force was assigned chiefly the task of destroying the locomotive and maintenance facilities. This Air Force began its attacks on these targets on 1 May when 314 of its bombers dropped 1007.5 tons of bombs on four French and two Belgian marshaling yards, with results varying from fair to excellent.

No more attacks were made until 7 May. On that data 67 bombers attempted to bomb the Liege yards through 8/10 to 9/10 cloud. Nineteen of the bombers dropped 54.5 tons of bombs with unobserved results. The following day 56 planes laid 16.5 tons on the yards at Brussels with fair results. On 9 May a return visit was paid to Liege, where 224 tons were left, and 53 aircraft put 132.5 tons on Luxembourg. The results were good and excellent respectively for these places. The Eighth's biggest day for transportation targets during the first half of the month was 11 May. On that day it hit three marshaling yards in France, two in Belgium, two in the Duchy of Luxembourg, and three in Germany with a total of 669 heavy bombers and 1944 tons of bombs. The results were fair to good for the French yards; poor for those in Belgium; good for Luxembourg, except Bettembury which was unobserved; and very good for two of the German targets, but poor at Saarbrucken where most of the bombs fell inside the town instead of on the railroads. An attack on the Canabruck yards by 177 airplanes on 13 May completed the Eighth Air Force's offensive against transportation for the first two weeks of May. In this raid 471.5 tons of high-explosive and incendiary bombs were dropped with good coverage of the marshaling yards and the steel mill of Klocknerwerke A.G.

During the last half of May the Eighth made 38 attacks on marshaling yards, all but eight of which were primary tarts. Twenty-three were located in France, Belgium, and Holland, and 15 were in Germany. A total of 6097.45 tons of mixed bombs were dropped on these places, with generally good results. This was nearly 17 per cent (16.77) of the total tonnage dropped on all targets for the whole month. The heaviest attacks were made on 27 May when a total of 1968 tons were dropped on one French and six German marshaling yards. The next two heaviest days were on 23 and 25 May. On the former, 4 French and 2 German targets were hit with 826 tons, and on the latter date 747 tons were laid on 12 French and Belgian yards.

During these same two weeks the RAF Bomber Command operated on five nights against seven French and two German marshaling yards. On 19/20 May, 350 planes dropped a total of 1909. Tons on Boulogne (627.2 tons), on Tours/St. Pierre des Corps (591.4 tons), and Orleans/Les

Aubrais (691 tons). This latter place was hit again on 22/23 May with 489.4 tons, and the same night 115 planes struck Le Mans with 432.3 tons. On the night of 24/25 May 401 RAF bombers raided Aachen marshaling yards, dropping 2021 tons with good results. On 27/28 May the yards at Aachen/ Rothe Erde received 905 tons and the Nantes railroad junction got 240 tons. The last raid for the month was on 28/29, when 114 aircraft dropped 40 tons on the Angers marshaling yards. Altogether 6457.3 tons of bombs were dropped in these nine attacks. This was 54 per cent of the total RAF Bomber Command tonnage for all targets in the last two weeks of May.

In June prior to D-day the Eighth attacked only three rail transportation targets. On 2 June, the railroad junctions of Massy-Palaiseau and Paris/ Acheres, and the Paris/Juvisy marshaling yards were attacked by 158 planes. At Massy-Palaiseau 46 of the aircraft wrecked tracks, buildings, and rolling stock and scored hits on the overpasses and flyovers with 71.5 tons of bombs. At Paris/Acheres, 76 planes dropping 208.25 tons cratered the area between the junction and the choke point of the marshaling yards and cut the main lines to the northwest and west. The Paris/Juvisy yards received 108 tons from 36 bombers which damaged the choke point, the bridge over the Orge River, and cut through-tracks to Paris. On D-day, 6 June, the Fougeres marshaling yards south of Avrnches were attacked but no bombs fell in the yards. Five hits were made, however, on the main line to the beachhead.

The RAF operated on three nights against transportation targets prior to the Normandy landings. On 31May/1 June, 235 tons were dropped on Saumur marshaling yards, inflicting moderate damage to the tracks. This important center on the Paris-Orleans-Nantes line was revisited the following night, ½ June, and an additional 282.24 tons completely destroyed the junction point. Trappes marshalling yards were also hit on 31 May/1 June with 837 tons, and bombed again on 2/3 June with 528.64 tons. In both attacks severe damage was inflicted. Ninety-nine RAF bombers also struck the Tergnier yards, a junction point on the Paris-Brussels and Abbeville-Chalons-sur-Marne routes, with very good results on 31 May/1 June.

By D-day a total of 114 rail centers in Northern France and adjacent areas had been attacked in accordance with the NEPTUNE plan by both the AAF and RAF in the ETO with 71,157 tons of bombs. Of this the

Eighth Air Force heavies were responsible for 10,008 tons and the RAF Bomber Command for 46,712 tons. In addition to these tonnages, the Eighth also dropped more than 5000 tons on rail targets in western Germany and on the France-German border which were included in the plan for OVERLORD. There is no doubt but that the attacks on French communications were a great help in making OVERLORD a successful operation, although in an over-all estimate it can be said that they did not accomplish as much as was hoped for. Between 1 March and D-day total French rail traffic was reduced by about 60 per cent from what it had been in January and February. In the latter two months traffic had averaged about what it had been in 1943. This reduction did not mean, however that this much essential military movement was out. As a rule, military traffic was mixed with civilian, and in early 1944 it was estimated that about two-thirds of the army freight was carried in this manner. This composed about one-third the total freight traffic of civilian trains. When the capacity of French railroads began to shrink in the spring a larger share was allotted to the Wehrmacht. The cut in nonmilitary traffic, of course, meant less carrying of materials for war production, less food for war workers, and less of other things essential to a war economy, and in the long run adversely affected the German ability to wage war.

It was in a tactical sense that the attack on rail transportation had most value. Lt. Gen. O. N. Bradley believed that the bombing of the French railroad system prior to D-day prevented the Germans from accumulating the full store of supplies necessary to meet the invasion and from shipping them to the front for immediate support. His belief is supported by captured German generals, such as Colonel General von Vietinghoff, Supreme Commander in the Southwest, and General Wolff, SS-Obergruppenfuehrer and general of the Waffen-SS, who stated that although a landing on the Continent would always have been possible with superior air and sea power, the failure of the transportation system, because of bombing, prevented bringing up adequate reinforcements to contain or liquidate the beachhead. Other generals maintained that a landing was not only possible but, because of a deteriorating German military situation, would have succeeded without attacks on transportation. Yet success would have required a much larger Allied commitment of troops, and losses would have been far heavier. An example of the immediate effect of Allied bombing on the bringing up of reserves is the case of the 9th and 10th SS Panzer Divisions. These units were moved by rail from Poland to Nanc, where they detrained and began to move by road some 400 miles to the front. It took them as long to get from eastern France to Normandy as it had taken to bring them from the Russian battle front to the railhead at Nancy. Some units of the Adolf Hitler Panzer Division took a week to get from Louvain to Caen because of the chaotic state of the railroads.

A third phase of the offensive against rail transportation was the attack on Balkan marshaling yards. Whereas the attacks against Italian, German, and French railroad systems were directly connected with American and British operations, the Balkan raids were primarily designed to aid the Russians and the Partisans. The attacks on the Balkan railroads were also much more simple operations than those against the French, German, and Italian systems whose complexity of organization often allowed for quicker resumption of business. Balkan transportation was one of the weakest links in Axis communications. Most of the main lines were single-tracked, and even before the war rolling stock and mileage were barely sufficient for peacetime needs. The heavy German demands severely taxed the capacity. And therefore attacks on a few key points could accomplish much to slow down traffic in and out of this area.

One of these key rail centers was Sofia, Bulgaria which had been attacked for the first time on 24 November 1943. The new year was only four days old when 108 B-17's from the Fifteenth set cut again to bomb the city and marshaling yards. Clouds completely obscured the target, however, and only five bombs were dropped. In fact, they were jettisoned, Eighty-one tons were dropped instead on Dupnitza on the line southward from Sofia to the Greek border, and six bombs were dropped on the Scutari highway bridge in Albania with moderate success. Another attempt was made on 10 January to hit the Sofia marshaling yards, and 418 tons were dropped on the city as a whole. The Skplje yards were also bombed by 35 B-24's with 82 tons of bombs. The results were fair. These two raids constituted the major part of the Fifteenth Air Force's first "500 tons day." Sofia on the rail line from the Bulgarian capital to Craiova, Rumania, was hit with 114 tons of bombs.

During February, MASAF, tied down by weather, commtments to the ground forces, and POINTBLANK, practically ignored the transportation system of the Balkans. No attacks against it occurred in the first half of the month and only three in the last half. On 24 February, 27 B-17's dropped 81 tons of bombs on the Fiume oil refinery and torpedo works as a secondary target. A small railroad yard and roundhouse adjacent to the refinery were damaged in the course of events. The next day the Fiume marshaling yards were struck as a secondary target by 16 B-24's which dropped 37 tons, scoring a number of hits in the center of the yards.

The first half of March was also devoid of attacks against Balkan transportation, but in the last two weeks of the month, the strategic Sofia marshaling yards were hit five times as a primary target, four of these times being by the 205 Group, RAF. The attacks came on 15/16 March, 24/25 March, 29/30 March, and 30 March. The last was the heaviest of all. A total of 367 tons were dropped, but not all with good results. Two of the raids were made through heavy overcast, with little or no damage resulting to transportation facilities. Other primary railroad targets in the last half of March were Plovdiv, Bulgaria (18/19 March), and Knin and Metkovic in Yugoslavia (19 March). At the former place, 37 Wellingtons, Halifax's, and Liberators dropped nearly 54 tons with poor results. At Knin, the 85 tons dropped cut all of the through lines, cratered the yards, damaged the station, and started many fires, but at Metkovic where 51 tons of bombs were left, there was practically no important damage and all of the through tracks were left open.

The transportation centers selected to be bombed were those whose destruction would aid either the Partisans or the Russians, and as the situation of either changed so did the bombing plans. On 9 March, Portal, who had the CCS authority to establish priorities in the Balkans, designated Sofia and other Bulgarian towns as topping the list. Then came Bucharest, and in third place was Budapest. On 21 March he announced to Spaatz and Wilson that in view of the Russian advance, German difficulty with Rumanian transportation, and the political situation in that country, Bucharest would be given highest priority. Sofia and other Bulgarian towns would be in second priority, and because of political developments Budapest would not be bombed without further orders. A week later, again because of the

Russian advance, Portal modified this directive. The Germans on this front were having plenty of trouble trying to get Rumanian railroads to function smoothly, and since they were developing facilities at Galatz and Constanta, and their communications were largely restricted to the railroad route through Hungary and Rumania, Ploesti would succeed Sofia as second priority. Budapest was once more added to the list and the rail priorities then became: (1) Bucharest; (2)Ploesti; (3) Budapest; (4) Sofia and other Bulgarian towns.

The more or less sporadic bombing of Balkan communications in the first quarter of 1944 gave way to a really concentrated attack in April. As the Russian Army advanced, MASAF's efforts against the railroads on which the Germans were dependent became more closely coordinated with the fighting front. By early April the Red Army had cut the rail communications between the north and south German forces, thus forcing the Nazi troops in the Ukraine and Bessarabia to be entirely dependent upon the Rumanian railroads or supplies, reinforcements, and withdrawal. Heavy bombing of these lines would reduce the enemy's ability to fall back and regroup his armies for a counterattack. In light of this tactical situation, Portal established on 4 April the following priorities: (1) Bucharest and Ploesti railroad facilities; (2) Budapest railroad targets, but temporarily much lower in importance; and (3) Bulgarian towns. These standings remained substantially the same for the rest of the north.

Toward the end of April it became apparent that the Germans might attempt a very large withdrawal from all of the Balkans when it became impossible to hold Galatz. The retreat from the Eastern Front would congest the Rumanian and Hungarian railroads north of the Danube, and preclude their use by the troops in Greece, Bulgaria, and Yugoslavia. These forces would be limited to the Orient Express route from southeastern Bulgaria through Sofia, Nis, Belgrade, and Zagreb. From Greece the escape route ran from Salonika through Veles and Skoplje where the line divided – the eastern branch joining the Orient Express at Nis and the western branch running north to Kraljevo, Lapovo, and thence to Belgrade. If these roads were blocked prior to any general withdrawal, the cause of the Partisans would be greatly aided. The enemy, isolated from supplies and reinforcements and prevented from moving out, could be more easily cut to pieces by the local patriots who at the same time would be supplied by the Allies, largely from the air. As a result MAAF intelligence section recommended the bombing of the following rail communication centers in the order named: Belgrade, Nia, Skoplje, Kraljevo, Veles, and Lapovo.

In addition to helping the immediate military situation, the bombing of rail lines would also aid in the war of industrial attrition. Germany received substantial shipments of chrome ore, copper, antimony, and lead from the Balkans and Turkey. Ambassador Steinhardt in Turkey requested late in April that the Orient Express route between Sofia and Turkey be bombed, particularly near the Turkish border, in order to strengthen the Allied position in the forthcoming negotiations with Turkey over chrome consignments to Germany. General Arnold believed, however, that the present bombing priorities were satisfactory to stop such freight movements and that the revision necessary to carry out Steinhardt's suggestion was not warranted.

The April offensive against transportation in southeastern Europe began on 2 April when 29 B-17's and 35 B-24's of the Fifteenth Air Force attacked the marshaling yards at Brod and Bihac respectively. The next day Brod received a return call, while other small formations struck the yards at Knin and Drnis. A much larger force of 268 B-24's caused wide-spread damage to the Budapest marshaling yards with 690 tons of bombs. This was in conjunction with an attack on the aircraft factories in that city. A few hours later planes of the 205 Group, RAF dropped 116.68 tons of mixed bombs in an area raid which further increased the already existing damage. This was the first time this Hungarian city had been bombed. The Fifteenth hung up another "first" on 4 April when it attacked Bucharest for the first time; 63 tons of bombs were dropped on the marshaling yards with excellent results by 220 B-24's and 93 B-17's. The next day Ploesti was hit by the Fifteenth for the first time. A total of 231 B-17's and B-24's left 444.5 tons of 500-pound GP and 144.2 tons of IB on the yards, against aggressive opposition and at a cost of 11 bombers. The same day, 179 tons were dropped on Nis marshaling yards and 7 tons on those at Leskovac. On 16 April, the Fifteenth bombed Turnu Severin on the main line from Belgrade to Craiova for the first time. Fair to excellent results were achieved with 375 tons. The preceding night the same target had been well covered with 151 tons left by the 205 Group, RAF. Also on 16 April, the Brasov marshaling yards were bombed for the first time with 316 tons and a return visit was paid to Nis, where 27 tons were dropped with poor results.

During the whole month of April the Fifteenth made 26 attacks and the 205th Group, RAF seven attacks against major Balkan transportation centers. Those hit more than once by the Fifteenth were: Brod and Bucharest four times each; Ploesti and Nis three times each; Drnis and Turnu Severin twice each; and Bihac, Knin, Budapest, Leskovac, Brasov, Zagreb, Sofia, and Belgrade/Sava marshaling yards once each. In the seven attacks by the 205 Group, RAF, Budapest was raided three times and Plovdiv twice. Turnu Severin was hit once as was Niksic. The latter was a daylight raid on 8 April by 11 Wellingtons which dropped 11 tons of bombs on the marshaling yards. In these 33 attacks severe damage was inflicted on most of the yards and large amounts of rolling stock were destroyed. Despite the ill effects resulting from these bombings, such as further strain upon physical capabilities, increasing labor difficulties, and a breakdown of telegraphic communication which slowed down forwarding by alternate routes, military traffic particularly in Rumania and Hungary remained very heavy. It was the economic traffic which suffered most, and the frequently changing embargoes, made to meet military exigencies, created much confusion among shippers, who found it almost impossible to do business.

Priorities for May remained practically the same, with Rumanian and Hungarian targets retaining first place. Also the mining of the Danube River became a top priority. Oil refineries were given priority next to transportation toward the end of the month, while chromium plants in Yugoslavia and the Tungaram electrical works in Budapest were put in third place. The May attacks against Balkan transportation were begun on the night of 3/4 and continued with little letup throughout the month. The heaviest attacks took place in the first two weeks, with the Fifteenth hitting Turnu Severin twice, and Bucharest, Ploesti, Brasov, Pitesti, Craiova, Campina, and Knin once each. The three biggest days in this period were 5-7 May. The former was celebrated as the first "1500 ton day" for the Fifteenth when 1564 tons of bombs were dropped on Rumanian and Yugoslavian targets, the largest portion of which (1255 tons) was laid on Ploesti. The three-day campaign of 5-7 May began on the night of 4/5 when 205 Group RAF Wellingtons and Halifax's dropped 89 tons of mixed bombs on the Budapest/Raos and Budapest/Ferenovakos marshaling yards. In the daylight attacks by the Fifteenth, 1255 tons were dropped on the Ploesti yards and pumping station in an outstandingly successful operation. Heavy damage was wrought on tracks, rolling stock, and other railway facilities, and huge fires were started in the near-by oil installations. In addition to the Ploesti raid, 117 tons of bombs were dropped with good results on the yards at Turnu Severin.

On 6 May the Fifteenth dropped 101 tons of bombs on the Turnu Severin marshalling yards, 344 tons on transportation facilities and an aircraft factory at Brasov, 140 tons on Craiova, and 328 tons on Campina. The oil installations at the latter place were bombed that night by the 205 Group, RAF. The same night other aircraft of this organization attacked the Bucharest industrial area with 76 tons of bombs, achieving several hits in the marshaling yards, and a few Wellingtons bombed the Pitesti and Filiasi railroad bridges. The following day, 7 May, the Fifteenth covered the Bucharest yards, choke points, roundhouse, repair sheds, and workshops and destroyed large quantities of rolling stock with 1114 tons of bombs. Other bombers of the Fifteenth tried to damage the Belgrade/Pancevo railroad bridge on this same day with 105 tons of bombs, but with little success. That night two Wellingtons returned to the Filiasi bridge with four tons, but no damage resulted. No further attacks were made on Balkan transportation until 10 May when Knin was bombed with little damage by 19 aircraft dropping 33 tons, and that night the 205 Group, RAF aimed 66 tons of bombs at the Budapest/Rakos yards by ETA methods.

Attacks in the last half of May were very light in comparison to the first half. With the emphasis on DIADEM, southern France, and other types of objectives the Fifteenth attacked only five Balkan transportation centers, some of them alternate targets, with a total of 570 tons of bombs. These places were Nis (131 tons), and Belgrade (280 tons) on 18 May; Varasdin (33 tons), located southeast of Maribor, on 24 May; Zagreb (93 tons) on 30 May; and Turnu Severin (33 tons) on 31 May. The 205 Group, RAF flew no missions against Balkan communication targets in this period.

By 1 June the attacks on the railroad centers in southeastern Europe had created a really serious transportation bottleneck which worried the Germans considerable. This was evidenced by the Nazi efforts to transfer large quantities of military traffic from the railways to the Danube River, and the increasing German control over Hungarian and Rumanian railroad administration. The Giurgiu-Ruse train ferry was also reserved exclusively for the army and it was operated on a 24-hour schedule. Likewise the enemy's order of battle in Yugoslavia revealed that his principal concern was for the safety of vital rail routes.

In June, prior to D-day, MASAF operated on one night and two days. On ½ June the 205 Group, RAF dropped 72 tons of bombs on Szolnok marshaling yards and bridge. Despite the fact that most of the bombs were dropped through thick haze by ETA a heavy concentration was scored on the yards, both choke points were cut, and all main-line tracks were obstructed by craters and wrecked rolling stock. The Fifteenth followed this up with another attack on Szolnok the next day, 2 June, along with raids on Miskoc, Szeged, Simeria, Cluj, Debreczan, and Oradea. A total of 1276 tons of bombs were dropped on these places with very good results. The next raids were made on 6 June. On that day, 28 aircraft of the Fifteenth, unable to bomb their primary target – the Iron Gate Canal – dropped 84 tons on Belgrade marshaling yards and a railroad bridge over the Sava River with good coverage, blocking most of the through lines. On another mission 13 B-24's loosed 333 tons on the Brasov yards, damaging portions heretofore untouched and destroying a considerable amount of rolling stock.

As a means of further impeding Balkan transportation, the Danube River was also mined. The possibility of attacking this traffic artery was discussed as early as January 1944, but at that time the project was not too favorably considered. It was believed that concentration on certain important river and rail junctions where goods were transshipped, such as Belgrade, would more effectively tie up river freight than the actual mining of the river. Likewise it would be more profitable to destroy certain engineering features, such as the locks and dam at Vilshofen above Passau, Germany, or the Iron Gate ship canal at Turnu Severin, Rumania, than to strike directly at shipping on the river. The best time to attack the latter was during the winter months when the Danube was frozen and the ships were packed hull to hull in the harbors at Giurgiu, Ruse, Budapest, Bratislava, and such places. Nevertheless, as the tide of war on the Eastern Front went against the Germans the Danube highway became more and more important, and in March con-

signments via the river exceeded rail dispatches by 200 per cent. By the
middle of May, bomb damage to Balkan railroads had increased the
enemy's reliance on the Danube and much of the armaments going to
Rumania went by this route as did coal for railroad use. At the same time the
entire fleet of a Hungarian river transportation company with carrying
capacity of 150,000 tons was taken over for military use.

The first of the mine laying operations began on 8/9 April when the 205
Group, RAF laid 12 half ton mines and 28 x 100-pounders in the Danube
below Belgrade. After the mines were laid the planes machine-gunned ships
and settlements. The next operation was on 12/13 April. Wellingtons and
Liberators of the same RAF outfit put 97 x 1000-pound and 10 x 1600-
pound mines in the Danube, again below Belgrade, and afterwards strafed
river shipping These two operations, in which 137 mines were laid, caused
so much disruption of traffic that Portal recommended continued mining of
the Danube along with the attacks on Rumanian rail centers. It was decided,
therefore, to employ up to one wing of Wellingtons and one squadron of
RAF Liberators for this work during the "moon period" (full moon) in May.
The decision as to the exact places where the mines were to be laid was left
to MASAF, except that none were to be below Turnu Seerin.

On 5/6 May the 205 Group, RAF dropped 105 mines, and on 9/10 put
48 more in the river in the Wovi Sad area. The next moon period suitable
for mine laying was set for 29 May-8June, and this time two wings of Wellingtons and one Liberator squadron of the British contingent of MASAF
were made available for this work. During the same period the Iron Gate
Canal was to be attacked with sufficient force to ensure a maximum amount
of damage to this structure. Again, however, no mines were to be laid below
Turnu Severin. The first attack in this period took place on 29/30 May
when 12 of the British Liberators successfully deposited 72 mines in the
Komarom (Komorn) region of the Danube. The next night 9 B-24's laid
129 mines in the river east of Belgrade, while 23 Wellingtons, 8 Halifax's
and 2 Liberators dropped 83 tons of GP bombs on the Iron Gate Canal with
good results.

By June, it was fully apparent that the mining of the Danube was paying
dividends. Although traffic continued to some extent there had been several
complete suspensions varying from a few days to two weeks in the areas

mined. These stoppages, even though temporary, had caused a congestion of goods at numerous points along the line, such as at Ruse, Svistov, Turnu Severin, Bratislava, Vienna, and Regensburg, which necessitated rerouting over the already overburdened Hungarian and Rumanian railroads. There had also been a considerable holdup of coke shipments to Bulgaria and of hard coal badly needed by the Rumanian railways. In addition, there had been, of course, the destruction of a number of barges and tankers.

The Danube was not the only place where mine-laying activities were carried out. The RAF Bomber Command extensively mined the waters along the coast of France and the Baltic to the Gulf of Danzig. From 1 April to 30 June this organization laid 7181 mines in these areas. The effect of British mine-laying projects was to strain seriously the German mine-sweeping service, , interfere with U-boat training, and endanger merchant shipping. It was estimated that the mining of the Kiel Canal and Helgoland Bight cost the enemy nearly 1,500,000 tons of imports in the first five months of 1944.

It is difficult to assess the value of the attacks on transportation. Attacks on transportation were of more immediate value when made in a tactical sense, that is, in support of some ground campaign, than when planned as a strategic blow at the war economy. This was especially true of the Italian, French, and German railways, which were much more complex than those in the Balkans, but even in the latter the greatest benefit to be derived from the bombing of the transportation system was the aid given the Russian advance. Yet all added up to a final collapse when taken in connection with all other factories. No one target system was exclusively vital.

There were several reasons why it was next to impossible to paralyze completely the enemy's transportation. The Germans entered the war with an excellent system. There was a planned overcapacity to take care of military needs, and maintenance standards were higher even than those I the United States. This overcapacity plus a network of rivers and canals to move slow and bulky freight, allowed for numerous alternate routes for essential traffic when a main line was blocked. The system was well administered, too, and as a rule the Germans were able to open at least one track within 2 to 48 hours after even a disastrous bombing. In spite of strains imposed upon the transportation system, it was more or less adequate until the late spring of 1944. It was also something of a paradox that regardless of the amount of damage to and destruction of rolling stock, the German position in this matter improved as the German armies were pushed closer and closer to the boundaries of the Reich. This was particularly true of locomotives. The shortage was serious at the beginning of 1943, but by the time of D-day it was estimated that the enemy had 63000 locomotives available while his requirements were only 60,000.

Tactically, the bombing transportation systems gave trouble in shipping military supplies and reinforcements or in making a withdrawal on an active front such as in the Italian or Russian battle areas. The heavy bombing of rail centers in France just prior to D-day prevented the Germans from moving troops quickly from one point to another to bolster sagging lines. The systematic destruction of the French and Belgian railways, coordinated with the land advance, did much to disrupt the plans of the Wehrmacht to make a strong defensive stand in France, but the density of the network prevented a total collapse and allowed for retreat to the Rhine. By strict curtailment of civilian requirements, it was possible to supply the German Army with most essential supplies until the Ardennes offensive. After that the system went to pieces rapidly. Milch claimed that the Allied progress was almost faultless. First, transportation to the west of the Rhine was destroyed and then by selected areas, east of this river until the Elbe was reached. By this time no transportation was possible. A million workers were taken out of the armament factories to make communication repairs, but the Allied ground advance was so rapid that the Germans lost the race.

Industrially, the immediate situation was not so bad as the tactical, but was serious enough to interfere with production schedules. Some German leaders stated that attacks on transportation were more disastrous than those on the factories, particularly after the dispersal program was initiated and production became more and more dependent upon the facility of movement of parts and raw materials. Combined with the attacks on oil the transportation situation grew steadily worse as the shortage of petrol greatly reduced the amount of trucking possible and the railroads were mired in torn track.

The results of attacks on water transportation varied. The mining of the Danube, as already pointed out, caused considerable worry to the Germans and some dislocation of their river traffic. In Germany, itself, with its vast network of waterways, the bombing of the system had little effect, except for the attacks on certain features like the Dortmund-Ems and Mitteland canals, until almost the very end of the war. RAF mining operations in the Baltic, however, were more effective, and despite the German attempts to clear shipping lanes, the mines gradually got the edge on the defense measures. U-boat training was also seriously interfered with, and the German Navy seemed unable to cope with the situation.

In the final analysis the attack on the German transportation system must be viewed in the light of all other phases of the CBO program and the tactical implications involved. It was a major but not the sole cause for German defeat. The collapse came finally as a result of many factors, including a coordination of effort by the Allied land, sea, and air forces.

13

ATTACK ON OIL, CHEMICALS, AND RUBBER

The third most important system attacked during the period covered by this study was that of petrol, oil, and lubricants (POL). Adequate oil supply had always been an important problem in the Nazi economy and despite all attempts to fill the shortages it remained tight and was a major controlling factor in military operations. The chief sources of supply were a small production of crude oil around Hannover which had met about 7 per cent of peacetime needs; a large refining industry around Hamburg and Bremen for imported crude; and a synthetic oil industry in the Ruhr, in Silesia, and around Leipzig.

The German government had realized that a war could very possibly cut off oil imports from the Western Hemisphere and the Middle East, and so as early as 1933 steps were taken to assure as much self-sufficiency as possible. Subsidies were granted to encourage exploratory drilling and in this manner several new fields were discovered and developed within Germany which increased crude production from 238,000 tons in 1933 to 1,052,000 tons in 1940. The development of a synthetic oil industry was another method adopted to assure the steady flow of POL products. Despite the extensive coal deposits on which it was based it was a high-cost enterprise, but the private business interests which operated it were protected by a high tariff on all imported oil, and the industry was thus able to expand from a yearly production of 1.3 million metric tons in 1938 to a rate of 4.5 million by early 1944.

The most important of the synthetic plants were those using the Bergius aviation gasoline was produced. In 1942 when it became apparent that the "blitzkrieg" was turning into a war of attrition, attempts were made to build additional hydrogenation plants and expand production in the already existing ones. The program was successful in part, at least until the second quarter of 194, as the amount of aviation gasoline produced by this process jumped from 845,000 metric tons in 1941 to 1,745,000 metric tons in 1943. The bombing program of 1944 reduced the output, however, to 996,000 tons for that year, although in the first quarter the plants were producing at a yearly rate of 2,012,000 metric tons.

In addition to increased production, the German plan also called for the accumulation of substantial surplus stocks, especially of aviation gasoline, and of Diesel and fuel oils. The reserve supply of the former was to be 1,500,00 tons and of the latter, 2,800,000. These goals were not reached, however, by the beginning of the war, and the Nazis entered the conflict with less than six months' supply of all liquid fuels based on wartime requirements. Yet, the first year of the war did not tax the German supply, but in fact supplemented it. The conquest of Poland added that country's crude oil production to the Nazi reserve, and after the fall of France it was discovered that the captured stocks of gasoline amounted to more than had been expended in the campaign. Likewise, pressure applied to Hungary and Rumania made available considerable amounts of additional POL. In 1943, about 2,000,000 tons, chiefly motor gasoline and Diesel oil, were imported into Germany from those countries.

As the war dragged on and German hopes for a quick victory vanished, further attempts were made to keep an adequate supply of oil flowing into the Reich. After the stalemate of the 1941 campaign against Russia, the Nazis turned their attention toward securing the Caucasian oil fields and also began their drive across northern Africa to reach the oil of the Middle East. The failure of these moves practically sealed the fate of Germany, and its oil situation grew progressively worse. The attacks by the strategic Air Forces on the production of oil, both crude and synthetic, therefore, were one of the greatest contributions of the Air Forces toward the defeat of Germany.

In spite of the vital position of German POL no real attempts were made to knock out production until almost the middle of 1944. In 1940, the RAF made five token attacks on the Leuna plant, but thereafter this important synthetic installation was left alone until 12 May 1944. Other raids against oil until the spring of 1944 were desultory and relatively ineffective. The most important of these was the daring and spectacular attack by the Ninth Air Force against Ploesti in August 1943, but it had only a temporary effect. Although an estimated 4,000,000 tons of refining capacity was knocked out for varying periods of time, this only eliminated a cushion of excess capacity, and except for about 70,000 tons of products estimated to have been destroyed, output was hardly affected. Actually, exports of Rumanian oil to Germany increased and allowed the Nazis to build up their stocks just prior to D-day to their highest level since May 1941.

There were several reasons for this delay in hitting the enemy's oil supply. First there was a large excess crude oil refining capacity and this would have to be destroyed first if output was to be reduced. This meant that there would have to be constant bombings to prevent recuperation, and if the job was to be thorough all refineries and synthetic plants should be attacked simultaneously. To do this required a larger number of heavy bombers and long-range escort planes than the Air Forces had available prior to the spring of 1944. Likewise bases were needed which were within range of all installations, and these were not secured in the MTO until late 1943 when the Fifteenth began operations out of Foggia and its satellite fields. Secondly, an economical campaign against oil demanded first that air supremacy be gained, and it was not until after the Big Week in February that the GAF could be dismissed as a serious threat to Allied freedom of the skies. As discussed in Chapter II, however, USSTAF in March 1944 did recommend that oil have priority over transportation in its plan for the completion of the CBO, but SHAEF finally decided in favor off transportation. Nevertheless, the Fifteenth Air Force began its attacks on Rumanian oil fields in April, and in the middle of May, 18 refineries were assigned to MAAF as non-POINTBLANK filler targets. In the latter part of this month, Portal definitely gave second priority in the Balkans to the Rumanian, Hungarian, and Austrian refineries. On 20 April the Eighth Air Force was directed to strike the Brux, Leuna, Magdeburg, Ruhland, Zeitz, and Bohlen synthetic plants, and it began the operations in May. On 8 June, Spaatz announced that the primary strategic aim of USSTAF was now to deny oil to the enemy's armed forces. The offensive against oil was on.

In 1944, prior to April, attacks on oil were practically nonexistent. In an attack on the Fiume torpedo factory on 21/22 January by the 205 Group, RAF, some bombs fell on the oil refinery, starting fires and damaging several of the storage tanks. The same night, 85 Lancasters, Halifax's, and Mosquitoes of the RAF Bomber Command attacked Magdeburg with 1138 tons of high-explosive and 1371 tons of incendiary bombs, causing damage to the Junkers aero-engine factory, synthetic oil plant, and ship canal. On the night of 31 January, 33 Wellingtons of the 205 Group, RAF aimed 56 tons at the Trieste oil refinery with rather unsatisfactory results. Most of the bombs were scattered and fell largely to the south of the target, although a few bursts were seen at the base of the oil pier. On 24 February, 26 Fifteenth Air Force B-17's, unable to reach their primary objective of Steyr, dropped 81 tons on the Fiume oil refinery, adding further damage. No attacks were made in March, although at the beginning of the month Spaatz told Arnold he was anxious to try oil now that the GAF had been disposed of, but as yet USSTAF was not cleared to hit Ploesti. Ploesti would have to be destroyed first, he said, or any other attacks on oil would be futile. About the middle of the month Arnold notified him that the CCS had no objections to attacking Ploesti at the first opportunity afforded by the weather, and the stage was now set for the Battle of Ploesti.

The first of the April attacks began on the third of the month when the Fifteenth hit the aircraft factory, marshaling yards, and oil refinery at Budapest, and the following day the Prahova refinery at Bucharest was damaged in an attack on that city's marshaling yards. Another marshaling yard attack on 16 April at Brasov inflicted some damage on the Mecum oil refinery, but the history-making raids had started on 5 April when the Battle of Ploesti had been launched. On that day, 95 B-17's and 136 B-24's from the Fifteenth Air Force directed 588.7 tons of mixed bombs at the marshaling yards, but some of the bombs spilled over into the refinery district and created so much havoc that the oil installations thereafter received the main weight of succeeding attacks. From 5 April to 19 August, 19 daylight heavy-bomber missions and one P-38 dive-bomb attack were made. The 205 Group, RAF flew four night raids. In the three months, April-June, 3183 bombers, or 38 per cent of the available bomber units in MASAF, were dispatched against this target and 6201 tons of bombs were dropped. Despite the fact that Ploesti was one of the most heavily defended spots in Europe, only 113 of the heavies were lost in these three months – 54 to enemy aircraft, 53 to flak, and 6 to other causes. The three April attacks eliminated the excess refining capacity, and the succeeding raids cut deeply into the current production, with the low point being reached in mid-June when only two small refineries were left active. The strengthening of ground defenses, particularly by an effective smoke screen, allowed for some recovery after this date until the capture of Ploesti by the Russians in August permanently denied this important source of oil supply to the enemy and made Germany more than ever dependent upon synthetic products.

The Ploesti installations were not the only crude oil refineries attacked. The Steau Romana company at Campina, the second largest Rumanian refinery, was hit by the 205 Group, RAF on the night of 5/6 May in the first of its raids against the Rumanian oil fields. Thirty aircraft dropped nearly 35 tons of bombs which blanketed the storage tanks, refinery plant, and railroad yards, and started fires which were visible for 60 miles. This group made no more attacks on Rumanian oil targets, however, until the latter part of July. The following day, 6 May, the Fifteenth Air Force's mission against the Campina marshaling yards also scored some hits on the refinery. On 14/15 May, the 205 Group, RAF dispatched eight Liberators against the Porto Marghera refineries near Venice. Five of the planes found the target and laid 14 tons on it. The Fifteenth visited the same place on 19 May and left 179.75 tons of GP. Porto Marghera was hit again on 25 May by the same Air Force with 168.25 tons of 500-pounders. The oil installations at La Spezia were also damaged on 19 and 22 May when the harbor and railroad facilities of that port were attacked.

Although the Eighth Air Force had some 20 German natural oil refineries on its target list none of these were attacked in the period covered by this study, but the bombing of such cities as Brunswick, Bremen, Berlin, and Essen indirectly affected the production of crude oil products by inflicting heavy damage on refining-equipment factories. One of the most important and disastrously hit of these plants was the Wilke Werke A.G. in Brunswick. Other such manufacturing establishments which suffered a similar fate were Karl Fischer, Julius Pintsch, and Rheinmeall Borsig in Berlin; Francke Werke A.G. at Bremen; and Drupp in Essen.

The biggest contribution of the Eighth was the destruction of the synthetic oil plants, most of which were within the range of this air force. Although its campaign did not get underway until May, two unsuccessful strikes were made in April. On the 11th of that month a large force of four-engine bombers (91) were dispatched against numerous targets in north and central Germany. Fifty-two of the aircraft dropped 120.5 tons of GP and IB on the Hydrierwerke Politz A.G. at Politz, but results were unsatisfactory. Another mission against aircraft factories and four synthetic oil plants on 21 April was recalled because deteriorating weather prevented assembly and rendezvous.

The real campaign against synthetic oil began on 12 May when the Eighth successfully struck five important plants in the Leipzig and Chemnitz areas. The most important of these were the I. G. Farbenindustrie A. G. works at Merseberg/Leuna. Here was not only the largest hydrogenation production in Germany but a place at which nitrogen and other important chemicals were manufactured. Over 220 planes raided this place, dropping a little over 500 tons of high-explosive bombs with such devastating results that the plant closed down completely for 10 days. This was the start of the Battle of Leuna which paralleled the Fifteenth's Battle of Ploesti, and before the end of the war Leuna was raided 20 times by the Eighth and twice by the RAF Bomber Command. A total of 6552 bombers made these attacks, dropping 18,328 tons of bombs.

Also on 12 May the Braunkohle Benzin factories at Zeitz and Bohlen were bombed, when 111 aircraft drooped 260 tons on the former place and 89 planes dropped 194 tons on the latter. A Pfc prisoner of war, captured in Italy, stated that when he was home on leave in Bohlen he learned that in this attack as many workers were drowned in the floods of oil loosed by the bombs as were killed and injured by the explosions. At Lutzkendorf 172 tons of bombs fell from 89 bombers, and 140 planes attacked Brux, southeast of Chemnitz in Czechoslovakia, with 311 tons of high explosives.

The events of 12 May were, according to Speer, the materialization of a nightmare that German leaders had had for over two years. They went to work immediately, however, to repair the damage and get the plants back into operation. Speer appointed one Edmund Geilenberg as General Commissioner for Immediate Measures and gave him priority on men and materials needed to bring the plants into production again. By the time of the next attacks on 28 May, production at Leuna, for example, had reached per cent of normal, and in spite of the second bombing was running at 75 per cent of capacity in early July.

The oil offensive was resumed on 28 May when Zeitz, Leuna, and Lutzkendorf were rebombed and Ruhland, Magdeburg, and Leipzig plants were struck for the first time in the new push. At the first place, 187 planes dropped 447 tons of GP on the Braunkohle Benzin works. The plant at Ruhland was hit with about 70 tons which severely damaged two of the three water gas installations. Lutzkendorf got another dose of 155 tons, and Magdeburg received 114 tons. The Moblis low-temperature, carbonization, and coal-tar treatment plant at Leipzig, a secondary target, was hit by eight planes and 20 tons of bombs. Leuna had only 151 tons dropped on it this time but this was sufficient to knock the plant out until 3 June, when it was able to resume partial operations. The next day, 29 May, 24 planes plastered the Hydrierwerke factory at Politz with 547 tons of bombs, achieving very good results. No more attacks were made on oil by the Eighth until 14 June, when raids were commenced against crude oil refineries at Emmerich, Hannover,, Bremen, Hamburg, Harburg, and Ostermoor. On the return trip from a shuttle bombing mission to Russia a refinery at Drohobyes, Poland, was also hit. The synthetic plants attacked in June were: Braunkohle at Magdeburg (20 June); Hydrierwerke at Politz (20 June); Braunkohle at Ruhland (21 June); and Braunkohle at Bohlen (29 June). Altogether in the first six months of 1944 the Eighth, Fifteenth, 205 Group, RAF, and the RAF Bomber Command dropped over 23,600 tons of bombs on Axis oil installations of all kinds.

Closely related to and often integrated in the oil industry were the chemical, explosive, and rubber industries. Chemicals, in spite of their importance, were not made a primary target system. There were 10 chemicals which were most vital to Germany's war economy – nitrogen, methanol, calcium carbide, sodium cyanide, ethylene, tetraethyl lead, sulphuric acid, caustic soda, chlorine, and sodium carbonate. The most important of these were nitrogen and methanol, and since over 90 per cent of these chemicals were produced by the synthetic oil plants the attacks on the latter also affected the supply of these products. Two synthetic oil complexes alone, Leuna and Ludwigshafen, accounted for about 60 per cent of the nitrogen and 40 per cent of methanol output, and they also manufactured 76 per cent of the enemy's ethyl chloride necessary for tetraethyl lead. Large tonnages of other chemicals were made in non-oil producing plants, but despite their importance they received very little attention from the strategic bombers.

Although important chemical plants were damaged in 1943 the production of chemicals and explosives was not seriously affected until the oil offensive was launched in May 1944. During the first five months of this year, the Eighth Air Force struck 14 times, damaging nine factories, and the RAF Bomber Command 21 times at 19 establishments, but the chief damage inflicted on the industry in this period stemmed not so much from precision attacks as from the PFF bombing of chemical centers by USSTAF and night area bombing by the RAF. From 1 May 1944 to the end of the war 62,915 tons of bombs were dropped on the chemical industry, but of this, 58,202 tons were aimed at the oil-chemical plants, and only 4713 tons fell on chemical factories which were not a part of the oil complexes. This 92 per cent of the total tonnage put on the chemical industry was incidental to the attack on oil.

Rubber, like chemicals, was intimately tied in with oil, and although it was a critical war item, it was left pretty much alone until affected by the campaign against synthetic oil. Germany had entered the war with practically no stock pile of rubber and the blockade soon cut off supplies of crude, so that the Germans became almost entirely dependent upon synthetic and reclaimed rubber. Nevertheless, the enemy was able to meet its requirements, even though at times supplies were dangerously low. Very early the Nazis had realized the necessity for rubber and the dangers which would confront them should the supply of crude be lost, and so they had begun an expansion program for synthetic manufacture. Synthetic rubber production was thus raised from 1100 tons in 1936 to 130,000 tons by 1944, and the industry reached an all-time high in March 1944 with a monthly output of

12,787 tons. To produce this amount Germany had only one small and three large synthetic plants – Schkopau, Hls, Ludwigshafen, and Leverkusen – and Ludwigshafen did not begin production until March 1943. The products of these plants plus reclaimed rubber and a negligible amount of crude were then manufactured into various articles by 278 processing factories of which 53 were major fabricators – 11 making tires, 13 manufacturing mechanical goods, and 29 fabricating other rubber products.

Despite the importance of rubber in modern warfare, the synthetic plants were not assigned a priority until 10 June 1943, when they were put in third place. On 10 November 1943, synthetic rubber was given a first-priority category,, and on 1 December the Eighth struck Leverkusen. The Eighth made five PFF attacks on Ludwigshafen (30 December 1943, 7 January, 11, 29 February, and 1 April 1944) prior to the opening of the synthetic oil offensive on 12 May, and the RAF also made several night area raids on this place. Altogether in the period 10 June 1943-12 May 1944 only 3367 tons of bombs were directed against synthetic rubber plants, but from this latter date to the end of the war an additional 15,736 tons were dropped. Out of this total of 19,103 tons, of which the Eighth was responsible for 10,805 tons, about 75 per cent fell on Ludwigshafen, where oil was the primary target. This did not mean that synthetic rubber did not suffer, because as the oil plants were put out of commission production in the rubber plants ceased. Schkopau relied entirely on Leuna for its supply of hydrogen, and when Leuna was bombed out Schkopau was eliminated. Hls lost production when its supply of gas from the Scholven and Gelsenberg synthetic oil plants was cut off. The destruction of the oil factories at Ludwigshafen and the chemical plants at Leverkusen stopped rubber production at these places.

The 278 fabricating plants did not offer much in the way of a good target system, since they were scattered. In fact, only 443 tons of bombs were aimed specifically at the rubber-processing plants from 1 September 1939 to 8 May 1945. Of this, 288 tons were dropped prior to 10 November 1943 and the remainder after 12 May 1944. The USAAF was responsible for 441 tons and the RAF for only two. Numerous tire and other rubber plants suffered varying degrees of damage, however, in area raids, and in this sort of operation the RAF played the larger role. The production of the fabricating plants was also limited as the supplies of raw materials were cut off through the bombing of the synthetic oil and rubber factories. Likewise as the transportation system deteriorated under Allied pounding it became next to impossible to move to the processing plants what raw materials there were. For example, in the middle of 1944, 1500 tons of Buna at Schkopau could not be shipped out because of lack of transportation, and supplies of raw materials at Continental Cumdwerke in Hannover were reduced from an equivalent of six weeks' production in January 1944 to two days' production in December for the same reason.

Since the campaign against oil and its allied industries did not get underway until April and May 1944, the real effects of the bombing program were not felt until the late summer and early autumn. Up to May the RAF and USAAF had dropped 509,206 tons of bombs on enemy targets in Europe, but only 1.1 per cent (5670 tons) were on German oil installations. None of these attacks caused an important loss in German oil production, however, and the developing shortages were due n large part to the enemy's inability to expand production at a rate commensurate with increasing needs. After the attention of the strategic bombers was focused on oil in the spring, production began to fall rapidly, and by July had dropped to 50 per cent of pre-attack levels. With the loss of Ploesti to the Russians and continued bombing of remaining refineries and synthetic plants, a low point of 3 per cent of pre-attack output was reached in September.

No single raid regardless of its severity, permanently stopped production, and it was the continually repeated bombings which caused the breakdown. At the start of the oil offensive recuperation was fairly rapid, and through the Geilenberg organization Germany was able to get individual plants into partial production in a remarkable short time. These quick repairs were accomplished by cannibalizing equipment from badly bombed installations and new plants under construction, but as the bombers kept returning, these sources of repair parts dried up and the time between production periods lengthened. According to Milch the bombing which was the most effective and which hindered recuperation in spite of cannibalization was that done by the American air forces. He did not mean to imply that the British were not good flyers, but the system, of day bombing made it possible to achieve greater accuracy and thus accomplish greater destruction. In night bombing each aircraft, as a rule, dropped its bombs individually, and while this ensured that not all bombs would miss the target "it also meant it was never possible to obtain a really concentrated effect." He estimated that on an average although between 25 and 30 per cent of American bombs completely missed the target at least 70 per cent hit it and resulted in "crater upon crater and that really smashed the target to bits."

The Germans had felt the need for additional oil, of course, two years before the great attacks began. The 1942 program for increasing the number of GAF pilots was seriously hampered by the inability to secure enough aviation gasoline. Thus while the Germans were losing an increasing number of pilots with only a small replacement, the American Air Forces were increasing in both personnel and equipment. By July 1944 the average American pilot had four to five times as much training in operational aircraft as the German pilot. This decline in pilot quality made for greater losses of aircraft and naturally curtailed operations. The lack of oil also affected the quality of the German aircraft. By August 1944 the final run-in time for airplane engines had to be reduced from two hours to one-half hour because of lack of aviation fuel. Some aircraft types, such as the He-177, had to be grounded because they consumed too much of the dwindling supplies of gasoline, and the emphasis placed on setting jet-propelled planes into production in 1944 was in part an effort to stretch this precious fuel.

In general, captured responsible army and government officials agreed that the attacks on oil were some of the most effective of the CBO program, and the loss of this vital product was one of the most decisive causes for Germany's defeat. Speer said the assault which began on 12 May "caused the first serious shortages of indispensable basic products and therefore the greatest anxiety for the future conduct of the war." Milch remarked that every day that passed without an attack on oil, the Germans said: "Thank God, they haven't bombed the synthetic oil plants yet! ... Let's hope they go on bombing air-frame factories; as long as they don't bomb the synthetic oil plants." Speer also testified that although a minimum of motor fuel and Diesel oil was produced to the very end of the war, aviation gasoline production was so limited from June 1944 onward that the Luftwaffe needs could not be anywhere nearly filled. By late summer and early fall, production of fuel was further cut because of the loss of the Rumanian fields; and the break-down in transportation, which prevented the transfer of oil from the refineries to the using agencies, along with the destruction of storage facilities, naturally affected the refinery output.

Some men, such as Keitel, placed the attack on chemical production as the second most important factor accounting for the fall of Germany. The two most vital chemicals in the war economy were nitrogen and methanol needed for the manufacture of explosives. Since chemicals were only slightly affected, however, prior to the beginning of the oil offensive, the Germans had ample ammunition until the middle of 1944. The severe losses resulting from the bombings after 12 May brought about revisions of allocations even to the principal users; and methanol, for example, used in making high explosives and chemical warfare items, was strictly rationed. The cut in nitrogen production by the end of July was so great that allocations for fertilizer were drastically cut and finally eliminated altogether. The situation became so serious that gradually more and more rock salt (used as an extender and filler) and less explosives were used in shells, mines, and bombs. By early 1945 heavy ammunition was adulterated with as much as 70 per cent salt.

As pointed out previously, production of synthetic rubber suffered as much or more from the bombing of the oil factories as from direct attacks, and the vast number of rubber fabricators did not offer a well-concentrated target system. The damage to these factories was not sufficient to be a major factor in defeat, and the lack of rubber did not seriously affect military operations, although at times inventories reached dangerously low levels. Despite the fact that production of synthetic rubber had fallen from a high of over 12,000 tons in March 1944 to a low of 2000 tons in December, there was an increase to 5500 tons by February 1945, which was a higher production rate than in 1939. In general the effect of the attack on oil, chemicals, and rubber can be summed up I a letter from Speer to the Fuehrer on 30 August 1944: "If the attacks on the chemical industries including synthetic oil continue in September in the same strength and with the same precision as in August, the production of chemicals will be still further decreased, and the last stocks will be consumed. Then those very materials essential for continuation of modern warfare will be unavailable in the most important fields."

CONCLUSION

The chief targets for the strategic bombers in the first six months of 1944 were the aircraft and ball-bearing factories, transportation, and the oil, chemical, and rubber industries, but in the course of bombing these targets, other industries were also sought out and attacked or they suffered incidentally from the raids on near-by installations or industrial areas. Steel and nonferrous plants, for example, were never priority targets, but in 1943 16 steel and 8 nonferrous plants were bomb-damaged, and in the first nine months of 1944 17 steel and 9 nonferrous factories suffered from Allied bombs. Most of the damage inflicted on these metal works came from area bombing by the RAF rather than from precision attacks. About 90 per cent of German steel production was centered in 36 cities, and during the war 167,000 tons, or 12 per cent of all tonnage dropped on Germany, were directed at these municipalities. Only 5924 tons were aimed at steel as a precision target. There were no precision attacks on steel during the first six months of 1944, but approximately 20,000 tons of bombs fell on the aforementioned 36 cities.

These attacks had little effect on the supply of steel for armaments, at least until the middle of 1944, because the Wehrmacht early overestimated its needs and because the occupation of western Europe in 1940 added 300,000 tons a month to the German output. Along with Swedish imports it was thus possible to allot more and more steel for nonmilitary uses and for the stock pile. By the second quarter of 1944, out of a total supply of slightly more than 2,000,000 tons only about 1,400,000 tons went directly to armaments programs. The greatest loss of production in the first half of 1944, too, was from air-raid alarms rather than air-raid damage. Thus, the steel situation did not become serious until late 1944 and early 1945 when the heavy attacks on the Ruhr and central Germany crippled the industry, but even then it was the breakdown of transportation which turned what ordinarily would have been a temporary disruption into a permanent collapse.

The nonferrous plants—particularly those working with copper, zinc, and aluminum—received very little damage, and since they were not singled out as specific targets but were included in area raids, their destruction was a more or less hit-and-miss proposition. Furthermore, there was an excess capacity in most of them, and therefore the damage inflicted did not materially affect war production. The Allies did show some concern over chrome, however, and I the spring of 1944 after the diplomats had succeeded in stopping Turkish shipments attention turned toward Balkan sources. In the middle of May, Arnold signaled Eaker that it might be worthwhile to attack the ore-concentrating plants around Skoplje, Yugoslavia. It was believed that German's sole source of chrome was then in those plants and that their destruction might eliminate the already low supply and impose and additional burden on the transportation system necessitating the shipment of raw ore to other plants. The Committee of Operations Analysts did not believe, however, that these factories were worth much of an expenditure of force, and therefore Arnold suggested such attacks be assigned to freshman missions. Shortly after this Portal put the chrome-concentration works at Radusa and Hanrijevo (both near Skoplje) and the Tung ram factory at Budapest on the list of targets of opportunity in the Balkans, but no attacks were made prior to 6 June.

Some of the chief users of steal – the tank, motor car (M/T), and armored force vehicle (AFV) industries—suffered very little from direct aerial bombardment until the late summer of 1944. In the early years of the war Germany had more than a sufficient supply of these items, and the few attacks in 1943 did no t affect production to any great extent. Nor did the sporadic attacks in the first six months of 1944 have much harmful effect. Like steel, these industries, during the period covered by this study, suffered most from the RAF area raids and it was not until summer, when they were given a high priority rating, that the Wehrmacht began to feel the pinch of shortages. The big decline in production and the resulting disastrous effects took place after July when German losses on all fronts exceeded supply, and much of the excess manufacturing capacity had disappeared because of its diversion to airplane manufacture. Even then the output of assembly plants was reduced not so much by direct attack as from shortages of such things as torsion bars, and drives. This condition had resulted from raids on components plants and the disruption of transportation which prevented the parts from flowing to final assembly centers.

Other large consumers of steel were the plants producing guns and shells, but they were never a primary target system. Heavy ordnance manufacture was generally carried on in the Ruhr, and again the area attacks by the RAF against the cities in this region usually resulted in some damage to these factories. The fabricators of lighter ordnance were widely scattered, and as in other countries many small engineering and light-metal plants were converted to this type of work. Altogether there were approximately 5000 heavy and light ordnance factories, many of which were unidentifiable as such from the air, and even the U.S. Strategic Bombing Survey was unable to determine the exact tonnage expended on this industry, although 8000 tons were specifically aimed at certain of the Ruhr plants during the course of the whole war. The over-all effects on the armament industry were insignificant, however, and production increased until very late in 1944.

Another industry which suffered very little from bombing was that of machine tools. Although there was discussion of its importance among the planners of strategic bombing it was never a priority target system and most of the damage it received was from spill-over's and area attacks. At no time did the enemy seem to be held up because of a lack of machine tools, and even when factories were damaged they were quickly put into operation again. This was due largely to the facts that: (1) Germany enjoyed an excess capacity; (2) Germany relied more upon general-purpose tools and highly skilled labor than on the highly complicated automatic and semiautomatic tools and semi-skilled labor commonly employed in the United States. However, severe damage resulted from fires which burned out the electric motors supplying the power.

The most effective attacks by the strategic bombers up to 6 June 1944, therefore were against the aircraft, ball-bearing, oil, chemical, and rubber industries and against transportation. Of these the ball-bearing industry was, perhaps, the most overrated as to importance and expected results of bombardment. Although the industry was concentrated and offered a good target, the failure to follow up with return attacks after the initial bombardment in 1943 allowed for recuperation and countermeasures. It was possible, therefore, for the Germans to adopt the slogan: "No equipment was ever delayed because bearings were lacking." Nevertheless the enemy was worried over the possible consequences of a shortage, and time and energy were spent in an attempt to meet such an eventuality. The chief countermeasures were redesign, salvage, and Swedish imports. The attacks on the aircraft industry combined with the campaign to knock the GAF out of the air were highly successful. Not only did the failure of the GAF to protect the homeland after the Big Week contribute to the breakdown of military economy, but its inability to support the ground forces left the infantry exposed to the merciless air attacks of the Allies. One captured general, Von Senger, the commanding general of the XIV Panzer Corps, stated that the lack of air support put the Germans in the same position as the Ethiopians had occupied when attempting to stop the mechanized Italian Army with ancient guns and spears.

Transportation, too, was a vital spot in Germany's armor, but for reasons stated in Chapter VIII it was a difficult target to destroy. Once battle was joined by the opposing ground forces, however, attacks on transportation bore more visible fruit. As the German armies retreated on all fronts and congested the railroads at the same time that the aerial attacks were stepped up, the transportation system could not stand the strain went to pieces.

Of equal importance with the attacks on the aircraft industry and on transportation was the campaign against oil and chemicals. To some of the Germans this was the death blow. It must be remembered that Seer had said that fear of attacks on synthetic oil had been a nightmare for two years. Despite the disaster heaped upon Germany by these raids, the U. S. Strategic Bombing Survey reported that still better results could have been obtained by a more careful selection of targets. The failure to destroy completely the ethyl plants was pointed out as a weakness because, without ethyl, high-grade aviation gasoline was impossible. Likewise more attention should have been paid to explosive and propellant plants. These factories were vulnerable to air attack and if struck hard enough their recuperation would have been very slow. As it was, the shortage of powder and explosives which developed in the latter part of 1944 was due to a lack of basic materials, such as nitrogen and methanol, rather than to direct bombing of the ammunition factories.

Despite the great weight of bombs dropped on German industry, the civilian economy was not so hard hit that war production had to be diverted to prevent disintegration of the home front. It was not until near the end of the war that the whole economy began to go to pieces and civilian discontent mounted rapidly. This was due, however, to the military collapse almost as much as to civilian bombing. The grumbling over the lack of coal for civilian production and domestic heating in late 1944, for example, was the result of the breakdown of transportation and of German inability under the circumstances to recuperate rather than the result of any direct attack on the population. The large-scale bombing of Germany did have a morale value of sorts, however, although in some cases it built instead of lowered morale. One captured German said the people regarded the attacks on cities as "Terror Raids" and this strengthened their determination to "see it through." Some army officers claimed that civilian bombing had a more pernicious effect on the morale of front-line troops because of worry over their home folk than it had upon the residents of the affected cities. Speer claimed that in those cities which were accustomed to air raids the citizens developed a fatalistic frame of mind, and fears and feelings were gradually dulled. Nevertheless, it is estimated that 305,000 civilians were killed in air attacks; 780,00 were wounded; between 18,000,000 and 20,000,000 were deprived of essential services such as gas, water, and electricity; and 5,000,00 were forced to evacuate their homes completely. So many people could not be affected without loosening to some extent the Nazi stranglehold on the populace and weakening the position of the government.

Generally speaking, the German army officers and government officials conceded that strategic bombing had a tremendously disastrous effect. Some even said the war could have been won entirely by the long-range heavy bomber, but the desire to end the war as soon as possible forced the combined use of air, land, and sea forces. From the enemy's point of view, however, Allied strategy had several defects. Speer criticized the lack of a logical system of attack. American and British efforts were too dispersed, and instead of expending time and energy on a number of targets, the Allies should have singled out one target system and completely flattened it so that recuperation would have been slow enough to allow bombing of another system until time to return to the first. The Allies had realized this, of course, and the concentrated campaigns against aircraft production in February and oil from May onward were examples of this type of bombing. But often weather or other factors, such as the necessity for supporting ground forces (as was frequently the case in Italy), prevented following this course without interruption. Another criticism was the priorities given by the Allies to the various target systems. In Speer's opinion, for example, the following should have been the priorities in the air war: (1) key points in basic industries; (2) transportation and communications; (3) front-line positions for psychological effect on troops; (4) final stages of manufacture, such as assembly plants; (5) tows; (6) naval installations, shipping, and air fields. Goering put oil first, then communications, aero-engines, airframes, ball-bearings, and airfields in that order. Goering's conviction that oil should have been first was shared by several other generals, but, as already pointed out, the Allies had good reason for waiting as long as they did. The skies had to be cleared of the GAF first.

Just as the American Civil War has been studied as an example of the first of modern wars, that is, where a fighting front extends over a very long line instead of a single point of contact between two armies, so will World War II be studied as a departure from orthodox warfare. Historically, the objective of any war is to destroy the enemy's army in the field. That was a prime goal in this war, but with an air arm capable of striking far behind the front lines it was possible to destroy the sources which supplied field armies and enabled them to fight. One German general hazarded the guess that at a future time it would not be necessary to put an army in the field if satisfactory methods of destroying the industry behind it could be found.

APPENDIX

BIBLIOGRAPHICAL NOTE

The sources for this study are varied and voluminous, and although many volumes have been turned over in order to get a few ounces of information, no claim is made to having exhausted all sources. The following depositories have been more or less thoroughly searched:

Archives of the AAF Historical Office

Office of the Cable Secretary, AAF

AAF Classified Files

AC/AS Plans

A-2 Library

AAF Operational Research Section

In each of these, however, the different methods of filing and the lack of subject indexes have denied the assurance that all pertinent records have been covered.

The most valuable sources may be narrowed down to comparatively few. Among the histories prepared by the different air forces in the field and forwarded to the Archives Section of the AAF historical Office, the History of the Mediterranean Allied Air Forces, 10 December 1943-1 September 1944, prepared by Lt. Col. James Parton and his staff, proved to be very valuable. This history consists of one volume of narrative and 33 volumes of supporting documents. The latter constitute something of a gold mine for information from the Mediterranean Theater of Operations. The monthly histories of the Eighth Air Force, although not so complete in supporting documents, were useful for the ETO theater. The final over-all histories of the Eighth Air Force and the Fifteenth Air Force are not yet complete. To date, no integrated history of the United States Strategic Air Forces in Europe has been prepared.

For the operations performed in connection with the strategic bombing of Europe, USSTAF Semi-Monthly Record of Results and USSTAF Air Intelligence Summaries were extremely valuable. The same can be said for the MAAF Central Mediterranean Operational Summaries, MAAF Air Intelligence Weekly Summaries, and special MAAF studies, such as "A Record Week of Strategic Bombing" and "Notes on MAAF Counter-Air Program," all of which are found among the supporting documents of the above-mentioned History of MAAF.

To these, the Tactical Mission Reports of the Fifteenth Air Force and the Eighth Air Force Air Operations Reports and Interpretation Reports should be added.

The results of the bombing program are well discussed in the U. S. Strategic Bombing Survey Over-all Report (European War), September 30, 1945 and the Survey's reports on individual industries, such as the Aircraft Division Industry Report (November 1945) or The German Anti-Friction Bearings Industry (November 1945). There are several objections to the use of these reports for this study, however, because they tend to discuss the whole war as an entity rather than by smaller chronological divisions. It is difficult, therefore, always to use the Survey for an evaluation of the success of the Combined Bomber Offensive for the period covered here. The Survey reports, however, have been supplemented by the various Intelligence Summaries, reports of Statistical Control Units, and special studies such as the "Strategic Bombing of Axis Europe, January 1943-September 1944," prepared by AC/AS Intelligence, Analysis Division, European Branch, in December 1944. The aforementioned sources, however, must be used with caution, since their evaluations are of the moment, and are often based on such things as photographs and sometimes on not fully tested ground reports. In this respect, the Survey reports are more reliable. They were based on examination of plants and production records by field teams and on interrogations of factory managers and other responsible persons, and could thereby arrive at sounder conclusions. A disadvantage of the Survey material, on the other hand, is that all reports are not yet completed. For example, there is at present no over-all report on the bombing of transportation and only two studies on two German rail divisions are available. An aid to interpretation are the various prisoner of war interrogations made by the U. S. Strategic Bombing Survey; the Captured Personnel and Material Branch, MID, U. S. War Department; MAAF; and other agencies.

Various correspondence files in AAF Classified Files, in AC/AS Plans, and among the supporting documents of the Eighth Air Force and MAAF histories have helped to fill in gaps. Other sources of value have been the cable files in both the Office of the AAF Cable Secretary and the Archives of the AAF Historical Office, and the reports in the files of the Operational Research Section. Information on the Royal Air Force has been gleaned from all the above-named sources in addition to the RAF Mediterranean Review and the RAF Bomber Command Review.

Unless otherwise noted, all citations are to materials in the Archives Section of the AAF Historical Office except in the case of cablegrams. For security reasons there is no notation as to whether the cable referred to is to be found in the Cable Secretary's Office or in the AFSHO files. In the case of prisoner of war interrogations the A-2 Library KO number has been added.

Appendix 1

UNUSED OR UNKNOWN ACTIVITY OF CRUDE OIL REFINERIES*

A. Major Refineries

Refinery	Capacity (In thousands of tons per annum)	Remarks
Confreville, France	1,600	Believed destroyed
Port Jérome, France	1,100	Believed destroyed
Martigues, France	900	Unused, inconveniently located
Petit-Couronne, France	800	Believed destroyed
Étang de Berre, France	500	Unused, incon. located
Rotterdam-Pernis	500	Very slight activity
Pauillac	500	Believed destroyed
Venice, Italy	450	Activity unknown, incon. located
Dunkirk, France	410	Believed destroyed
L'Avera, France	400	Unused, incon. located
Aquila, Trieste, Italy	350	Activity unknown, incon. located
Bec d'Ambes, France	250	Unused, incon. located
La Spezia, Italy	310	Unused, incon. located
Ebeno, Hamburg, Germany	300	Unused
Courchelettes, France	250	Activity unknown
Gravenchon, France	250	Believed destroyed
Frontignan (Sète)	200	Unused, incon. located
Leghorn, Italy	185	Believed destroyed
Donges, France (2 plants)	320	Unused, incon. located
Ostermoor, Hamburg, Germany	150	Unused
Ramsa, Fiume, Italy	120	Believed destroyed
SIAP, Trieste, Italy	120	Activity unknown, incon. located
Antwerp (Fedeventza), Belgium	120	Believed destroyed
Limanowa, Poland	90	Used for storage
Ghent, Langerbrugge (Shell), Belgium	85	Activity unknown
Novy Bohumin (Oderberg), Czechoslovakia	65	Activity unknown

Total capacity excluding refineries destroyed or inconveniently located,
940,000 tons.

---

* Plan for the Completion of the Combined Bomber Offensive, 5 Mar 44,
Sup. No. 10.

Appendix 1 (Cont'd.)

B. Minor Refineries

Refinery	Capacity (In thousands of tons per annum)	Remarks
Rumania		
Noris	50	Activity unknown
Brasov-Vacuum	35	Partial operation
Austria		
Schwechat	50	Capacity operation
Korneuburg	45	Capacity operation
Vösendorf	40	Capacity operation
Drösing	35	Activity unknown
Hungary		
Fanto Budapest	50	Capacity operation
Hazaii	50	Capacity operation
Munkacs	25	Major portion in use
Petfurdo	20	Major portion in use
Nyirbogdány	15	Major portion in use
Szöreg	10	Major portion in use
Czechoslovakia		
Dubové	60	Major portion in use
Prwoz (Moravská-Ostrava)	55	Activity unknown
Kralup	40	Activity unknown
Yugoslavia		
Smederevo	50	Activity unknown
Osijek (Ipoil)	25	Activity unknown
Poland		
Maglowice (Jaslo)	60	
Gliñik-Mariampolski	60	Major portion in use
Drohóbycz (Nafta)	35	Major portion in use
Krosno	30	Used for storage
Lwów	30	Major portion in use
Italy		
Fornovo di Taro	50	Activity unknown, inconveniently located
Germany		
Düsseldorf	25	Activity unknown
Regensburg (4 targets)	80	Activity unknown
Schönberg	18	Activity unknown
Templehof	15	Activity unknown
France		
Autun	15	Shale oil operation
Norway		
Valió-Toneberg	50	Activity unknown, inconveniently located

```
Belgium
     Antwerp-Kiel               50        Believed destroyed
     Ghent Langerbrugge         20        Activity unknown
     Hoboken (Socony)           20        Believed destroyed
     Antwerp-Darse              20        Activity unknown
Holland
     Flushing asphalt           40 (?)    Activity unknown

     Total, excluding the few
     believed destroyed or in-
     conveniently located     1,253

     Percentage of total
     usable capacity
     suitably located             9%
```

SUPPORT OF GROUND OPERATIONS BY MASAF, FEBRUARY-MARCH 1944*

1-29 February

Target	Date	Target	Date
Sulmona M/Y	3	Ferrara M/Y	14
Stimigliano M/Y	3	Verona & Mantua M/Y	14
Antheor viaduct	4	Vicenza RR	14
Padua M/Y	7/8	Pontedera A/D	14
Verona M/Y	8	Brescia	14
Prato M/Y	8	Modena M/Y	14
Piombino M/Y	8	Verona M/Y	14
Orvieto A/D	8	Albano/Cecina &	
Tarquinia A/D	8	Cecina/Canpoleone roads	14/15
Viterbo A/D	8	Poggibonsi M/Y	15
Rimini M/Y	8/9	Monte Cassino Monastery	15
Albano town	10	Grottaferrata/Albano/	
Tivoli & Vicovaro towns	10	Velletri roads	15/16
Manteratonde road junction		Pontassieve M/Y	16
& RR	10	Pontassieve T/0's	16
Campoleone M/Y	10	Certaldo	16
Velletri town	10	Poggibonsi M/Y	16
Cecina town & RR	10	Rieti road & RR	16
Cisterna town	10	Siena M/Y	16
Troop concentrations		Cecina bridge	16
(Anzio)	12	San Stefano harbor	16/17
Cisterna, Velletri & Cori		Anzio area	16/17
towns	12/13	Anzio area	17
Campoleone/Cecina roads	12/13	Anzio area	17/18
Campoleone/Cecina roads	13/14	Anzio area	18/19
Albano/Cecina roads	13/14	Sante Marie/Tagliacozzo	
Arezzo M/Y	14	area	20
Pisa A/D & M/Y	14		
Prato M/Y	14		
Pontedera A/D	14		

1-15 March

Target	Date	Target	Date
Anzio area	1/2	Castelfiorentino M/Y	7
Anzio area	2	N. Central Italy T/0's	7
Montalto di Castro	2/3	Viterbo A/D	7
San Stefano	2/3	Fabrica di Rome A/D	7
Orbetello M/Y	2/3	Orvieto A/D	7
Viterbo A/D	3	San Stefano	7/8
Camino L/G	3	Prato M/Y	11
Fabrica di Roma A/D	3	Pontassieve M/Y	11
Littorio and Tiburtina M/Y	3	Iesi A/D	11
Pontassieve M/Y	7	Padua M/Y	11
Prato M/Y	7	Cassino and area	15
Poggibonsi M/Y	7		

Appendix 5

DISPOSITION OF GAF OPERATIONAl FIGHTER STRENGTH FOR ALL FRONTS
JANUARY-MAY 1944'**

Month	Total	Western Front	South German Front	Mediterranean and Balkan Front	Russian Front
January	2,638	60.0%	10.6%	13.9%	15.5%
February	2,607	61.0%	14.4%	8.9%	15.7%
March	2,613	62.8%	12.2%	8.7%	16.1%
April	2,646	58.6%	13.0%	8.6%	19.7%
May	2,721	23.1%*	49.3%**	7.7%#	19.8%##

*   Excluding Germany
**   Changed to German and Central European Front
#   Including Bulgaria
Including East Hungary, Rumania, Bessarabia
***   USSTAF, Semi-Monthly Record of Results, January-May 1944

PRE-ATTACK SOURCES OF GERMAN SUPPLY OF BALL BEARINGS*

Plant	Location	Per Cent of Pre-attack Supply
Germany		
Kugelfischer	Schweinfurt	19.7
VKF	Schweinfurt	18.0
Fichtel and Sachs	Schweinfurt	.9
Norma (VKF)	Stuttgart	5.1
VKF	Berlin/Erkner	4.3
VKF	Berlin/Neukölln	3.4
NDK	Berlin/Lichtenberg	.9
DKF	Leipzig	3.4
Jaeger	Wuppertal	2.6
Muller	Nuremburg	1.7
Robert Kling	Wetzlar	.9
Gebaur and Moller	Fulda	.9
Geb. Heller	Marienthal	.8
All others		1.7
Austria-Poland-Czechoslovakia		
Steyrwaffen Walzlager Werke	Steyr	9.4
SKF	Pürnstein	.9
All others		.8
Italy		
RIV	Turin	5.5
RIV	Villar-Perosa	1.4
IMI	Ferrara	.9
All others		.8
France		
CAM	Paris/Blois Colombes	2.6
CAM	Paris/Ivry-sur Seine	2.6
SRO	Annecy	1.7
All others		.8
Total Axis Europe		91.7

Plant	Location	Per Cent of Pre-attack Supply
Imports		
Sweden		7.9
Switzerland		.4
Total		100.0

ATTACKS ON GERMAN ANTIFRICTION BEARING INDUSTRY
JANUARY-MAY 1944*

Plant	Location	Date	Air Force
RIV	Villar-Perosa	3 Jan	15th
Kugelfischer	Elberfeld	30/31 Jan 2/3 Feb 4/5 Feb 7/8 Feb 8/9 Feb 9/10 Feb 11/12 Feb 12/13 Feb	RAF
DKF	Leipzig (area)	20 Feb	8th
VKF	Stuttgart	21 Feb 25 Feb	8th
Steyrwaffen Walzlager Werke	Steyr	23 Feb 2 Apr	15th
Kugelfischer VKF, Werke I and Werke II Deutsche Star Kugelhalter Fichtel und Sachs	Schweinfurt	24 Feb 24/25 Feb 25/26 Feb 24 Mar 30/31 Mar 13 Apr 26/27 Apr	8th RAF RAF 8th RAF 8th RAF
VKF	Berlin/Erkner	8 Mar	8th
Nadella	La Ricamarie	10/11 Mar	RAF
RIV	Turin	29 Mar	15th
SRO	Annecy	9/10 May	RAF

* AC/AS Intel., Analysis Div., European Br., "Strategic Bombing of Axis Europe, January 1943-September 1944," 1 Dec 44, in 353.41--Bombing, Bulk (Classified Files). U. S. Strategic Bombing Survey, The German Anti-Friction Bearings Industry, Nov 45, Exhibit D.

GERMAN DIFFICULTIES WITH RUMANIAN RAILROADS
As Told by POW Oberst Han Koeffner*

P/W has had a long and varied experience with the Wehrmacht which opens many corridors of information not probed into in this report. He served in Southern Russia, Italy and Rumania in charge of transportation and incidental remarks made during the interrogation show that there is an ample field in his experiences in these regions for further interrogation.

Throughout these times P/W made the observation that blueprints and actual performances remained far apart. In Italy, in Russia, and in the Balkans the German general staff had not figured with certain imponderables.

For example, there is the affair of the bored buffaloes. The Herr Oberst had faced and resolved many transport problems before he came to Rumania, but the shunting of freight cars by means of buffaloes who nudged the cars into place along the switch-tracks on the banks of the Danube was a bit of a poser. Rumanian railways were not noted for their efficiency at their best, and the impatient Germans sought means of vitalizing these services. With mere human beings, this was a simple problem, for the German methods of stimulating greater exertions in their behalf were by this time well if not favorably known. The buffalo-drivers were readily convinced that their interest lay on the side of faster freight car marshalling for the Germans. They belabored the buffaloes mightily with iron goads.

But the buffaloes, secure in a dignity quite superhuman, were not having any. They simply walked off the job, and plumped themselves down in the riverbed in a sort of lie-down strike. Threats, cajolery, goads, were all tried in vain, the buffaloes lay in the riverbed indifferent to the problems of any living space but their own. Not for two days, when hunger at last presented the winning argument, did they emerge to resume their former task under their vastly relieved drivers.

However, notes the Herr Oberst with a shrug, they did precisely as much work as previously, no more and no less, thus recording one of the earliest of the now culminating series of triumphs over the Wehrmacht.

---

* AAF Evaluation Board in ETO, Effectiveness of Air Attack against Rail Transportation in the Battle of France, Jun 45, p. 151.

MAJOR RUBBER FABRICATING PLANTS DAMAGED BY AREA RAIDS,
JANUARY-MAY 1944*

Plant	Location	Date	Air Force
Continental Gummiwerke	Hannover	31 Jan	8th
Michelin	Clermont-Ferrand	16/17 Mar	RAF BC
Clouth	Cologne	20/21 Apr	RAF BC
Cologne Gummifadin Fabrik	Cologne	20/21 Apr	RAF BC
Paguag	Düsseldorf	22/23 Apr	RAF BC
Metzler	Munich	24/25 Apr	RAF BC
Wilhelm Pahl	Dortmund	22/23 May	RAF BC
Semperit	Neunkirchen	24 May	15th
Englebert	Aachen	24/25 May 27/28 May	RAF BC

---

* U. S. Strategic Bombing Survey, Oil Division Final Report, App., Table C-9;
USSTAF, Semi-Monthly Record of Results, Jan-Jun 44.

MAAF OPERATIONS IN SHINGLE, CASSINO, AND DIADEM

The Anzio beachhead campaign was divided into three phases as far as
the air forces were concerned. The first phase, 2-13 January, was a cover
operation consisting of attacks in northern Italy to divert enemy attention
from the proposed landing site. The second phase, 13-22 January when the
beachhead was established, was devoted to disrupting communications and
isolating the battle area. The third phase, 22 January-25 May when the Anzio
forces were united with the main body of the Fifth Army, concerned aerial
cover for the landing and subsequent necessary protection.[1]

During the first period, the Fifteenth attacked the marshalling yards
in northern Italy, striking such railroad centers as Bolzano, Vicenza, Padua,
Ferrara, and Turin.[2] It also gave direct support to the Eighth Army by hitting the tracks at Pescara, the nearest point to the front lines yet to be
bombed by four-engine aircraft,[3] although except in cases of emergency, the
general line of demarcation for the strategic and tactical air forces was Pisa-
Rimini.[4]

In the second and third phases, the heavy bombers kept up their attacks
on marshalling yards.[5] For the most part a line roughly from Pisa to Rimini
still marked the boundary for normal operations of the Fifteenth and Twelfth
Air Forces, although the former did occasionally employ its forces south of
this line in a role usually played by the light bombers of the tactical air
forces. During the last week of January, for example, Fortresses and Liberators were used to bomb enemy motor transports on the way to Anzio and to
create road blocks by destroying bridges and railroad junctions between Rome
and the beachhead.[6]

43
1. History of MAAF, 10 Dec-1 Sep 44, I, 155.
2. Ibid., VI, MAAF, Air Intelligence Weekly Summary, No. 59, 3 Jan 44; ibid.,
   XIII, MAAF, Central Mediterranean Operational Summary, No. 12, 3 Jan 44;
   Fifteenth Air Force, "Villar-Perosa Ball Bearing Factory and Turin-Lingotto
   Marshalling Yards Operation of 3 January 1944."
3. History of MAAF, 10 Dec 43-1 Sep 44, VI, MAAF, Air Intelligence Weekly Summary
   No. 59, 3 Jan 44.
4. MAAF, Air Power in the Mediterranean, November 1942-February 1945, 49.
5. The following marshalling yards were attacked by the Fifteenth Air Force
   and the 205th Group, RAF in the last half of January in support of Anzio
   and the general Italian campaign: Empoli, Arezzo, Ferrara, Verona, Foligno,
   Bologna, Siena, Fabriano, Rimini, and Ancona. USSTAF, Semi-Monthly Record
   of Results, 16-31 Jan 44.
6. History of MAAF, 10 Dec 43-1 Sep 44, VI, MAAF, Air Intelligence Weekly Summary,
   No. 63, 31 Jan 44; ibid., XIII, MAAF, Central Mediterranean Operational Summary, No. 30, 22 Jan 44.

CONFIDENTIAL

In addition to assaults against the railroads, large-scale attacks were started on the airdromes and landing grounds furnishing fighter and bomber bases to the enemy for launching air assaults against Anzio and the rest of the battle line. This part of the program, although designed to support the Italian campaign, also served to carry out the intermediate objective of POINT-BLANK, which was the destruction of the GAF wherever it could be found. The airfields affected were located in Italy, southern France, and southern Germany.[7]

In the remaining months before the junction of the Fifth Army and Anzio, the Fifteenth Air Force continued to support the beachhead and general land operations, and as late as May was still engaged in such tactical operations.[8] The bulk of continuous close support by MASAF, however, was done by the 205th Group, RAF in its night work. In the critical month following the landing, the planes of this organization were dispatched almost every night to bomb troop concentrations, roads, and towns in the beachhead area.[9]

Since the CCS had given top theater priority to the Italian battle in the MTO, there was generally no objection to the use of the Fifteenth to push this campaign except when it came in conflict with POINTBLANK.[10] In the latter part of February the bad weather which had slowed up POINTBLANK operations gave promise of clearing. Spaatz was extremely anxious to take advantage of the opportunity thus offered to stage a series of concentrated and heavy attacks which would vitally cripple the enemy's remaining aircraft-production facilities. He therefore planned a number of missions, several of which were to be joint or coordinated attacks by the Eighth and Fifteenth Air Forces. One such mission was planned for 20 February, but on 19 February the ground situation and overriding priority of the Italian campaign threatened to interfere. Eaker notified Spaatz that both Clark and Cannon believed that

7. The airdromes and landing grounds attacked by the Fifteenth during the last half of January were: Ciampino, Centocelle, Montpellier/Frejorgues, Istres Le Tube, Salon-de Provence, Aviano, Maniago, Villaorba, Lavariano, Udine/Campoformido, Klagenfurt, Osoppo, Perugia, Guidonia, Rieti, and Aquila. USSTAF, Semi-Monthly Record of Results, 16-31 Jan 44; History of MAAF, 10 Dec 43-1 Sep 44, XIII, MAAF, Operational Summary No. 24, 16 Jan 44, No. 27, 19 Jan 44, No. 28, 20 Jan 44; ibid., VII, Opsum, Eaker to Arnold, Portal, Spaatz, 24 Jan 44.
8. For example, in the first half of February operations were confined chiefly to hitting marshalling yards, roads, airfields, and bridges in support of the ground effort. Between 12 February and 2 March the Fifteenth dispatched 799 planes and dropped 1,457 tons of bombs against troop concentrations, motor transport parks, stores depots, and bivouac areas. On 5 May, 116 B-24's attacked the Podgorica troop concentration, dropping 276 tons of bombs. History of MAAF, 10 Dec 43-1 Sep 44, X, Fifteenth Air Force, "Operations in Close Support of Ground Forces, 12 February-15 August 1944"; ibid., XII, Opsum, Eaker to Arnold, Spaatz, Portal, DeFord (Ref. No. AI-369), 6 May 44; USSTAF, Semi-Monthly Record of Results, 1-15 Feb. 44.
9. History of MAAF, 10 Dec 43-1 Sep 44, XII, Opsum, Eaker to Spaatz, Arnold,

20 February would be a critical day at Anzio and that they had expressed hope that the Fifteenth would give full heavy-bomber support. Furthermore, the weather over southern Germany did not hold any promise for visual bombing, and area bombing, as suggested by Spaatz if such a condition existed, was out of the question since the Fifteenth lacked H2X equipment. Baker asked if the Eighth needed the Fifteenth for diversionary purposes anyway. If so, he would split his forces, but he wished to avoid the formal declaration of a tactical emergency by Wilson. He did not want a precedent to be established.[11]

Spaatz replied that he would leave the matter to Eaker's discretion, but that he was concerned over the possible development in Italy of a "continuous emergency" which would prevent the use of the strategic air forces for the purposes for which they were organized.[12] Eaker finally decided to divide his force and the next day 105 heavies operated over the beachhead and 126 attempted to reach Regensburg. The latter planes, however, were forced to return because of icing conditions over the Alps and never reached their target. But they did furnish diversion which allowed the Eighth to proceed as planned, and for this Spaatz was grateful.[13] Although the mission to Regensburg was abortive, Eaker had been able to satisfy both of his superiors and prevent a formal declaration of an emergency. In the next few months there were several other instances when major heavy-bomber support was given to the ground forces, but each time it was done by request and Wilson never had to declare a tactical emergency.[14]

In at least one instance, however, the strategic forces were used, not only at the request of Wilson but also on the suggestion of General Arnold, to give very heavy support to the ground army. This was at Cassino. Arnold, worried because of the impasse which existed at this place and which held up the union with the Anzio forces, suggested that all available air power be concentrated in an attack which would blast this enemy anchor off the map and "break up every stone in the town behind which a German soldier might be hiding." As long as this stalemate existed, the part of MASAF in the CBO would be of limited value because of the diversions necessary to aid the land campaign. Once the ground armies were free to move, the strategic air forces could resume their primary mission without interruption. Because of the success of similar strategy used in the Desert and Tunisian campaigns--although, to be sure, Cassino

11. History of MAAF, 10 Dec 43-1 Sep 44, XXII, CS IE, Eaker to Spaatz, #29, 19 Feb 44.
12. Ibid., I, 145, Redline, Spaatz to Eaker, 19 Feb 44.
13. Ibid., Redline, Spaatz to Eaker, 20 Feb 44.
14. Ibid.; for the method of requesting tactical aid of MASAF, see ibid., VIII, Operations Instructions, No. 11, 4 Mar 44.

presented a different terrain—Arnold believed that such a maneuver would be successful.[15]

Eaker replied that the air and ground forces had already worked out a plan coinciding almost exactly with that proposed by Arnold, but weather had delayed its execution. At first it had been lack of suitable flying weather, but now the troops were so mired down that they were unable to move. Eaker warned Arnold not to be disappointed if the operation failed to connect the present line of battle with the Anzio beachhead. He himself did not think such bombing would shake the Germans from their current position or compel them to abandon their defensive role, particularly if they followed their orders to hold to the last man. As to whether or not the Italian campaign was likely to jeopardize FOINTBLANK, Eaker pointed out that there had never been a day on which the heavies h d participated in the land battle when weather would have allowed them to reach south German targets.[16]

For one month before the big raid, the Fifteenth had been aiding in the battle for Cassino. On 15 February, after giving the monks due warning, 142 planes dropped approximately 353 tons of bombs on the monastery, which the Germans were using for military purposes. On the morning of 15 March began the big air assault on the town itself. A force of 263 Fortresses and Liberators dropped 300 tons of bombs on Cassino, and including that dropped by the B-25's and A-20's the total tonnage was over 1,100 tons.[17] As a result of these operations Cassino was reduced to rubble, but as Eaker had feared, the Germans were not dislodged, and it was not until some time later that the army was able to open a hole in the line and continue its advance.

For the most part, however, the aid given by the Fifteenth to the Italian campaign was strategic rather than tactical. It consisted largely of attacking important railroad centers through which supplies and men were being funnelled to the front. Although the Fifteenth did aid the Twelfth Air Force in interdiction,[18]

---

15. Ibid., II, ltr, Gen. H. H. Arnold to Lt. Gen. Ira C. Eaker, undated.
16. Ibid., II, ltr, Lt. Gen. Ira C. Eaker to Gen. H. H. Arnold, 6 Mar 44.
17. Ibid., VI, MAAF, Air Intelligence Weekly Summary, No. 70, 20 Mar 44; ibid., X, Fifteenth Air Force, "Operations in Close Support of Ground Forces, 12 February-15 August 1944"; ibid., XII, Opsun, Eaker to Arnold, Spaatz, Portal (Ref. No. AI-302), 16 Mar 44.
18. AC/AS, Intel., Analysis Div., European Br., "Strategic Bombing of Axis Europe, Jan 43-Sep 44," 1 Dec 44, 353.41—bombing, Bulk (Classified Files). For example, MAAF attacked the marshalling yards at Orbetello and the track at Montalto di Castro on the night of 2/3 March and Littorio and Tiburtina on 3 March in order to block traffic leading immediately into Rome and the battle front. The attack on Pontassieve, southeast of Florence, on 11 March cut all through tracks to the battle front except one, and on this one track derailed cars and debris temporarily blocked the line. USSTAF, Semi-Monthly Record of Results, 1-15 Mar 44; History of MAAF, 10 Dec 43-1 Sep 44, VI, MAAF, Air Intelligence Weekly Summary, No. 69, 13 Mar 44.

its primary interest was in the railroad control of the Po Valley--the crossroads
for Italian traffic to Germany and the Balkans.[19] In the early part of 1944,
the Germans were able to limit serious tie-ups to the area south of Rimini-Pisa
where the Twelfth Air Force kept battering the roads leading to the battle front.
The plans of the Fifteenth promulgated in early March called for concentrated
attacks on the north Italian yards to complement those of the tactical air forces.
The slowness of the ground advance, however, led Devers to suggest that the Fifteenth
"thicken the bombings of the mediums" by striking Rimini, Bologna, Florence, and
Pisa and thereby more quickly cut off the supplies to the Germans south of Rome.
What he wanted was immediate rather than long-range results.[20]

The hub of enemy communications was Florence, whose marshalling yards were
important to the Germans for final handling of both troops and equipment to the
battle fronts over the main lines to Rome. The Allies, however, were hindered
in their efforts to choke off this traffic by their policy of not endangering or
destroying cultural or historical sites unless absolutely necessary. The result
was that the allies left Florence alone and attempted to accomplish the same
results by bombing the yards of numerous surrounding cities, such as Pontassieve,
Prato, Poggibonsi, Castelfiorentino, Pontedera, and Arezzo.[21] The attacks on these
yards and the work of interdiction on the part of the tactical air forces south
of Florence hard pressed the enemy, although traffic inched forward as the Germans
repaired cuts in their lines. This traffic, however, was insufficient for the
full battle needs. Prisoners of war taken from late March to June all reported
that soldiers came by rail as far as Florence but from there were forced to go by
foot or motor transport.[22]

The fact that the rail lines to Florence were able to function without
too much delay led the strategic forces to try to knock out the yards in the
Po Valley and destroy the considerable amount of freight which had accumulated in
them. For the most part MASAF used these targets as alternates when POINTBLANK
operations were not feasible,[23] although during the last week of March it was

---

19. After the withdrawal of Italy from the war in September 1943, the Germans
     organized an Army Transport Control (Wehrmacht Verkehrsdirecktion) at
     Verona, the southern terminus of the Brenner line. This organization con-
     trolled all freight traffic entering Italy over the five main routes and by
     shifting the load from one line or marshalling yard to another was able to
     keep congestion down when bombing was not too heavy. U. S. Strategic Bombing
     Survey, Transportation Report No. 1, Nov 45, pp. 4-5, KO-33545.
20. History of MAAF, 10 Dec 43-1 Sep 44, II, memo, Eaker to Director of Operations,
     MAAF, 11 Mar 44.
21. For example, the following marshalling yards were attacked by MASAF during
     the first half of March: Orbetello on the night of 2/3 March; Littorio and
     Rome/Tiburtina on the 3d; Fontassieve, Prato, Poggibonsi, and Castelfiorentino
     on the 7th; and Prato, Pontassieve, and Padua on the 11th. USSTAF, Semi-
     monthly Record of Results, 1-15 Mar 44.
22. History of MAAF, 10 Dec 43-1 Sep 44, VI, MAAF, Air Intelligence Weekly Summary,
     No. 85, 3 Jul 44.
23. Ibid., II, ltr, Lt. Gen. Ira C. Eaker to Gen. H. H. Arnold (Round-up Item
     No. 7), 7 Apr 44.

role be meant some of the heaviest actions on these northern yards. In two days alone, 28 and 29 March, 974 heavies and 344 fighters of the Fifteenth loaded with 2,218 tons of bombs were airborne against enemy communications. They were aided at night by the 205th Group, RAF. Among the targets hit during that week, were important yards at Turin, Milan, Verona, Vicenza, Padua, Bolzano, Bologna, Mestre, and Rimini. In the course of these operations some industrial targets also suffered. For example, the Fiat aero-engine factory at Turin was set afire and burned for 24 hours after the attack, and the Breda shipbuilding and armaments works, a benzine and petrol depot, and chemical plant, all at Mestre, were seriously damaged.[24] The intense attacks were carried on through April with all rail approaches to Italy from Trieste to Allessandria being harassed, and with traffic south of the Po Valley being broken up by repeated assaults on marshalling yards, rail junctions, and bridges.[25]

After DIADEM was begun on the night of 11 May, much of the effort of the strategic air forces was directed to support this project. On D-day plus 1 the day bombers were instructed to employ their maximum number on the first mission. Double sorties would be flown and the force of the second mission was to be on a maximum sustained-operations basis. The targets to be attacked on D-day plus 1 were: enemy headquarters at Monte Soratto and enemy command posts; the harbors at San Stefano, Piombino, Porto Ferrajo, Leghorn, La Spezia, and Genoa; the Leghorn marshalling yards; and the Genoa-La Spezia rail line. The remainder of the bombing effort would be expended on the marshalling yards north of Rimini-Pisa. Subsequent operations would be against similar targets, but with the possibility of sudden new assignments depending upon the tactical situation. The night bombers were to bomb the harbors at Porto Ferrajo, Piombino, and San Stefano on the nights of D-day plus 1 and 2, and otherwise were subject to the same general regulations as the day bombers.[26]

The strategic attack opened with an assault on the corps headquarters at Massa d'Albe, but for the next three days emphasis was put on the enemy's lines of communications. These consisted of raids on such places as Arezzo, Avisio, Bologna, Bolzano, Bronzolo, Borgo, Cesena, Castelmaggiore, Civitavecchia, Fidenza, Faenza, Ferrara, Genoa, Modena, Mestre, Orbetello, Padua, Piacenza, Parma, La Spezia, Vicenza, and numerous other points.[27] Constant attacks, by day and night, on enemy communications were continued throughout the month and the first part of June. Railroad centers and harbors bore the brunt of these raids, although the 205th Group, RAF dropped considerable tonnage on highways

---

24. Fifteenth Air Force, Tactical Mission Report, 28-29 Mar 44; History of MAAF, 10 Dec 43-1 Sep 44, VI, MAAF, Air Intelligence Weekly Summary, No. 71 (27 Mar 44), No. 72 (3 Apr 44); ibid., XII, Opsum, Eaker to Arnold, Spaatz, Portal, (Ref. No. AI-370), 25 Mar 44, (Ref. No. AI-397), 28 Mar 44, (Ref. No. AI-305), 29 Mar 44, (Ref. No. AI-312), 30 Mar 44.
25. USSTAF, Semi-Monthly Record of Results, 16-30 Apr 44.
26. History of MAAF, 10 Dec 43-1 Sep 44, VIII, MAAF, Operations Order No. 35, 12 May 44.
27. Ibid., MAAF, Air Intelligence Weekly Summary, No. 79, 22 May 44.

between Rome and the battle front.[28]

Support of DIADEM was not confined solely to Italian operations. After the Germans had attacked Tito's headquarters with the hope of capturing him and ending the Yugoslav Partisan activities, MAAF began a series of Balkan raids designed to aid the guerrillas and thus keep the Germans busy on another front. Although these raids were not primarily a MAAF project, the strategic forces aided the tactical and coastal commands in these Balkan forays. The Fifteenth made attacks on German troop concentrations on 26, 28, and 29 May, using 593 planes and dropping approximately 1,077 tons of bombs.[29]

The scope of operations also extended to France. In order to disorganize the movement of reinforcements to Italy, the heavies began to hit the marshalling yards of southern France. On 25 May, the yards in the Lyon area and at Toulon were successfully attacked, leaving the through lines blocked, workshops wrecked, and many cars destroyed.[30] The operations in southern France, however, were not only for aiding DIADEM but also in preparation for the forthcoming DRAGOON. These attacks, combined with the increasingly heavy raids (for OVERLORD) on communications in northern France by the England-based air forces, pounded the enemy until he was almost punch-drunk.

---

28. In the last half of May the Fifteenth Air Force dropped 1,125 tons of bombs on nine Italian railroad centers. Some of the harbors attacked during this same period were: San Stefano, Piombino, Genoa, Leghorn, La Spezia, Porto Ferrajo, and Porto Marghera. The bombing of highways included the roads through and around such places as Frosinone, Valmonte, Terracina, Viterbo, Subiaco, and Rome environs. USSTAF, Semi-Monthly Record of Results, 16-31 May 44; History of MAAF, 10 Dec 43-1 Sep 44, VII, Opsum, Baker to Arnold, Spaatz, Portal (Ref. No. AI-399),18 May 44, (Ref. No. AI-307), 19 May 44, (Ref. No. AI-326), 20 May 44, (Ref. No. AI-351), 23 May 44, (Ref. No. AI-376), 25 May 44, (Ref. No. AI-385), 26 May 44, (Ref. No. AI-317), 28 May 44, (Ref. No. AI-327), 29 May 44, (Ref. No. AI-338), 30 May 44, (Ref. No. AI-357), 1 Jun 44, (Ref. No. AI-315), 5 Jun 44.
29. The places attacked were: Bihac, Miksic, and Podorica. Ibid., X, Fifteenth Air Force, "Operations in Close Support of Ground Forces, 12 February-15 August 1944."
30. Ibid., VI, MAAF, Air Intelligence Weekly Summary, No. 80, 20 May 44.

COORDINATED ATTACKS BY USSTAF, FEBRUARY-JUNE 1944

The first of USSTAF's coordinated attacks was set for 9 February with the object of hitting 14 targets, but the deterioration of the weather in the MTO made it necessary for the Fifteenth to cancel its part of the operation. The Eighth got 848 bombers in the air, but prior to departure from the English coast they were also recalled because of increasing cloud conditions over the target areas.[1] Another coordinated attack for 15 February was also canceled by the Fifteenth because of weather. A third such mission planned for 20 February conflicted with the request for Fifteenth Air Force support of the Anzio battle, but Taker split his force and sent part to the beachhead and dispatched the other to participate in the planned coordinated attack. The latter mission proved abortive for the MTO forces, however, since weather turned the planes back in the vicinity of Trieste.[2] Another joint mission for 21 February was also canceled by the Fifteenth because of weather.

The first successful coordinated attack took place on 22 February. The targets for the Fifteenth were the Regensburg aircraft factories. These had last been attacked by the Eighth Air Force in August 1943. The damage inflicted at that time had reduced the output of Me-109's from 200 to 250 a month to an estimated 50. Repairs were under way almost immediately and by the end of January 1944 the plants at Regensburg/Prüfening and Regensburg/Obertraubling apparently were in full operation again.[3] It was, therefore, imperative that these factories be again put out of commission. Over Prüfening the bombers encountered solid overcast, but 65 B-17's dropped 153 tons of bombs with unobserved results. Fifteen aircraft returned their bombs to their bases, and 21 dropped 42 tons on the marshalling yards and town of Petershausen. At Obertraubling, 132 B-24's dropped 178 tons of general-purpose 500-pound bombs and 47 tons of incendiaries with good results. The bombers experienced heavy and accurate flak over Klagenfurt, Pola, and Trieste and encountered about 120 enemy fighters, some of which were rocket-firing twin-engine planes. The Fifteenth lost 19 bombers and two fighters and claimed a score of 42-17-6. As a diversion to the main force, freshman missions bombed Zagreb airdrome and Sibenik and Zara harbors, but in all of these there was no encounter with enemy aircraft nor any losses.[4]

The Eighth Air Force met with weather trouble which prevented six combat wings from assembling and necessitated recalling two more before they reached

---

1. CM-IN-6221 (9-2-44), Spaatz to Arnold, UK-3578, 9 Feb 44; ltr, Maj. Gen. F. L. Anderson to Brig. Gen. L. S. Kuter, 11 Feb 44, in 312.1--Operations Letters (Classified Files).
2. History of MAAF, 10 Dec 43-1 Sep 44, VIII, MAAF, Central Mediterranean Operational Summary, No. 59, 20 Feb. 44.
3. Ibid., VI, MAAF, Air Intelligence Weekly Summary, No. 67, 28 Feb 44.
4. Ibid., I, 149; ibid., II, Opsum, Taker to Spaatz, Arnold, Portal (Ref. No. AT-302), 23 Feb 44; ibid., XIII, MAAF, Central Mediterranean Operational Summary, No. 61, 22 Feb 44; ibid., XVI, MAAF, PRO Air Communique, 23 Feb 44.

enemy home territory. The latter, however, dropped nearly 234 tons of bombs on Dutch targets of opportunity on their return to England after receiving their recall. Some 289 B-17's of the 1st Bombardment Division were able to proceed to their targets in central Germany and about 175 dropped 379 tons of bombs with good results on the aircraft factories at Aschersleben, Bernburg, Wernigerode, Halberstadt, Magdeburg, Marburg, and Bünde. Here also, rocket-firing planes were encountered, and a total of about 200 enemy aircraft attacked, many being vicious and persistent. The Eighth lost 38 bombers and 11 fighters but claimed 91 enemy planes destroyed, 25 probable, and 43 damaged.[5]

The next coordinated attack was on 24 February. On this date 87 B-17's of the Fifteenth dropped 201 tons of bombs on the Daimler-Puch factory at Steyr, causing severe damage to the machine and assembly shops, foundry, offices, power plant, and transformer station. Again the Germans put up aggressive opposition, about 110 fighters meeting the bomber formations. Some of the enemy planes fired rockets or used aerial bombs. Sixteen bombers and three fighters were lost as against 35-12-5.[6] The Eighth dispatched 809 bombers against Gotha, Schweinfurt, and Rostock. The Messerschmitt factory at the first-named city felt the weight of 382 tons of bombs delivered by 169 bombers of the 2d Bombardment Division, and an additional 44 B-24's of the same division laid 78 tons on the town of Eisenach. A force of 236 B-17's of the 1st Bombardment Division reached Schweinfurt and dropped 573 tons on the Kugelfischer, VKF Werke I, and Fichtel and Sachs ball-bearing factories. At the city of Rostock, 255 B-17's plastered the shipbuilding and aircraft factories with about 604 tons of incendiaries and GP bombs. Again the enemy put up stiff opposition, which cost the U.S. forces 49 bombers and 10 fighters in exchange for 120-27-55.[7]

The next successfully completed coordinated attack was on the following day, 25 February. The previous night, Wellingtons of the 205th Group, RAF unloaded almost four tons of bombs on the Daimler-Puch factory at Steyr and nearly 53 tons on the Sels marshalling yards and vicinity. No respite was to be allowed the enemy. On 25 February, Regensburg was again the target, but this time for both the Eighth and Fifteenth. This was the first instance when both air forces were over the same target on the same day. The Fifteenth dispatched a force of 132 B-17's and 264 B-24's against this city, but only 46 B-17's and 103 B-24's were able to reach their objectives. Although aggressively attacked by approximately 200 fighters, the bombers were able to destroy their targets almost entirely. An hour later 266 B-17's of the

5. Ibid., I, 149; Narrative History of Headquarters, Eighth Air Force, Feb 44; Eighth Air Force Operations Report.
6. History of MAAF, 10 Dec 43-1 Sep 44, XII, Opsum, Eaker to Spaatz, Arnold, Portal (Ref. No. AI-324), 25 Feb 44; ibid., VIII, MAAF, Central Mediterranean Operational Summary, No. 63, 24 Feb 44; ibid., VI, MAAF, Air Intelligence Weekly Summary, No. 67, 23 Feb 44.
7. Narrative History of Headquarters, Eighth Air Force, Feb 44; ibid., Annex C.

Eighth Air Force completed the destruction of Regensburg/Obertraubling and
Regensburg/Prüfening with 640 tons of bombs. The earlier assault by the
Fifteenth had taken some of the sting out of the opposition to the Eighth,
only 35 to 50 fighters being encountered. The former air force lost 32
bombers while the latter lost only 12. The claims of the Fifteenth were
52-10-9 and those of the Eighth were 13-1-7. The MASAF forces which failed
to reach Regensburg attacked Graz/Thalerhof and port installations at Zara,
Fiume, and Pola as secondary targets and with good results.[8]

In addition to the attack on Regensburg, the Eighth also sent forces
against the Bachmann von Blumenthal & Co. (Me-110 and Me-410 components and
final assembly) factory at Fürth near Nuremburg; the Messerschmitt factory at
Augsburg; and the ball-bearing center at Stuttgart. At the latter place bombs
struck not only the Vereinigte Kugellager Fabrik (VKF), but also the Fortuna
Werke Spezial Maschinen Fabrik, manufacturers of grinding machines, gauges, and
measuring instruments, and the piston ring, submarine, and temperature-gauge
plant of the J. P. Weisemann Co. Crippling damage was inflicted on all targets
in the three cities.[9]

This was the last successfully completed coordinated attack until after
D-day (6 June). In the period covered by this study 15 were proposed, all of
them by the Eighth Air Force, and two were implied. Of this total of 17, 9
were canceled because of weather, 1 was declined, and 4 were abortive. The
last proposed attack before D-day was on 12 April, but was canceled because of
weather. After that date both air forces were busy with either OVERLORD preparations or the support of the Italian and Balkan campaigns, and POINTBLANK operations in general were uncoordinated except for the filing of daily bombing
intentions. The next coordinated attack after April was proposed for 16 June,
but again weather forced cancelation. The first coordinated attack to be completed after 25 February was on 7 July.[10]

---

8. History of MAAF, 10 Dec 43-1 Sep 44, VIII, MAAF, Central Mediterranean
    Operational Summary, No. 64, 25 Feb 44; ibid., XII, Opsum, Baker to Spaatz,
    Arnold, Portal (Ref. No. AI-332), 26 Feb 44; ibid., VI, MAAF, Air Intelligence
    Weekly Summary, No. 66, 6 Mar 44; Narrative History of Headquarters, Eighth
    Air Force, Feb 44, Annex C; Eighth Air Force, Air Operations Report, Mission
    235, 25 Feb 44.

9. Narrative History of Headquarters, Eighth Air Force, Feb. 44; ibid., Annex
    C; Eighth Air Force, Air Operations Report, Mission 235, 25 Feb 44; Eighth
    Air Force, Interpretation Report No. S.A. 1061, Mission 235, 25 Feb 44.

10. For the list of proposed coordinated attacks, see Table 7, this study.

AAFRH-19

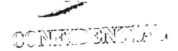

A P P E N D I X E S

(The source of all data in these Appendixes is: "Statistical Summary
of Eighth Air Force Operations, European Theater, 17 Aug 1942-8 May 1945.")

AAFRH-19 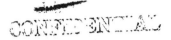 203

Appendix 1

Eighth Air Force 1943 Order of Battle
Heavy Bombardment Groups Operational at End of Each Month

Total
Operational

Jan 1943   B-17 Groups:
              92d (Tr only), 306th, 91st, 303d, 305th
              B-24 Groups: 6
              93d, 44th

Feb 1943   B-17 Groups:
              92d (Tr ohly), 306th, 91st, 303d, 305th
              B-24 Groups: 6
              93d, 44th

March 1943   B-17 Groups:
              92d (Tr only), 306th, 91st, 303d, 305th
              B-24 Groups:
              93d, 44th   6

April 1943   B-17 Groups:
              92d (Tr only), 306th, 91st, 303d, 305th
              B-24 Groups:
              93d, 44th   6

May 1943   B-17 Groups:
              92d, 306th, 91st, 303d, 305th, 95th, 96th,
              351st, 94th, 379th
              B-24 Groups:
              93d, 44th   12

June 1943   B-17 Groups:
              92d, 306th, 91st, 303d, 305th, 95th, 96th,
              351st, 94th, 379th, 100th, 381st, 384th
              B-24 Groups dispatched to Mediterranean   13

July 1943   B-17 Groups:
              92d, 306th, 91st, 303d, 305th, 95th, 96th,
              351st, 94th, 379th, 100th, 381st, 384th,
              385th, 388th
              No B-24 groups operational   15

Aug 1943   B-17 Groups:
              92d, 306th, 91st, 303d, 305th, 95th, 96th,
              351st, 94th, 379th, 100th, 381st, 384th,
              385th, 388th, 390th, 482d (3 sqdns PFF)
              No B-24 groups operational   16-3/4

AAFRH-19   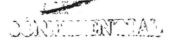   204

                                                        Total
                                                        Operational

Sep 1943   B-17 Groups:
             92d, 306th, 91st, 303d, 305th, 95th, 96th,
             351st, 94th, 379th, 100th, 381st, 384th,
             385th, 388th, 390th, 482d (3 sqdns, PFF)   20-3/4
             B-24 Groups:
             93d, 44th, 389th, 392d

Oct 1943   B-17 Groups:
             92d, 306th, 91st, 303d, 305th, 95th, 96th,
             351st, 94th, 379th, 100th, 381st, 384th,
             385th, 388th, 390th, 482d (3 sqdns, PFF)   20-3/4
             B-24 Groups:
             93d, 44th, 389th, 392d

Nov 1943   B-17 Groups:
             92d, 306th, 91st, 303d, 305th, 95th, 96th,
             351st, 94th, 379th, 100th, 381st, 384th,
             385th, 388th, 390th, 482d (3 sqdns, PFF),
             401st   21-3/4
             B-24 Groups:
             93d, 44th, 389th, 392d

Dec 1943   B-17 Groups:
             92d, 306th, 91st, 303d, 305th, 95th, 96th,
             351st, 94th, 379th, 100th, 381st, 384th,
             385th, 389th, 390th, 482d (3 sqdns, PFF),
             401st, 447th   25-3/4
             B-24 Groups:
             93d, 44th, 389th, 392d, 445th, 446th, 448th

AAFRH-19 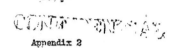 205

Appendix 2

Eighth Air Force
1943 Personnel Strength by Months

Strength as of Last Day of Each Month of 1943	Officers Assigned	Enlisted Men Assigned	Total Assigned
Jan 31	4,525	31,716	36,241
Feb 28	4,608	31,990	36,598
March 31	5,169	35,111	40,280
April 30	6,499	37,984	44,483
May 31	8,981	65,567	74,548
June 30	11,664	89,685	101,349
July 31	11,966	87,366	99,332#
Aug 31	14,761	115,213	129,974
Sep 30	16,780	129,747	146,527
Oct 31	16,792	127,289	144,081##
Nov 30	21,845	151,312	173,157
Dec 31	22,945	173,382	196,327

July drop in assigned strength due to Mediterranean diversion.

October drop in assigned strength due to loss of personnel to Ninth Air Force, which was established 15 Oct in United Kingdom.

AAFRH-19

206

Appendix 3

Eighth Air Force
Aircraft and Crew Strength
Daily Average by Month--1st Line Tactical Aircraft
Heavy Bombers

Month 1943	Asgd to Air Force	On Hand in Opnl Tac Units	Fully Opnl in Opnl Tac Units	Crews Asgd	Crews Avail	Effective Strength for Combat
Jan	225	155	80	147	85	80
Feb	209	146	84	143	74	74
March	257	190	112	151	87	87
April	337	231	153	187	140	140
May	547	340	200	318	178	178
June	775	459	287	419	222	232
July	800	589	378	464	315	279
Aug	761	582	406	509	341	291
Sep	881	656	461	661	409	373
Oct	1000	763	535	820	479	417
Nov	1254	902	705	1085	636	578
Dec	1503	1057	752	1556	949	723

AAFRH-19 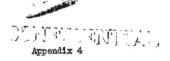 207

Appendix 4

Eighth Air Force
1943 Bombing Operations

Month 1943	Days Operations Carried Out	Total Sorties	Credit Sorties	Effective Sorties	Tons of Bombs on Targets Visual	Tons of Bombs on Targets PFF
Jan	4	358	279	263	665.6	
Feb	5	526	298	250	636.6	
March	9	956	716	610	1662.5	
April	4	450	373	353	962.5	
May	9	1640	1340	1217	2851.8	
May M/B		23	23	11	10.7	
June	7	2154	1447	1128	2610.4	
July	10	2828	2334	1609	3698.3	
July M/B		283	245	184	193.4	
Aug	8	2267	2058	1653	3570.5	
Aug M/B		1190	996	679	908.4	
Sep	11	3419	2561	2088	4728.6	748.9
Sep M/B		3033	2344	1897	2777.0	
Oct	7	2690	2159	1911	3528.5	1169.4
Oct M/B		579	485	266	396.0	
Nov	11	4490	2916	2483	2030.4	4395.1
Dec	10	6337	5618	4730	4456.1	7467.6
Total 1943	95	33223	26192	21332	35687.2	13781.0

First PFF Bombing Mission 27 Sep 1943

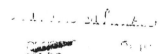

AAFRH-19   CONFIDENTIAL   208

Appendix 5

Eighth Air Force
Types of Bombs Dropped by Heavy Bombers

1943 Months	High Explosive	Fragmentation	Incendiary	Total Tons
Jan	665.6			665.6
Feb	636.6			636.6
March	1662.5			1662.5
April	962.5			962.5
May	2727.3		124.5	2851.8
June	2610.4			2610.4
July	3186.1		512.1	3698.2
Aug	3140.4	80.7	349.4	3570.5
Sep	4810.7	318.4	348.4	5477.5
Oct	3405.3		1292.6	4697.9
Nov	4042.6		2382.9	6425.5
Dec	7734.1		4189.6	11923.7
1943 Totals	35,584.1	399.1	9199.5	45182.7

CONFIDENTIAL

AAFRH-19  209

Appendix 6

Eighth Air Force
Bomb Tonnage by Country
Bombers and Fighters

Month 1943	Germany	France	Belgium	Holland	Norway	Poland	Shipping and Other	Total
Jan	202.0	463.6						665.6
Feb	259.3	377.0					.3	636.6
March	532.0	961.5		169.0				1662.5
April	267.0	450.0	245.5					962.5
May	1294.0	1232.0	325.8	10.7				2862.5
June	1748.8	721.1	95.5				45.0	2610.4
July	1967.3	1268.6	14.6	80.2	495.3		45.6	3891.6
Aug	1335.9	2633.8	32.3	474.4			2.5	4478.9
Sep	1215.1	6538.1	448.7	12.0			39.9	8253.8
Oct	4023.9	291.8		420.6		358.3		5094.6
Nov	5385.0	16.8		32.0	1001.3		7.2	6442.3
Dec	8901.2	3022.5		10.5				11934.2
1943 Totals	27151.5	17976.8	1162.4	1209.4	1496.6	358.3	140.5	49495.5

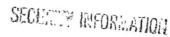

AAFRH-19 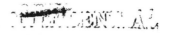 210

Appendix 7

Eighth Air Force
1943 Heavy Bomber Loss Rate on Combat Operations

Month 1943	Combat Unit Credit Sorties	A/C Lost MIA, and Cat E	Losses as % of Credit Sorties
January	279	21	7.5
February	298	24	8.1
March	716	23	3.2
April	373	29	7.8
May	1340	73	5.4
June	1447	93	6.4
July	2334	128	5.5
August	2058	124	6.0
September	2561	101	3.9
October	2159	198	9.2
November	2916	114	3.9
December	5618	200	3.6
Totals 1943	22099	1128	5.1

MIA--Missing in Action.

Category E--Damaged beyond economical repair.

AAFRH-19   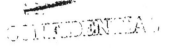   211

Appendix 8

Eighth Air Force
1943 Bomber Command Units Missing in Action and Claims

Month 1943	Bombers MIA	Enemy Aircraft Claims		
		Destroyed	Probably Destroyed	Damaged
Jan	18	40	42	26
Feb	22	71	24	12
March	19	147	41	53
April	28	148	41	31
May	68	389	82	175
May M/B	10	—	—	—
June	85	300	81	146
July	109	542	155	325
July M/B	2	3	2	2
Aug	107	440	56	162
Aug M/B	4	4	2	3
Sep	84	273	45	125
Sep M/B	7	13	6	6
Oct	176	790	131	348
Nov	93	134	46	81
Dec	163	227	89	133
1943 Totals	995	3521	843	1628

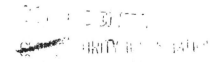

CONFIDENTIAL

Appendix 9

Eighth Air Force
Heavy Bombers Missing in Action by Cause

1943 Months	Enemy A/C	Flak or Flak & E/A	Accident	Other and Unknown Cause	Total
Jan	11	3	2	2	18
Feb	12	4	2	4	22
March	14	-	-	5	19
April	18	1	-	9	28
May	25	14	1	28	68
June	46	7	1	31	85
July	41	22	8	38	109
Aug	50	13	7	37	107
Sep	16	12	5	51	84
Oct	71	11	1	93	176
Nov	14	8	10	61	93
Dec	30	25	4	104	163
1943 Totals	348	120	41	463	972

AAFRH-19

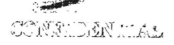

213

Appendix 10

Eighth Air Force
1943 Heavy Bomber Battle Damage by Category

Month 1943	Combat Unit Credit Sorties	Category of Damage				Total Heavy Bombers Damaged	
		A	AC	B	E	Number	% of Credit Sorties
Jan	279	110	20	2	3	135	48.4
Feb	298	100	10	1	2	113	37.9
March	716	127	15	1	4	147	20.5
April	373	67	19	0	1	87	23.3
May	1340	304	100	4	5	413	30.8
June	1447	391	66	8	8	473	32.7
July	2334	876	126	4	19	1025	43.9
Aug	2058	756	90	6	17	869	42.2
Sep	2561	669	59	3	17	748	29.2
Oct	2159	770	95	13	22	900	41.7
Nov	2916	540	83	5	21	649	22.2
Dec	5618	1005	222	12	37	1276	22.7
1943 Totals	22099	5715	905	59	156	6835	30.9

Cat A--An airplane which, by nature of the damage, may be repaired within
  36 hours, and is repairable by a combat unit.
Cat AC--An airplane which, by nature of the damage, requires 36 or more
  hours to repair, and is repairable by a subdepot or service sq.
Cat B--An airplane which, by nature of the damage, is repairable by a
  repair depot activity or establishment, regardless of whether the
  work is done on site or in a depot.
Cat E--An airplane damaged beyond economical repair while in performance
  of an operational mission.

Chart I

ORGANIZATION OF THE FIFTEENTH AIR FORCE
DECEMBER 1943 AND JUNE 1944*

December 1943:

    5th Bomb Wing
        1st Fighter Group (P-39), 27th, 71st, 94th Squadrons
        14th Fighter Group (P-38), 37th, 48th, 49th Squadrons
        325th Fighter Group (P-47), 317th, 318th, 319th Squadrons
        2d Bomb Group (B-17), 20th, 49th, 96th, 429th Squadrons
        97th Bomb Group (B-17), 340th, 341st, 342d, 414th Squadrons
        99th Bomb Group (B-17), 346th, 347th, 348th, 416th Squadrons
        301st Bomb Group (B-17), 32d, 352d, 353d, 419th Squadrons
    47th Bomb Wing
        154th Squadron of the 68th TR Gp. (P-39 and F-4A)
        82d Fighter Group (P-38), 95th, 96th, 97th Squadrons
        98th Bomb Group (B-24), 343d, 344th, 345th, 415th Squadrons
        376th Bomb Group (B-24), 512th, 513th, 514th, 515th Squadrons
        449th Bomb Group (B-24), 716th, 717th, 718th, 719th Squadrons
        450th Bomb Group (B-24), 720th, 721st, 722d, 723d Squadrons
        451st Bomb Group (B-24), 724th, 725th, 726th, 727th Squadrons
    304th Bomb Wing
        454th Bomb Group (B-24)
        455th Bomb Group (B-24)
        456th Bomb Group (B-24)
    XV Air Force Service Command

June 1944:

    5th Bomb Wing
        2d Bomb Group (B-17), 20th, 49th, 96th, 429th Squadrons
        97th Bomb Group (B-17), 340th, 341st, 342d, 414th Squadrons
        99th Bomb Group (B-17), 346th, 347th, 348th, 416th Squadrons
        301st Bomb Group (B-17), 32d, 352d, 353d, 419th Squadrons
        463d Bomb Group (B-17), 772d, 773d, 774th, 775th Squadrons
        483d Bomb Group (B-17), 815th, 816th, 817th, 840th Squadrons
    47th Bomb Wing
        98th Bomb Group (B-24), 343d, 344th, 345th, 415th Squadrons
        376th Bomb Group (B-24), 512th, 513th, 514th, 515th Squadrons
        449th Bomb Group (B-24), 716th, 717th, 718th, 719th Squadrons
        450th Bomb Group (B-24), 720th, 721st, 722d, 723d Squadrons

* History of MAAF, 10 Dec 43-1 Sep 44, XI/23d SCORU, Monthly Statistical Summary
of Mediterranean Allied Air Forces, No. 2 (Dec 43), No. 8 (Jun 44).

Chart I (Cont'd)

49th Bomb Wing
    451st Bomb Group (B-24), 724th, 725th, 726th, 727th Squadrons
    461st Bomb Group (B-24), 764th, 765th, 766th, 767th Squadrons
    484th Bomb Group (B-24), 824th, 825th, 826th, 827th Squadrons
55th Bomb Wing
    460th Bomb Group (B-24), 760th, 761st, 762d, 763d Squadrons
    464th Bomb Group (B-24), 776th, 777th, 778th, 779th Squadrons
    465th Bomb Group (B-24), 780th, 781st, 782d, 783d Squadrons
    485th Bomb Group (B-24), 828th, 829th, 830th, 831st Squadrons
304th Bomb Wing
    454th Bomb Group (B-24), 736th, 737th, 738th, 739th Squadrons
    455th Bomb Group (B-24), 740th, 741st, 742d, 743d Squadrons
    456th Bomb Group (B-24), 744th, 745th, 746th, 747th Squadrons
    459th Bomb Group (B-24), 756th, 757th, 758th, 759th Squadrons
306th Fighter Wing
    1st Fighter Group (P-38), 27th, 71st, 94th Squadrons
    14th Fighter Group (P-38), 37th, 48th, 49th Squadrons
    31st Fighter Group (P-51), 307th, 308th, 309th Squadrons
    52d Fighter Group (P-51), 2d, 4th, 5th Squadrons
    82d Fighter Group (P-38), 95th, 96th, 97th Squadrons
    325th Fighter Group (P-51), 317th, 318th, 319th Squadrons
    332d Fighter Group (P-47), 99th, 100th, 310th, 302d Squadrons
    (Group composed of Negroes)
XV Air Force Service Command
←——305th Bomb Wing (nonoperational)
←——885th Bomb Squadron (SP) (B-17's and B-24's)
←——154th Weather Reconnaissance Squadron (P-38)

CRUDE OIL REFINERIES SELECTED AS PRIMARY TARGETS**

Refinery	Annual Capacity (In thousands of tons)	Activity	% of Total Usable Capacity Suitably Located
*Astra Romana, Ploesti	1750	capacity operation	14
*Concordia Vega, Ploesti	1300	major portion in use	10
*Romana Americana, Ploesti	1100	capacity operation	9
*Phoenix Unirea, Ploesti	800	major portion in use	6
*Harburg, Germany	550	capacity operation	4
*Petrol Block, Ploesti	550	major portion in use	4
*Lobau, Austria	350	capacity operation	3
*Hannover, Germany (Misburg)	300	capacity operation	2
*Snell, Budapest, Hungary	220	capacity operation	2
*Dacia Romana, Rumania	220	major portion in use	2
*Prahova Petrolul, Bucharest	200	major portion in use	2
Pardubice, Czechoslovakia	180	capacity operation	1
Almasfuzito, Hungary	170	capacity operation	1
*Bratislava	150	capacity operation	1
Columbia Aquila, Ploesti	135	capacity operation	1
Floridsdorf, Austria	100	capacity operation	1
Bremen Oslebshausen, Germany	100	capacity operation	1
Caprag, Yugoslavia	120	major portion in use	1
Merkwiller, Pechelbronn, France	130	major portion in use	1
Drohobycz (Polmin), Poland	120	major portion in use	1
Magyar, Budapest, Hungary	90	capacity operation	1
Drohobycz, Galica, Poland	90	major portion in use	1
Trbzebinja, Poland	90	major portion in use	1
Czechowice (Dziedzice), Poland	90	major portion in use	1
Kolin	80	capacity operation for lubricating oil, not crude	1
Kegran, Austria	75	capacity operation	1
Speranta, Ploesti	400	unknown	3
*Eurotank, Hamburg, Germany	400	unknown	3
Xenia, Ploesti	260	unknown	2
Redeventza, Rumania	230	unknown	2
Lumina Petrolmina, Rumania	140	unknown	1
Total	10,490		45

TARGETS SELECTED FOR ATTACK BY THE 8TH AND 15TH AIR FORCES**

Aircraft:

Factory	Location	Attacking Force
Erla--Me-109	Leipzig/Heiterblick	8th
Erla--Me-109	Leipzig/Möckau	8th
Messerschmitt--Me-109	Regensburg/Prüfening	8th & 15th
Messerschmitt (Wiener Neustadt)--Me-109	Fischamend	15th
Steyr-Daimler-Puch--Me-109	Steyr	15th
Focke Wulf--FW-190	Poznán (Posen)	8th
Focke Wulf--FW-190	Krzesinki (Kreising)	8th
Focke Wulf--FW-190*	Tutow	8th
Fiesler--FW-190	Kassel/Waldau	8th
Gothaer--Me-110	Gotha	8th
Messerschmitt--Me-110	Brunswick/Wilhelmitor	8th
Messerschmitt--Me-110	Brunswick/Neupetritor	8th
Messerschmitt--Me-410	Augsburg	15th
Manfred Weiss--Me-410	Szigetszentmiklós	15th
Junkers--Ju-88	Bernburg	8th
Junkers--Ju-88	Halberstadt	8th
Junkers--Ju-88	Aschersleben	8th
Siebel--Ju-88	Leipzig/Schkeuditz	8th
Heinkel--He-219	Schwechat	15th

Ball Bearings:

Kugel-Fischer	Schweinfurt	8th & 15th
VKF, Werke I	Schweinfurt	8th & 15th
VKF	Berlin/Erkner	8th
Steyrwaffen Walzlagerwerke	Steyr	15th
Deutsche K.F.	Leipzig	8th
Norma (VKF)	Stuttgart/Bad Cannstadt	8th or RAF
Jaeger	Wuppertal	8th or RAF

---

* Listed in original as an Arado plant.
** History of MAAF, 10 Dec 43-1 Sep 44, VIII, ltr, Air Ministry to RAF Bomber Command, USSTAF, MAAF, 28 Jan 44.

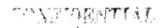

Table 4

FIRST-PRIORITY POINTBLANK TARGETS AUTHORIZED
FOR JANUARY-FEBRUARY 1944[**]

Fighter Aircraft:

1. Messerschmitt-109 assembly plant   Regensburg/Prüfening
2. Messerschmitt-410 assembly plant   Augsburg
3. Steyr-Daimler-Puch Messerschmitt
   Components   Steyr
4. Messerschmitt-109 components plant   Fischamend
5. Messerschmitt-410 assembly plant   Szigetszentmiklós
6. Heinkel-219 assembly plant   Schwechat

Ball Bearings:[*]

1. VKF, Werke I   Schweinfurt
2. Steyr-Daimler-Puch and Walzlagerwerke   Steyr
3. VKF   Stuttgart/Bad Cannstadt

---

[*] The ball-bearing factories were to have equal priority with the aircraft
factories.
[**] History of MAAF, 10 Dec 43-1 Sep 44, VIII, Precis of Present Bombing
Directives other than Areas Authorized in Operation Instuction No. 8,
22 Feb 44.

MAAF POINTBLANK PRIORITIES FOR APRIL 1944*

First Priority:

1. Wiener Neustadter Werke I (Me-109 components), Wiener Neustadt
   (Werke II to be attacked also if force permits).
2. Wiener Neustadter Flugzeugwerke (Me-109 components), Fischamend
3. Me-109 Factory Airfield, Bad Vöslau
4. Duna Aircraft Factory (a/c components), Szigetszentmiklós
   Duna Factory Airfield (Me-210 assembly), Tököl
5. Messerschmitt Plant (Me-410 assembly), Augsburg
6. Norma Ball-bearing Factory (VKF), Stuttgart/Bad Cannstadt
7. Dornier Factory Airfield (Me-410 and Do-217 assembly), Oberpfaffenhofen
8. Hungarian Wagon Works (Me-109 assembly), Gyor
9. IAR Aircraft Factory (Me-109 assembly), Brasov
10. Heinkel Factory Airfield (He-219 assembly), Schwechat

Secondary Priority (to be attacked when first priority targets weathered out):

1. Macchi Aircraft Factory, Varese
2. Fiat Aeritalia Factory, Turin
3. Breda Works, Bresso Airfield, Milan
4. Wiener Neustadter Flugzeugwerke, Klagenfurt
5. Wiener Neustadter Flugzeugwerke, Zemun
6. Muller Ball-bearing Factory, Nuremberg

Subsidiary Targets not Warranting Individual Attack (to be attacked in connection
with above targets when size of force permitted or when grouped together to
constitute mission objectives on a secondary priority):

1. Industrial Targets:
   a. Kammgarnspinnerie, Bad Vöslau
   b. Enzesfelder Metal Works, Enzesfeld (near Wiener Neustadt)
   c. Textile Mill, Ebreichsdorf (near Wiener Neustadt)
   d. Rohrbeck Spinning Mill (a/c components), Neunkirchen
   e. Pottendorfer Spinnerei (Me-109 components), Pottendorf
   f. Aircraft Factory, Neaubing /Neuaubing?/ (near Munich)

2. A/C Concentrations on the Ground, A/C Servicing Facilities, Air Parks:
   a. Wallersdorf A/D, Wiener Neustadt
   b. Fildex Factory A/D, Budapest/Vecses No. 1
   c. Erding A/D, Munich
   d. Gablingen A/D, Augsburg
   e. Landsberg A/D, Munich
   f. Leipheim, A/D, Ulm
   g. Munich/Neubiberg A/D
   h. Munich/Riem A/D
   i. Graz/Thalerhof A/D

Table 6

MAAF POINTBLANK PRIORITIES FOR MAY 1944*

First Priority:

1. Wallersdorf A/D, Wiener Neustadt
2. Amme-Luther-Seck (Me-109 components), Atzgersdorf
3. Dornier (Me-410, Do-217 assembly), Oberpfaffenhofen
4. Munich/Neubiberg A/D
5. Zwölfaxing A/D
6. Budapest/Vecses A/D
7. Munich/Riem Air Park
8. Dornier Factory, Neuaubing
9. Graz/Thalerhof A/D

Secondary Priority (to be attacked when first priority targets weathered
out):

1. Erding A/D and Air Stores Park
2. Budaörs A/D
3. Muller Ball-bearing Factory, Nuremberg
4. Wiener Neustadter Flugzeugwerke, Klagenfurt
5. Steyr-Daimler-Puch Factory, Steyr
6. Rohrback Spinning Mill, Neunkirchen
7. Pottendorfer Spinnerei, Pottendorf
8. Textile Mill, Ebreichsdorf
9. Kammgarnspinnerie, Bad Vöslau
10. Steyr-Daimler-Puch, Graz/Neudorf

MAAF POINTBLANK PRIORITIES FOR MAY 1944

Subsidiary Targets not Warranting Individual Attack (to be attacked in connection with above targets when size of force permitted or when grouped
together to constitute mission objectives on a secondary priority):

    1. Industrial Targets:
        a. Wiener Neustadter Factory, Neudörfl, Austria
        b. Duna Factory, Szigetszentmiklós, Hungary
        c. Siebel Co., Phaleron, Greece
        d. Enzesfelder Metal Works, Enzesfeld, Austria

    2. A/C Concentrations on the Ground, A/C Servicing Facilities, Air
Parks:

        a. Zemun A/D
        b. Brasov A/D
        c. Münchendorf A/D
        d. Klagenfurt A/D
        e. Markersdorf A/D
        f. Tököl A/D and Duna Assembly Plant
        g. Vienna/Aspern A/D
        h. Vienna/Tulln A/D
        i. Hörsching A/D
        j. Wels A/D
        k. Neuberg A/D
        l. Memmingen A/D
        m. Kalamaki A/D
        n. Gyor A/D

Non-POINTBLANK Filler Targets (recommended for use where tactical considerations required supplementary targets in same general area as POINTBLANK
targets):

    1. Refinery and/or Oil Storage Facilities:
        a. Ploesti Area (including Câmpina), Rumania
        b. Giurgiu, Rumania
        c. Bratislava, Czechoslovakia
        d. Vienna-Floridsdorf, Austria
        e. Vienna-Kagran, Austria
        f. Vienna-Korneuburg, Austria
        g. Vienna-Schwechat, Austria
        h. Lobau, Austria
        i. Winterhafen, Austria
        j. Budapest-Csepel, Hungary
        k. Almasfuzito, Hungary
        l. Budapest, Hungary
        m. Caprag, Yugoslavia
        n. Brod, Yugoslavia
        o. Ipil, Yugoslavia
        p. Porto Marghera, Italy

Table 7

USSTAF COORDINATED ATTACKS
1 JANUARY-6 JUNE 1944***

Date	Coordinated Attacks		Cancelled or Declined		Results	
	Proposed	Implied*	Weather	Other Reasons	Abortive	Completed
9 Feb	8th		15th			
15 Feb	8th		15th			
20 Feb	8th				15th	
21 Feb	8th		15th			
22 Feb	8th					8th/15th
23 Feb	8th		8th			
24 Feb	8th					8th/15th
25 Feb	8th					8th/15th
26 Feb	8th			15th**		
4 Mar	8th				15th	
17 Mar		X	15th			
			8th			
24 Mar	8th				15th	
26 Mar	8th				15th	
29 Mar	8th		8th			
7 Apr	8th		8th			
11 Apr		X	15th			
12 Apr	8th		8th			

*   "Coordinated Attack Implied" means that if the intentions of both air forces
     had been carried out as announced, a coordinated attack would have resulted,
     though neither had specifically requested the support of the other.
**   Planes had been forced by weather to land away from base on previous day's
     attack.
*** MAAF, Preliminary Study of Coordinated Attacks by USSTAF, Sup. B.

Table 9

HEAVY BOMBERS ON HAND AND OPERATIONAL
JANUARY-MAY 1944*

Month	Air Force	Type of Plane	No. on Hand	No. Operational	Per Cent Operational
January	8th	B-17	938	657	70
	8th	B-24	244	186	76
	15th	B-17	234	186	80
	15th	B-24	458	300	66
Total			1,874	1,329	71
February	8th	B-17	1,129	786	70
	8th	B-24	352	260	74
	15th	B-17	192	159	83
	15th	B-24	518	341	66
Total			2,191	1,546	71
March	8th	B-17	1,100	792	72
	8th	B-24	399	302	76
	15th	B-17	324	279	86
	15th	B-24	734	570	78
Total			2,557	1,943	76
April	8th	B-17	1,129	908	80
	8th	B-24	485	379	78
	15th	B-17	324	245	76
	15th	B-24	853	607	71
Total			2,791	2,139	77
May	8th	B-17	1,190	949	80
	8th	B-24	836	675	81
	15th	B-17	326	264	81
	15th	B-24	936	605	65
Total			3,288	2,493	76

Table 10

HEAVY BOMBER CREWS ASSIGNED AND OPERATIONAL
JANUARY-MAY 1944**

Month	Air Force	Type of Crew	Crews Assigned	Crews Operational	Effective Strength
January	8th	B-17	1,190	805	*
	8th	B-24	454	308	
	15th	B-17	201	172	169
	15th	B-24	583	492	300
Total			2,428	1,777	
February	8th	B-17	1,171	812	*
	8th	B-24	512	343	
	15th	B-17	151	121	121
	15th	B-24	687	497	339
Total			2,521	1,773	
March	8th	B-17	1,091	699	650
	8th	B-24	548	364	292
	15th	B-17	278	223	223
	15th	B-24	883	715	514
Total			2,800	2,001	1,679
April	8th	B-17	1,134	711	694
	8th	B-24	583	393	355
	15th	B-17	312	270	232
	15th	B-24	966	826	604
Total			2,995	2,200	1,885
May	8th	B-17	1,299	848	805
	8th	B-24	807	534	499
	15th	B-17	309	249	241
	15th	B-24	1,008	870	597
Total			3,423	2,501	2,142

Table 14

ACTUAL DAYS OF OPERATION IN THE EIGHTH AIR FORCE
JANUARY-JUNE 1943 and 1944*

Month	1943	1944
January	4	11
February	5	18
March	9	23
April	4	21
May	9	25
June	7	28

Table 15

MISSION FAILURES IN THE EIGHTH AIR FORCE
JANUARY-JUNE 1944**

Month	No. of Attacks	Mission Failures	Per Cent
January	154	29	19
February	261	71	27
March	232	51	22
April	529	53	10
May	639	93	15
June	832	111	13

---

* Eighth Air Force, _Tactical Development, August 1942-May 1945_, 86.
** Eighth Air Force, ORS, Bombing Accuracy of the Eighth Air Force Bombardment
Divisions, Combat Wings and Groups, in ORS Archives.

G L O S S A R Y

AAF/MTO	Army Air Forces/Mediterranean Theater of Operations
AC/AS	Assistant Chief of Air Staff
A/D	Airdrome
AEAF	Allied Expeditionary Air Forces
AFAEP	AC/AS Plans
AFDAO	Air Ordnance Officer
AFV	Armored Force Vehicle
AGO	Office of the Adjutant General
AGWAR	Adjutant General, War Department
AIA	Atelier de L'Air Industriel
BTO	Bombing through overcast
BMW	Bayerische Motoren Werke
C/AS	Chief of Air Staff
CBO	Combined Bomber Offensive
CCRC	Combat crew replacement center
CCS	Combined Chiefs of Staff
CEP	Circular Probable Error
COPC	Combined Operational Planning Committee
DB	Daimler-Benz
DKF	Deutsche Kugellager Fabrik
ETO	European Theater of Operations
ETOUSA	European Theater of Operations, United States Army
GAF	German Air Force
GO	General Order
HBS	Heavy Bombardment Squadron
JCS	Joint Chiefs of Staff
L/G	Landing Ground
MAAF	Mediterranean Allied Air Forces
MASAF	Mediterranean Allied Strategic Air Force
MEW	Ministry of Economic Warfare (British)
MIAG	Muhlenbau u. Industrie A. G.

MID	Military Intelligence Division, WDGS
MIS	Military Intelligence Service
MM&D	Material, Maintenance, and Distribution
M/T	Motor Transport
MTO	Mediterranean Theater of Operations
M/Y	Marshalling yard
OC&R	Operations, Commitments, and Requirements
Opsum	Operational Summaries
ORS	Operational Research Section
PFF	Pathfinder Force
POL	Petrol, oil, and lubricants
POW	Prisoner of War
PRO	Public Relations Officer
RAF	Royal Air Force
SAC	Supreme Allied Commander
SCORU	Statistical Control Unit
SHAEF	Supreme Headquarters, Allied Expeditionary Forces
SRO	J. Schmidt-Roost ball-bearing company
T/O	Target of Opportunity
USAFIME	U. S. Army Forces in the Middle East
USSAFE	U. S. Strategic Air Forces in Europe
USSTAF	U. S. Strategic Air Forces in Europe
VKF	Vereinigte Kugellager Fabrik

Premiere
http://premiere.fastpencil.com